THERAPY WARS

Nolan Saltzman

——————— *and* ———————

John C. Norcross,
Editors

THERAPY WARS

Contention
and Convergence in
Differing Clinical Approaches

Jossey-Bass Publishers

San Francisco • Oxford • 1990

THERAPY WARS
Contention and Convergence in Differing Clinical Approaches
by Nolan Saltzman and John C. Norcross, Editors

Copyright © 1990 by: Jossey-Bass Inc., Publishers
350 Sansome Street
San Francisco, California 94104
&
Jossey-Bass Limited
Headington Hill Hall
Oxford OX3 0BW

The excerpt in the Concluding Remarks of Chapter Eleven is from "Little Gidding" in *Four Quartets*, copyright 1943 by T. S. Eliot and renewed 1971 by Esme Valerie Eliot, reprinted by permission of Harcourt Brace Jovanovich, Inc. Permission for reprinting outside of the United States obtained from Faber and Faber Limited, Publishers.

Library of Congress Cataloging-in-Publication Data

Therapy Wars : contention and convergence in differing clinical
approaches / [edited by] Nolan Saltzman and John C. Norcross.
p. cm. — (The Jossey-Bass social and behavioral science
series)
Includes bibliographical references.
Includes index.
ISBN 1-55542-259-4 (alk. paper)
1. Psychotherapy—Case studies. I. Saltzman, Nolan, date.
II. Norcross, John C., date. III. Series.
[DNLM: 1. Psychotherapy—case studies. 2. Psychotherapy—
methods. WM 420 T3988]
RC465.T48 1990
616.89′14—dc20
DNLM/DLC
for Library of Congress   90-4637
                                                            CIP

Manufactured in the United States of America

The paper in this book meets the guidelines for permanence and durability of the Committee on Production Guidelines for Book Longevity of the Council on Library Resources.

JACKET DESIGN BY WILLI BAUM

FIRST EDITION

Code 9066

For information about our audio products, write us at:
Newbridge Book Clubs, 3000 Cindel Drive, Delran, NJ 08370

The Jossey-Bass
Social and Behavioral Science Series

Contents

◉

Foreword

Therapy Wars is unique. To the best of my knowledge, no other book assembles so many eminent clinicians who specifically address focal treatment strategies and eschew abstract theorizing across such wide-ranging case vignettes. It is a distinct honor for me to write the foreword to a book that may be considered a distinguished work of art and science. Drs. Saltzman and Norcross have cleverly selected and organized point-counterpoint debates, followed by compelling amplifications and rebuttals. The result is a range of challenging notions, provocative ideas, enlightening observations, and, at times, poignant insights into the creative tactics of some of the best thinkers and doers in our field. This is no dry academic tome. I cannot imagine how committed students or practitioners of counseling or psychotherapy could fail to experience surges of excitement as they read through the book or how they could miss what Norcross, Saltzman, and Giunta term the "downright educational" impact of this rich material.

The format of responses to case vignettes by therapists of different persuasions, followed by their commentaries on one another's perspectives, is exciting, but it is also frustrating at times. I wish the contributors had had the opportunity to react to their colleagues' points of contention. Of course, rejoinders to rebuttals and rebuttals to rejoinders can probably proceed ad infinitum, but perhaps one more round might not have made this book too ungainly. For instance, I have a lot to say to Dr. Davis about his reactions to my multimodal position in the case of "The Wallflower," and I have no doubt that he would have no less to offer in response to my criticisms of his approach. I feel pretty certain that many of the other contributors have similar reactions and would have welcomed the opportunity to set the record straight and perhaps to "go a few more rounds."

In some instances, I feel that the contributors overresponded to the editorial mandate to find areas of convergence and that they underplayed their particular points of departure. Yet, as Dr. Doug Powell underscored, the integrative therapy movement, which is the focus of this book, has had little impact in many quarters, and prominent clinicians are still inclined to adhere to a single or unitary perspective. Frankly, I gained a lot more from the technical and conceptual differences that were addressed than I learned from areas of agreement. Nevertheless, readers will have many "ah-ha" experiences (insight), "ha-ha" reactions (amusement), "oh-no" responses (disagreement), "uh-huh" perceptions (reflection), and many others.

This book can be sampled at many different points, and it will immediately rivet one's attention. There is much to ponder; and the editors' cogent comments underscore some of the significant conclusions to be drawn. Thanks to Drs. Norcross and Saltzman, we have a tour de force that stands alone in the annals of psychotherapy.

June 1990   Arnold A. Lazarus, Ph.D.
                               Distinguished Professor
                               Graduate School of Applied
                               *   and Professional Psychology*
                               Rutgers University

Preface

The title of this book, *Therapy Wars,* is deliberately provocative and ironic. It is provocative in appearing to advertise bloody professional warfare; and it is ironic in that this book fosters open inquiry and transtheoretical dialogue without resorting to the mutual antipathy and "dogma-eat-dogma" ambience that characterized earlier decades of psychotherapy. Warfare is antithetical to the healing spirit of psychotherapy, a field that achieves progress through an informed and respectful, not ignorant and destructive, clash of perspectives. *Contention and Convergence in Differing Clinical Approaches,* our subtitle, more accurately reflects our goals in organizing this project. And it reflects the goals of the *Journal of Integrative and Eclectic Psychotherapy (JIEP),* from whose Clinical Exchange section the present book is derived.

As detailed in Chapter One, this volume provides a forum for eminent clinicians of diverse persuasions to share, in ordinary language, their clinical formulations of and treatment plans for the same psychotherapy patient—one not selected or nominated by those therapists—and then to discuss points of convergence and divergence in their recommendations. Imagine! In each of nine chapters, a different panel of three or four distinguished psychotherapists consults on a patient's case and subsequently tries to learn from colleagues on the panel. This was our original fantasy and inspiration. The contributors' courage in responding to these demanding assignments helped make our fantasy a reality.

Audiences

The novelty and potency of the enterprise make *Therapy Wars* attractive to a wide variety of audiences. The book is intended, primarily, for psychotherapists of all persuasions and professions. The conception of the book was guided by clinical research and experience indicating that mental health professionals learn mainly from actual case material—theirs as well as others'—and from human interchange, as in case conferences. This volume follows that pedagogical tradition. *Therapy Wars* is intended, secondarily, for psychotherapists in training. Clinical illustrations from multiple perspectives help students ground soaring metapsychology and combat the pervasive "one-truth, only-truth" method of theorizing. We avoid such abstract theorizing in favor of a uniquely readable, practical "view from the trenches."

Instructors of psychotherapy, counseling, psychology, psychiatry, and social work can profitably integrate this book into their courses as an adjunct text. Table 1.1 in Chapter One lists the theoretical distribution of the contributors and demonstrates how the cases can be assigned in conjunction with coverage of the major theoretical orientations. Table 1.2 presents patient demographics and consensual diagnostic impressions as aids to instructors who wish to organize their assignments around diagnostic categories and mental disorders.

Overview of the Chapters

The organization of the book is straightforward. In Chapter One, we explicate the context in which the volume is embedded—the psychotherapy integration movement—and articulate the development of the clinical exchanges, which stand in sharp contrast to the cases in most psychotherapy casebooks. Chapters Two through Ten constitute the heart of the book: nine psychotherapy cases analyzed with the wisdom of thirty-four distinguished psychotherapists.

Each chapter in this main section was created in three steps, and, correspondingly, each chapter contains three parts. The first part, labeled "Case Presentation," is a summary of the patient's history and presenting problems. It gives a sense of his or her interpersonal style through vignettes of actual in-therapy dialogue. The second part, "Formulations and Treatments," consists of three or four psychotherapists' independent responses to core questions regarding the client's diagnosis and characterization, the therapeutic relationship, the treatment methods, and the therapy process. Each of these responses is published under the respective therapist's name. The third part, "Points of Contention and Convergence," consists of subsequent essays by the contributors noting agreements and disagreements with the recommendations of the other respondents to the same case.

The closing chapter is our effort to extract salient patterns of convergence and divergence throughout the volume in particular and throughout clinical practice in general. We review the outcome of the enterprise and, equally important, the process of respectfully exploring commonalities. Qualitative impressions and quantitative data are presented to inform future dialogues on clinical material as well as research studies on psychotherapy integration.

Acknowledgments

Two groups of people deserve special acknowledgment for their assistance in completing this book. We thank our wives and children, without whose patience and encouragement we could hardly have engaged ourselves so wholeheartedly in this project. And we acknowledge the inspiration of pioneers in integrative and eclectic psychotherapies, particularly Jusuf Hariman, founder of the *JIEP*; Arnold A. Lazarus, father of technical eclecticism in psychotherapy; and charter members of the Society for the Exploration of Psychotherapy Integration, many of whom have contributed to this volume.

June 1990   Nolan Saltzman
                                            New York, New York

                                            John C. Norcross
                                            Mt. Cobb, Pennsylvania

The Editors

NOLAN SALTZMAN is director of the Bio Psychotherapy Institute in New York City and was formerly clinical exchange editor of the *Journal of Integrative and Eclectic Psychotherapy*. He received his B.A. from Columbia College in biological sciences, his M.A. from Columbia University in biophysics, and his Ph.D. from Indiana Northern University in human relations psychology. He has published extensively for clinicians and is a fellow of the International Academy of Eclectic Psychotherapists.

Dr. Saltzman has taught at New York University, Pace University, and the New School for Social Research. He has made presentations on integrative psychotherapy at Downstate Medical Center, State University of New York, and at the National Institute of Mental Health. He maintains his strong scientific interests through research and teaching at the City University of New York, where he gave the "Brain, Mind, Behavior" lectures in conjunction with the Public Broadcasting System. He lives in New York City with his wife and son.

JOHN C. NORCROSS is chair and professor of psychology at the University of Scranton, a clinical psychologist in part-time independent practice, and past editor-in-chief of the *Journal of Integrative and Eclectic Psychotherapy*. He received his B.A. from Rutgers University in psychology, his M.A. and Ph.D. from the University of Rhode Island in clinical psychology, and he completed his internship at the Brown University School of Medicine.

Author of more than eighty publications, Dr. Norcross's main research interests pertain to integrative psychotherapy, self-change, and the person of the therapist. He has authored/edited several books, most recently the *Casebook of eclectic psychotherapy* (1987). He has served as a clinical and research consultant to a number of organizations, including the National Institute of Mental Health and "CBS This Morning." He resides in Mt. Cobb, Pennsylvania, with his wife and two children.

The Contributors

JANET L. BACHANT, PH.D., is a supervisor and faculty member at the Post Graduate Center for Mental Health and the Institute for Contemporary Psychotherapy and is a visiting faculty member at the Westchester Center for the Study of Psychoanalysis and Psychotherapy. She has been an adjunct assistant professor of psychology at several colleges in the New York area and maintains a full-time psychoanalysis and psychotherapy practice.

BERNARD D. BEITMAN, M.D., is author of *The structure of individual psychotherapy* (1987) and coeditor of *Combining pharmacotherapy and psychotherapy in clinical practice* (1984, with G. Klerman). He is director of the Panic/Cardiology Research Project at the University of Missouri, Columbia, where he is professor in the Department of Psychiatry.

LARRY E. BEUTLER, PH.D., is professor of psychiatry and psychology and chief of the psychology programs at the University of Arizona College of Medicine. He is editor of the *Journal of Consulting and Clinical Psychology* and author of approximately 200 papers and articles. His six books include *Eclectic psychotherapy: A systematic approach* (1983) and *Systematic treatment selection: Toward prescriptive psychological treatments* (1990, with J. Clarkin).

JAMES F. T. BUGENTAL, PH.D., is visiting distinguished professor at the California School of Professional Psychology, adjunct professor at the Saybrook Institute, and clinical lecturer at the Stanford University Medical School. He retired from active practice in 1987 to devote his time to writing and teaching. Among other books, he is author of *The art of the psychotherapist* (1987) and *The search for authenticity* (1965/ 1981). He is past president of the Association for Humanistic Psychology.

JOHN D. DAVIS, PH.D., is senior lecturer in psychology at the University of Warwick, where he directs the university's psychotherapy training program. He practices psychotherapy within the National Health Service. He also chairs the British Psychological Society's advisory committee on psychotherapy and represents the society on the council of the United Kingdom Standing Conference for Psychotherapy. He is author of *The interview as arena: Strategies in standardized interviews and psychotherapy* (1971).

GERALD C. DAVISON, PH.D., is chair of the Department of Psychology and professor of psychology at the University of Southern California. His books include *Clinical behavior therapy* (1976, with M. R. Goldfried), *Case studies in abnormal psychology* (1986, with T. F. Oltmanns & J. M. Neale), and *Abnormal psychology: An experimental clinical approach* (1990, with J. M. Neale). His research is on the development of new cognitive assessment procedures and on methods of cognitive-behavior therapy.

CARLO C. DICLEMENTE, PH.D., ABPP, is associate professor of psychology at the University of Houston, where he directs the Change Assessment Research Program. He is author of numerous articles and book chapters on addictive behaviors and other clinical problems. He has directed an outpatient alcoholism treatment program and maintains a part-time private psychotherapy practice. He is coauthor of *The transtheoretical approach: Crossing the traditional boundaries of therapy* (1984).

ALBERT ELLIS, PH.D., is president of the Institute for Rational-Emotive Therapy in New York City. He has given numerous talks and workshops throughout the world and has authored or coauthored over 600 papers and more than 50 books on psychotherapy, sex, love, and marital relationships, including *Reason and emotion in psychotherapy* (1962), *A new guide to rational living* (1975, with R. Harper), and *The practice of rational-emotive therapy* (1987, with W. Dryden).

SPENCER ETH, M.D., is acting chief of psychiatry at the West Los Angeles Veterans Administration Medical Center, Brentwood Division. He also serves as assistant professor of psychiatry at the University of California, Los Angeles (UCLA), and as clinical associate professor of psychiatry at the University of Southern California. Dr. Eth is an editor of and contributor to *Post-traumatic stress disorder in children* (1985).

JANUS M. G. FRAILLON, M.B.B.S., FRACGP, is a general practitioner who has worked in Melbourne, Australia, since 1956. He has held various clinical and academic posts during that time and was cofounder of the Logotherapy Society in Australia. He also represents the International Academy of Eclectic Psychotherapy in Melbourne and lectures on both logotherapy and counseling in general practice to various professional groups.

ALLEN FRANCES, M.D., is professor of psychiatry at the Cornell University Medical College and chair of the task force on *DSM-IV.* He is coauthor of numerous volumes and editor of several book series and audio seminars.

MARVIN R. GOLDFRIED, PH.D., is professor of psychology and psychiatry at the State University of New York, Stony Brook. In addition to his teaching, supervision, and research, he maintains a limited private practice in New York City. He is coauthor of *Clinical behavior therapy* (1976, with G. C. Davison) and editor of *Converging themes in psychotherapy* (1982).

LESLIE S. GREENBERG, PH.D., is professor of psychology at York University in Toronto and director of the Psychotherapy

Research Centre. He is cofounder and codirector of the Vancouver Gestalt Experiential Training Institute and maintains a part-time private practice. He is author of *Emotion in psychotherapy* (1987, with J. Safran), coauthor of *Emotionally focused therapy for couples* (1988, with S. Johnson), and coeditor of *Patterns of change* (1984, with L. Rice) and *The psychotherapeutic process* (1986, with W. Pinsof).

BERNARD G. GUERNEY, JR., PH.D., is a diplomate in clinical psychology (ABPP), behavioral medicine (AABM), and marital and family therapy (ABFam. P). He is professor of human development and head of the Individual and Family Consultation Center, Pennsylvania State University. He has practiced and taught family therapy for over thirty years and has been corecipient, with his wife Louise, of several national awards for developing the Relationship Enhancement Approach.

SAUL I. HARRISON, M.D., is professor and director of child and adolescent psychiatry at Harbor-UCLA Medical Center and professor emeritus at the University of Michigan. He is author or editor of seven books and approximately 100 articles and book chapters.

DIANA A. KIRSCHNER, PH.D., maintains an independent private practice. Together, the Kirschners have coauthored *Comprehensive family therapy: An integration of system and psychodynamic treatment models* (1986), as well as numerous papers on integrative theory and practice.

SAMUEL KIRSCHNER, PH.D., serves as an adjunct faculty member at the Wharton School of Family Business and is in independent private practice.

MILTON V. KLINE, PH.D., is director of the Morton Prince Mental Health Center of the Institute for Research in Hypnosis and Psychotherapy in New York City. He is in full-time private practice in psychotherapy and was the founding editor of the *International Journal of Clinical and Experimental Hypnosis*.

He is author of *Freud and hypnosis* (1966) and *Multiple personality: Facts and artifacts in relation to hypnotherapy* (1984).

ARNOLD A. LAZARUS, PH.D., holds the rank of distinguished professor in the Graduate School of Applied and Professional Psychology, Rutgers University. He has a private practice in Princeton, New Jersey, and serves on the editorial boards of seven scientific journals. He has authored many articles and books, of which *The practice of multimodal therapy: Systematic, comprehensive and effective psychotherapy* (1989) is his most recent.

ELISABETH A. LEDERMAN, M.A., is coordinator of the Family Violence Program at Barrier Free Living, a mental health clinic for disabled people in New York City. As part of the comprehensive Family Violence Program, she was involved in establishing the first battered women's shelter for deaf women. She has often spoken in the United States and in her native Canada on sexual and physical abuse.

ALVIN R. MAHRER, PH.D., is professor in the School of Psychology, University of Ottawa. Author or editor of ten books and numerous articles, his primary work is aimed toward the development of the practice and theory of experiential psychotherapy, and his secondary work is aimed at discovering how psychotherapy works.

JUDD MARMOR, M.D., is professor emeritus of psychiatry at the University of Southern California and past president of both the American Psychiatric Association and the American Academy of Psychoanalysis. He maintains a limited practice in psychotherapy. He is author of over 300 articles and author or editor of six books, the most recent being *The interface between the psychodynamic and the behavioral therapies* (1980) and *Homosexual behavior: A modern reappraisal* (1980).

STANLEY B. MESSER, PH.D., is professor of psychology in the Graduate School of Applied and Professional Psychology,

Rutgers University. He maintains a part-time independent practice in psychoanalytic psychotherapy and consults on forensic cases to offices of the public defender. He is coeditor of and contributor to *Psychoanalytic and behavior therapy: Is integration possible?* (1984) and *Hermeneutics and psychological theory* (1988).

DOUGLAS H. POWELL, ED.D., ABPP, is a psychologist and lecturer at Harvard University. He coordinates the Behavior Therapy Program at the Harvard University Health Services. In addition, he is president of Powell Associates, a group providing psychological consulting to individuals, schools, and corporations. He is author of *Teenagers: When to worry and what to do* (1986) and numerous articles on integrative psychotherapy.

LAURA N. RICE, PH.D., is professor emeritus in psychology at York University in Toronto and is currently a consultant to the University Counseling and Development Center. She is coeditor of *Innovations in client-centered therapy* (1974, with D. A. Wexler) and *Patterns of change: Intensive analysis of psychotherapy process* (1984, with L. S. Greenberg).

JEREMY D. SAFRAN, PH.D., is associate professor of psychiatry at the University of Toronto and director of the Cognitive Therapy Unit at the Clarke Institute of Psychiatry in Toronto. He is coauthor of *Emotion in psychotherapy* (1987, with L. S. Greenberg) and *The process of cognitive therapy: An interpersonal approach* (1990, with Z. V. Segal). In addition to his academic duties, he maintains a part-time psychotherapy practice.

SHRIDHAR D. SHARMA, M.D., is deputy director general of health services, coordinating medical education in India. He was formerly director of the Central Institute of Psychiatry, Ranchi, and was professor of psychiatry at Goa Medical College. He is chairman of the World Association of Social Psychiatry and former president of the Indian Psychiatric Society. He is author of five books, including *Mental hospitals in India* (1984).

ROBERT N. SOLLOD, PH.D., is associate professor in the Department of Psychology, Cleveland State University. He also conducts a part-time psychology practice. His areas of academic interest and contribution include psychotherapy integration, literacy training, and the relevance of transpersonal concepts to psychotherapy.

GEORGE STRICKER, PH.D., is professor of psychology and dean of the Derner Institute of Advanced Psychological Studies, Adelphi University. A diplomate in clinical psychology, he maintains a part-time independent practice in clinical psychology. He is past president of both the Society for Personality Assessment and the National Council of Schools of Professional Psychology. Stricker's most recent book is the *Handbook of quality assurance in mental health* (1988, with A. Rodriguez).

MARTIN R. TEXTOR, PH.D., is a researcher at the State Institute of Early Education and Family Research in Munich, West Germany. He has authored two books and edited six, among them *Helping families with special problems* (1983) and *The divorce and divorce therapy handbook* (1989).

J. KEVIN THOMPSON, PH.D., is associate professor in the Department of Psychology, University of South Florida. He is author of *Body image disturbance: Assessment and treatment* (1990), and he has guest edited issues of the *Journal of Cognitive Psychotherapy* (on client-therapist relationship and cognitive psychotherapy) and *Behavior Modification* (on cognitive-behavioral treatment of anorexia nervosa and bulimia nervosa).

GERTRUD B. UJHELY, PH.D., R.N., is a Jungian analyst in private practice in New York City and Long Island, New York. She was formerly professor and director of the graduate psychiatric nursing program at Adelphi University and is now on the faculty of both the C. G. Jung Institute and the Long Island Institute of Psychoanalysis. She has published two books for nurses and numerous articles, primarily in nursing journals.

PAUL L. WACHTEL, PH.D., is distinguished professor of psychology at City College of New York and the Graduate Center of
the City University of New York. He is author of *Psychoanalysis and behavior therapy* (1977), *The poverty of affluence,* and
Action and insight (1987); coauthor of *Family dynamics in
individual psychotherapy* (1986, with E. Wachtel); and editor
of *Resistance: Psychodynamic and behavioral approaches.*

THERAPY WARS

1

The Clinical Exchange: Toward Integrating the Psychotherapies

⊡

John C. Norcross
Nolan Saltzman

A metamorphosis is occurring in the mental health profession—the integration of the psychotherapies (Gurman, 1980; London, 1988; Moultrup, 1986). The last decade in particular has witnessed the stirrings of therapeutic rapprochement and a decline in the ideological cold war. The debates across theoretical systems appear to be less polemical or, at least, more issue specific. Clinicians of all persuasions are coming out of their theoretically monogamous closets (Held, 1986) to acknowledge the inadequacies of any one theoretical system and the potential value of others (Norcross, 1986).

The psychotherapy integration movement has experienced dramatic and unprecedented growth of late (Beitman, Goldfried, & Norcross, 1989). Consider, for example, that the plurality of American psychotherapists, between one-third and one-half, now identify themselves as eclectics or, increasingly, as integrationists (Norcross & Prochaska, 1988). Specific eclectic therapies (e.g., Beutler, 1983; Lazarus, 1981; Prochaska & DiClemente, 1984) and compilations of prescriptive treatments (e.g., Beutler & Clarkin, 1990; Goldstein & Stein, 1976; Frances, Clarkin, & Perry, 1986) have appeared before receptive professional audiences. Leading counseling and psychotherapy textbooks (Brabeck & Welfel, 1985) demonstrate a growing trend toward an eclectic perspective, and when one evaluates the predictions of psychotherapy experts (Prochaska & Norcross, 1982), one discovers that eclecticism is likely to increase in popularity more than any other therapy system in the 1990s. Several interdisciplinary organizations committed to advancing the movement have been formed in the past ten years, notably the Society for the Exploration of Psychotherapy Integration (SEPI). (SEPI membership information may be obtained from George Stricker, Derner Institute of Advanced Psychological Studies, Adelphi University, Garden City, New York 11530.)

Even the federal government has gotten into the act. The National Institute of Mental Health (NIMH) sponsored a workshop on research in psychotherapy integration (Wolfe & Goldfried, 1988) in the expectation that treatments of greater efficacy, efficiency, and safety will result from efforts to integrate the best elements of different schools of psychotherapy. In addition, research on integrated treatment models may well lead to the development of a comprehensive model of psychotherapy process that will have solid empirical backing.

The notions of integrating various therapeutic approaches and of securing an empirical base for clinical practice are hardly new. Indeed, eclecticism as a point of view has probably existed as long as philosophy and psychotherapy. In philosophy, a third-century biographer, Diogenes Laertius, referred to an eclectic school that flourished in Alexandria during the second century A.D. (Lunde, 1974). In psychotherapy, as is well known, Freud consciously struggled with the selection and integration of diverse methods (Frances, 1988).

However, it is only recently that integration has developed into a clearly delineated area of interest (Goldfried & Newman, 1986). A confluence of mutually reinforcing factors has produced the contemporary preoccupation with psychotherapy integration (see London, 1983; Norcross & Grencavage, 1989). Briefly stated, these factors are as follows:

1. The proliferation of brand-name therapies, leading to fragmentation, a deafening cacophony of rival claims, and excessive choice

2. The nascent consensus that no one approach is clinically adequate for all problems, patients, and situations

3. The equality of therapeutic outcomes, with some exceptions, ascribed to empirically evaluated therapies or, in the words of Perry London (1988, p. 7), "Meta-analytic research shows charity for all treatments and malice towards none."

4. The resultant search for convergence and common components across diverse schools

5. Socioeconomic pressures, such as the growth of the therapy industry and escalating demands for accountability, which have led to more intertheoretical cooperation and a more unified psychotherapy community

Three main thrusts have become evident in the contemporary movement to integrate the psychotherapies (Arkowitz, 1989; Norcross & Grencavage, 1989). *Eclecticism* refers to the technical, relatively atheoretical combination of clinical methods. As exemplified by the work of Lazarus (1967, 1989b) and Beutler (1983, 1986) among others, technical eclecticism is empirical in that it involves the pragmatic selection of extant procedures on the basis of their demonstrated efficacy, not their theoretical heritage. By contrast, *integration* denotes the conceptual synthesis of diverse theoretical systems. Theoretical integration, as manifested in the work of Wachtel (1977, 1987), Prochaska and DiClemente (1984, 1986), and others, is more conceptual than empirical in developing superordinate or metatheoretical models of psychotherapy. *Common-factor approaches*, as represented by Frank (1973) and Garfield (1980, 1986), seek to determine the core ingredients different therapies may share in common, with the eventual goal of constructing more efficacious treatments based on these components.

Consensual distinctions among these three thrusts have been established in the minds and practices of psychotherapy researchers (Wolfe & Goldfried, 1988), editorial consultants (Norcross & Napolitano, 1986), and most important, self-designated eclectic and integrative clinicians (Norcross & Prochaska, 1988). Accordingly, throughout this volume we will preserve these semantic distinctions. However, when referring to the general concern of synthesizing the psychotherapies, which includes technical eclecticism, theoretical integration, and common factors, we will use the terms *integration movement* and *psychotherapy integration*.

The Clinical Exchange Arrives

In 1982, the movement toward integrating the psychotherapies was marked and solidified with the founding of the *International Journal of Eclectic Psychotherapy* by Australian Jusuf Hariman. Beginning in 1986 with the journal editorship of John Norcross, a section called "Clinical Exchange" was launched under the stewardship of Nolan Saltzman. The journal's title was subsequently modified to the *Journal of Integrative and Eclectic Psychotherapy (JIEP)* to reflect the multiple paths toward synthesizing therapies, including theoretical integration and technical eclecticism. Over the years and despite improvements in the journal, the "Clinical Exchange" section has been consistently rated the most popular in *JIEP*.

The present book derives from the "Clinical Exchange" of the *Journal of Integrative and Eclectic Psychotherapy*. In the four years from 1986 through 1989, fourteen challenging cases were sent to panels typically composed of four authorities of differing clinical approaches. Their responses were compiled and published in the "Clinical Exchange" without benefit of dialogue or debate. In preparing this volume, we recontacted the panel members and asked them to review their original contributions for accuracy, clarity, and possible additions. More important, we enclosed reprints of their fellow panel members' journal contributions, and we asked them all to write to tell us where they agreed and disagreed regarding the therapeutic relationship, method, and process. Which of their colleagues' recommendations did they accept? Which did they reject? How much overlapping or blending of techniques did they acknowledge? We requested brief explanations for agreements and disagreements from their theoretical perspectives so that we could move beyond glib generalizations to fundamental convergences and divergences. This second round of responses was aggregated and is here published for the first time in the "Points of Contention and Convergence" sections at the ends of Chapters Two through Ten.

Virtually no opportunity exists for highly esteemed psychotherapists to consult with the same patient at the same stage of his or her treatment. (Note that we will employ the terms *patient* and *client* interchangeably because neither term satisfactorily describes the therapeutic relationship and because we wish to remain theoretically neutral on this point.) "The Clinical Exchange" simulates this kind of situation by offering clinicians from various orientations a written account of a client at a particular time in therapy—typically at the initial consultation or at a moment of impasse. While the prospect of responding to a vignette on paper rather than to a person in the flesh may seem daunting, there are benefits in such an exercise. One is that the level playing field allows the reader to see what each panel member found or construed in the client or, as some might argue, projected onto the client. Furthermore, the reader begins on the same level playing field. Identical information is provided to everyone, and as the reader finishes the vignette, he or she is in exactly the same place as the contributors—facing the challenges of understanding patients and of assisting them. The potential for education, interchange, and dialogue is evident.

The "Clinical Exchange" section began with the brief case of a young man—Ken, the Spaceman (see Chapter Two)—who had already been seen by several mental health professionals and had been variously diagnosed as suffering from paranoid personality disorder, bipolar personality disorder, and schizophrenia. While the first panel was grappling with Ken and his extraterrestrials, we solicited future case material from the editorial board of the *JIEP* and selected members of SEPI. We also decided to include more information on each patient and to ask standard questions of each contributor in subsequent exchanges.

Case contributors were reminded to alter the patients' names and to omit identifying information, while retaining characterological details and a close-enough depiction of circumstances. Since the cases were to be sent to practitioners using different approaches, there had to be enough data for everyone—enough history for the psychodynamicists to explore, enough behavior for the behaviorists to modify, enough thought for the cognitive therapists to restructure, and enough lively emotion to make the experiential therapist resonate with empathy. As "Clinical Exchange" editor, Saltzman persuaded clinicians to stow diagnostic jargon and replace it with the vivid original material of the sessions.

Saltzman also favored vignettes that retained some ambiguity as to diagnosis or severity of the disorder. It was anticipated—and hoped—that there would be different interpretations and recommendations. Specifically, an implicit premise was that the cases would, in most instances, be suitable for psychological treatment on an outpatient basis, but medication or even hospitalization could not be ruled out if a panelist's reading of a case required it.

We followed five general ground rules in choosing contributors. First, the panels were composed of clinicians recognized as effective in dealing with the kind of challenge offered by the client in terms of possible diagnosis, demographic variables, and conditions of therapy. In selecting contributors, we recognized that some authors are proficient at describing an ideal version of their therapy but only fair to middling with real persons before them, while there are clinicians who, although less published, are well regarded by their peers for achieving exemplary outcomes. Both types had something to offer our enterprise and were invited to participate. Second, we made a conscious attempt to approximate current statistics on the prevalence of the various schools; thus, exponents of psychodynamic, eclectic/integrative, and cognitive-behavioral theories were invited relatively often because there are more practitioners working from these orientations. (Refer to Table 1.1 for the theoretical orientations of the case contributors.) Third, each panel member was to approach the case differently; that is, not more than one behaviorist or one psychodynamicist should be on any given panel. Fourth, we attempted to have at least one woman on each panel. And fifth, to help preserve the international flavor of the journal and to enhance perspective, Saltzman attempted to include foreign authorities on most panels.

Our original list of authorities to be solicited for contributions comprised clinicians who had published on integration and eclecticism and recognized exponents of one or another of the major approaches. In our attempt to have at least one woman on each panel, we added the names of several women who had published less but who had stellar reputations as psychotherapists or supervisors in the training process. Nevertheless, since the list of potential panel members still included more males than females, the approximately even attrition of males and females from the list of invited contributors (individuals who generally cited inabilities beyond their control to respond within our publication deadlines) led to a mathematically determined consequence—an increase in the ratio of male contributors to female contributors.

For the purpose of this book, we have selected nine "Clinical Exchanges" from a pool of fourteen existing sections. Judging any exchange as more informative than another is admittedly a subjective and difficult matter. We were guided in our decisions by the vitality of case material, prominence of the contributors, diversity of the patient's demographics and presenting problems, and representativeness of the panel members' theoretical orientations and professional affiliations. In a few instances, we decided against publishing a response from an original contributor in the interest of length, and in two instances (Rice and Beitman), we invited new contributions to the original cases in the interest of balance.

In all instances, members of the panels were asked to address four central issues. These are as follows.

I.   Diagnosis and characterization
   A.   What is your diagnostic impression or problem formulation?
   B.   What else would you need to know, and how would you typically obtain the information?
II.   Therapeutic relationship
   A.   What type of therapeutic relationship would you strive to create?
   B.   How would you anticipate the client responding to this relationship?
III. Treatment methods
   A.   What format or modality would you recommend?
   B.   What would be your principal techniques or interventions?
IV.   Therapy process
   A.   How would therapy proceed from the first session?
   B.   What would you expect and be wary of as therapy progressed?

Our Purpose

Within the context of the integration movement, this book was designed to foster open inquiry and transtheoretical dialogue in terms of actual psychotherapy cases. Specifically, the purpose is for *eminent clinicians of diverse persuasions to share, in ordinary language, their clinical formulations and treatment plans for the same psychotherapy patient—one not selected or nominated by those therapists—and then to discuss points of convergence and divergence in their recommendations.* The novelty and popularity of the "Clinical Exchange" can, perhaps, be best understood by considering the constituent elements of its purpose.

First, we sought the participation of *eminent clinicians* who were widely recognized as authorities in the field. The objective was to compile responses not merely from representative, competent clinicians, but from prominent practitioners, authors, and researchers of psychotherapy. The list of contributors reads like a virtual *Who's Who in Psychotherapy;*

Table 1.1. Theoretical Representation of Case Contributors.

Theoretical Orientation	Chapter Number	Contributor
Psychoanalytic/Psychodynamic	2	Marmor
	2	Kline
	3	Stricker
	4	Wachtel
	5	Sharma
	7	Bachant
	7	Ujhely
	8	Messer
Person-Centered	3	Rice
Cognitive/Rational-Emotive	2	Ellis
	5	Davison
	7	Goldfried
	8	Thompson
	9	Safran
Behavioral	3	Powell
	5	Davison
	7	Goldfried
Experiential/Gestalt	3	Mahrer
	6	Saltzman
	7	Greenberg
Humanistic/Existential	5	Bugental
	8	Lederman
	10	Fraillon
Systems/Family	9	Textor
	10	Guerney
	10	Kirschners
Eclectic/Integrative	2	Frances
	4	Lazarus
	4	Davis
	4	Wachtel
	5	DiClemente
	6	Beutler
	6	Eth and Harrison
	8	Beitman
	9	Sollod
	10	Guerney

few experienced therapists will fail to recognize immediately the names of Arnold Lazarus, Judd Marmor, Albert Ellis, Allen Frances, James Bugental, and Paul Wachtel, among others.

Second, the invited contributors were purposefully of *diverse persuasions,* because meaningful transtheoretical dialogue and knowledge acquisition require the active interplay of various tenaciously held views (see Feyerabend, 1970; Kuhn, 1970). Our thirty-four members represent all the leading systems of psychotherapy, as is evident in Table 1.1. Indeed, the proportional theoretical representation closely parallels that found among mental health professionals throughout the United States. Eclectic/integrative and psychoanalytic/psychodynamic vie for the most common orientation, followed by family/systems, cognitive, behavioral, and humanistic approaches closely grouped together (cf. Norcross, Strausser, & Faltus, 1988).

Both the editors and the contributors experienced difficulty in placing psychotherapists under a single, crude rubric of theoretical orientation. The result of this necessary, categorical evil was to list contributors under two theories or under eclectic/integrative at times. In ten years, and in subsequent books of this nature, we hope the impact of the psychotherapy integration movement will have made such classification along theoretical lines unnecessary and obsolete.

Representative diversity of two other sorts—professional discipline and biological gender—was also desired. With regard to the former, our contributor list comprises twenty-three psychologists, seven psychiatrists, three psychotherapists, and one psychiatric nurse. However, for reasons previously mentioned, only six of the contributors are women.

Third, each psychotherapeutic tradition has its own jargon, a clinical shorthand among its adherents that widens the precipice across differing orientations. The so-called language problem, as it has become known, confounds understanding of one another's constructs and, in some cases, even leads to active avoidance of those constructs (Goldfried, 1980). Isolated language systems encourage clinicians to wrap themselves in semantic cocoons from which they cannot escape and which others cannot penetrate. Code words are used to express one's theoretical identity, one's sharing in the brotherhood, one's expertise with the rituals (Colby & Stoller, 1988). As Lazarus (1986a, p. 241) tartly concluded, "Basically, integration or rapprochement is impossible when a person speaks and understands only Chinese and another converses only in Greek!"

Accordingly, contributors to this volume were asked to write in *ordinary language* in order to facilitate communication and comprehension. Ordinary, descriptive language by itself will not establish theoretical consensus, of course (Norcross, 1987a). However, before we can agree or disagree on a given matter, we need to ensure that we are in fact discussing the same phenomenon. Punitive superego, negative self-statements, and poor self-image may indeed be similar phenomena, but we cannot know with certainty until they are defined operationally and consensually (Stricker, 1986).

Fourth, responses to each case from the "Clinical Exchange" focus on *the same psychotherapy patient—one not selected or nominated by those therapists.* Many observers have lamented the failure of psychotherapists to concentrate on the specific issues and circumstances of particular patients (cf. Siberschatz, Curtis, & Nathans, 1989). Strupp (1986a), among others, has concluded that psychotherapy research will advance to the extent it is geared to the specific dynamics of particular patients and in-therapy interactions. Much of the apparent disparity among theoretical prescriptions is precisely this neglect of idiographic case material and the concomitant proliferation of nomothetic formulation. We can begin to compare psychotherapies intelligibly and to examine their potential convergence in terms of treatments of the same patient with identical information available to all.

As psychotherapy trainees, we were impressed that the clinical cases presented by textbook authors were, invariably, beautifully formulated and successfully treated. We were rarely apprised in our readings of clients who were referred elsewhere, who terminated prematurely, or who were unsuccessful in their therapeutic quests. Little did we realize back then that these idyllic outcomes were as much due to the psychotherapist's biased reconstruction and selective recall as they were to the facts of the case.

One colleague, after listening incredulously to his cotherapist's tale of clinical heroics with a mutually known client, quipped, "Any resemblance of this case presentation to any actual case is purely coincidental." It is a sad but accurate observation on many published psychotherapy cases.

The cases in *Therapy Wars,* by contrast, were not handpicked by the contributors to illustrate a theoretical point or to validate a therapy system. These cases feature complicated clients, realistic clients, frequently resisting therapy or at an impasse in their treatment—just as one encounters daily in clinical practice.

Finally, after sharing their clinical formulations and treatment plans of the same patient, these psychotherapists *discuss points of convergence and divergence in their recommendations.* This dialogue stands in marked contrast to the overwhelming bulk of case material, which does not afford alternative conceptualizations or opportunities for consensual validity of the posited conclusions. Our format makes a clean break with what Spence (1982) has labeled the "Sherlock Holmes tradition" by developing case presentations that allow the reader to participate in the dialogue, to evaluate the proposed links between evidence and conclusions, and to consider the possibility of alternatives, even of refutations. Collectively, this format increases learning opportunities, explanatory force, and respectful exchange.

The Cases

Case material rightfully counterbalances soaring metapsychology and concretely illustrates technical concepts. Cases provide a coupling of the abstract with the concrete, the intellectual awareness and the felt experience. Theorizing becomes pragmatic (Driscoll, 1984) and consequential (Berger, 1985)—relevant to what transpires in clinical practice. Clinical data render books more readable, interesting, and most of all, useful (Norcross, 1987b).

Table 1.2 provides an overview of the nine cases in terms of title, patient demographics, and diagnostic impressions. Demographically, the cases concern young and middle-aged adults presenting for therapy individually. The cases are primarily, but not exclusively, middle-class Caucasians. The patients range in age from nine to forty-four. There are no clients past middle age, which is probably a shortcoming. In

Table 1.2. Patient Demographics and Diagnostic Impressions by Case.

| Chapter Number | Case Title | Patient Demographics | | Diagnostic Impressions |
		Age	Gender	
2	The Spaceman	20	male	Paranoid or Borderline Personality Disorder
3	The Diplomat	28	male	Anxiety Disorder Passive-Aggressive Personality Disorder
4	The Wallflower	30	female	Dysthymic Disorder Borderline or Masochistic Personality Disorder
5	The Envious Lover	29	male	Substance Abuse Mixed Personality Disorder
6	The Survivor	28	female	Post-Traumatic Stress Disorder Depersonalization Disorder
7	The Don Juan	44	male	Panic Disorder Schizoid or Borderline Personality Disorder
8	The Make-Up Artist	27	female	Borderline or Narcissistic Personality Disorder
9	The Returning Hero and Absent Wife	38 32	male female	Marital Problem Hypertension Compulsive or Schizoid Personality Disorder Post-Traumatic Stress Disorder
10	The Adopted Sister	9	female and family	Family Problem Attention Deficit Disorder with Hyperactivity

seven of the cases, one individual is the focus of the interview; one case each addresses a married couple and an intact family. Three women and four men make up the seven individual cases. This gender ratio is a refreshing change from the traditional reliance on female cases presented by male therapists.

Diagnostically, these cases run the gamut of common presenting problems and psychopathology, excluding psychotic disturbances. The diagnostic impressions presented in Table 1.2 are the product of the coeditors' consensus based on the case material available. These diagnoses are not necessarily those advanced by the contributors, who often disagreed among themselves on the specific disorder and even the utility of formal diagnoses.

Significantly, six of the seven individual therapy patients carried the consensual diagnosis of a personality disorder. Our penchant for these difficult and challenging cases may have contributed to the prevalence of Axis II diagnoses. Nonetheless, personality disorders are being diagnosed with increasing frequency in clinical practice, whether due to artifactual or real increases in their prevalence, and a sizable portion of contemporary clinical practice concerns itself with these clients.

Here, then, are nine stimulating psychotherapy cases and the instructive responses of first-rate clinical minds. We hope that you will find the cases as intriguing, and the exchanges of the panelists as enjoyable, as we did.

2

The Spaceman

🔲

Judd Marmor
Albert Ellis
Allen Frances
Milton V. Kline

Case Presentation

Ken is twenty years old and, at first impression, gentle, conscientious, likable. He is a college junior majoring in chemistry, "taking hard courses and doing well." Lately he has dropped out of school, unable to study ("my thoughts not clear, my past whipping by"). He began to talk to his classmates about extraterrestrials among us, or, alternatively, being an extraterrestrial himself. He was treated with Thorazine by a psychiatrist at his university before he returned to his hometown.

You note that Ken is extremely angry and afraid. He has guilt feelings and nightmares of his own execution, is counterphobic, and tends toward macho pursuits and Rambo-like vengeance fantasies. He reports that he is skilled in karate and that he exercises several hours a day. Ken does not use marijuana or other nonprescription drugs, and he says his friends regard him as a compulsive student.

Ken has a deficient sense of himself and is attracted to authoritarian organizations ranging from the Marines to fundamentalist cults. His thought tends to be filled with symbolic imagery. He is impulsive and is likely to commit himself to three different paths in two days. The combination of rage, macho fantasy, and impulsiveness make him appear violently dangerous, although he has never attacked anyone.

In describing himself, Ken's phrasing and affect are often stagy. You remark on that to see how he responds, and he admits that his friends have noticed the same trait.

Ken has had no mature sexual experience. He appears slow to recognize that he is attractive. He is heterosexually oriented but expresses anxiety that others may doubt his masculinity.

At moments, Ken hates his mother and, far more, her mother. He describes his grandmother and her whole family as Nazis. He likes his father, and you gather that his father tends to remove himself from family stress. In your conversations with his mother, she appears to be concerned, responsible, and realistic, quite unlike Ken's description of her. In Ken's early years, her work required her absence from Ken for weeks at a time. Ken has one younger brother, whom he likes, but Ken disapproves of his pot smoking and irresponsibility. You sense Ken may have an infantile dependence on his parents—a dependence that he does not recognize.

Ken does not seem committed to his extraterrestrial fantasies. You suggest to him that they are ways of explaining to himself his feelings of alienation. He readily agrees, and he adds that they are also a way to keep people at a distance. Then, he offers that he thinks he can trust you and would like to try psychotherapy with you.

Formulations and Treatments

Judd Marmor (Psychoanalytic)

My initial reaction to the consultation is that I need considerably more information about Ken before I arrive at a definitive diagnosis and plan of treatment. In particular, I would like to know much more about his developmental history, from early childhood on. I need to know more about why he hates his mother and grandmother, in contrast to the positive feelings he has for his father. What kind of relationship did he have with them during his childhood and adolescence? What was his reaction to the birth of his brother, and what was the nature of their early interaction? Also, what kind of peer relationships did he have growing up, and why is it that he seems to be rather inhibited sexually? It is clear that he has an impaired self-image and feelings of masculine inadequacy. But how and why did this occur?

My first tentative impression, subject to revision when I get more information about him, is that we may be dealing with a borderline personality disorder. My reasons for suspecting this diagnosis include his chronic anger, his impulsiveness, his histrionic tendencies, his emotional immaturity, his impaired self-image, and what appears to have been a transitory schizophrenia-like episode. I would not be too quick to fault the psychiatrist who first saw him for prescribing Thorazine—without receiving a report from that psychiatrist as to what his findings were at that time. With Ken's permission, I would be inclined to write to that psychiatrist for information. We must keep in mind also that we are seeing him after he was treated with Thorazine, which may well have produced a remission in his apparent psychotic break.

If further exploration of Ken's developmental background and personality patterns were to confirm my initial impression, I would be inclined to place him in a program of dynamic psychotherapy, seeing him face-to-face on a twice-a-week basis. The initial goal of such therapy would be to try to develop a strong working alliance in which Ken's fragile sense of trust can be strengthened. I would work toward helping him achieve a better understanding of how and why his difficulties have developed and of the way his perceptions, both of himself and of significant others, may have been distorted. Depending on how the situation evolves, it might well be that some family therapy sessions including his mother, his father, his brother, and his maternal grandmother, if she is still alive, would also be indicated and useful. In any event, I tend to see Ken's therapy not as a short-term prospect, but as one that might well extend over a longer time. At the moment, I would see no indications for adjunctive psycho-pharmacological therapy, but I would not rule it out as a possibility, if subsequent circumstances indicated that kind of treatment.

Albert Ellis (Rational-Emotive)

I would suspect from the initial consultation that Ken is in the borderline personality range but would refrain from making a more definitive diagnosis until after I had had a few more therapy sessions. In using rational-emotive therapy, or RET (Ellis, 1962, 1988a; Ellis & Dryden, 1987), I find that the best mode of diagnosis is therapy itself, since the ways in which the client reacts to the first few therapy sessions usually tell much more about him than any amount of objective or projective tests.

I would take each of Ken's major symptoms and look for the main irrational beliefs—his core *masturbatory* philosophies—that probably lie behind them and that tend to produce them. I would hypothesize that his extreme anger stems from his absolutistic insistence that others (including his family members and therapists) *must* treat him in the manner that he considers fair and proper. I would guess that his fears and macho defenses against them tend to be produced by his commands that he has to perform well and be competent and powerful. I would tentatively assume that his guilt feelings follow from his dogmatic demands that he do the right thing with regard to his responsibilities and his actions toward others. I would hypothesize that his deficient sense of himself and his need to join authoritarian cults originate in his *necessitizing* about his being all-powerful and having mighty associates and identities. I would guess that his impulsiveness largely stems from his low frustration tolerance, underlain by his beliefs that he must get what he wants when he wants it and that under no conditions should he be seriously balked or frustrated.

While checking out Ken's absolutistic demands on himself, on others, and on the universe, and while determining his specific "tyranny of the shoulds" (Horney, 1950), I would quickly begin to show him that he had better keep his goals, ideals, and purposes as his choices rather than as Jehovian demands. At the same time, I would give him unconditional acceptance, in spite of his failings and deficiencies, and show him how fully to accept himself. I would encourage him to use some of RET's shame-attacking exercises (such as deliberately acting foolishly or unmasculinely in front of others and managing to feel unashamed and unembarrassed while doing so). I would work with him behaviorally to help him do several things that he is irrationally afraid of doing—such as approaching attractive females and trying to win their favor. I would also try to encourage him to stay in uncomfortable situations—such as returning to school—until he works on his low frustration tolerance and begins to feel, first, comfort and, later, enjoyment. I would particularly try to show him that although masculinity has certain advantages in our culture, it is hardly the be-all and end-all of human existence and that he can fully accept himself whether or not he is totally masculine and whether or not significant others approve of him.

Allen Frances (Integrative)

The patient's diagnosis is most likely paranoid disorder or paranoid personality, the choice depending on how seriously one takes his possibly delusional beliefs. In either case, many factors in his presentation resemble the profiles of individuals at risk to commit violent acts, and most especially murders or assassinations. The crucial initial problem is establishing a visible and enduring therapeutic relationship with an individual who is often suspicious, resentful, frightened, and likely to quit impulsively situations he regards as dangerous. Ken's reaction to the therapist's first interventions are encouraging: he accepts the confrontation concerning the extraterrestrial fantasies, volunteers that he likes the therapist, and wants to try therapy.

The psychotherapist should point out that the therapy will

be uncomfortable for Ken and predict that he will at times feel angry and fearful and want to stop. The therapist should educate Ken about what will be expected and about how to deal with feelings as they emerge in the treatment. Psychoeducation should also include as much about the patient's risk for violence as can be imparted without threatening the therapeutic alliance. Often patients like Ken have long been frightened by their violent impulses and fantasies and are relieved by the opportunity to discuss them openly.

The therapeutic relationship with a paranoid/dependent patient like Ken is usually most useful if the therapist maintains distance and avoids challenging the patient too directly or attempting too great a closeness. An unobtrusive and educational approach is usually best tolerated. Interviews should be conducted in large rooms, with easy exits for the patient, chairs at equal distances, and a willingness to end early if the patient becomes upset.

The ongoing treatment plan (Frances, Clarkin, & Perry, 1986) might combine varying proportions and sequences: direct advice (that guns be disposed of, that the grandmother be avoided, that decisions about joining cults be postponed); ventilation; exploration of cognitions that the world is inherently dangerous and that only the strong and heavily armed survive; behavioral exposure to anxiety-provoking situations in very gradual and easy-to-take steps; and again, in very gradual steps, psychodynamic exploration of his underlying wishes, fears, and defenses (particularly, that his fears of being harmed by others constitute a projection of his own hostile impulses).

Which techniques are used, and in what order, would depend on the intuition of the therapist and on the patient's capacity to respond to gentle trials of each. Perhaps the most important agent of change in the treatment of patients like Ken is the corrective emotional experience that occurs in the interpersonal relationship with the therapist, so the choice of techniques should always be influenced by the effects they will have on that relationship. Family or group treatment is occasionally helpful. Medications to reduce violence have been and are being tested—most particularly lithium, Propanolol, and anticonvulsants. Results are encouraging but inconclusive. Medication for paranoid personality is unavailable; neuroleptics are often effective for patients with paranoid disorders, but these patients are more than usually noncompliant with the treatment regimen because of their general suspiciousness about medication and their specific intolerance of side effects. It is beyond our scope here to discuss the legal implications raised by treatment of Ken or the risks and countertransferences occasioned by such treatment, but these issues are likely to be of considerable importance.

Milton V. Kline (Psychoanalytic)

Since Thorazine was administered to Ken prior to some of the case material reported, psychotic features that may have been present in the earlier, active phase of the illness may not be present now; but there are characteristic symptoms involving multiple psychological processes.

I am not able to ascertain from the material presented the degree of deterioration. Schizophrenic reactions always involve some deterioration from a previous level of functioning, so additional collateral information from the family and from observations, particularly by the psychiatrist at school, would be important in making this assessment.

I am not certain whether Ken's talk about the presence of extraterrestrials or, alternatively, of being an extraterrestrial himself is a fantasy, whether it represents a major dissociative disturbance, or whether it reflects an underlying, multiple-process schizophrenic illness. There appears to be some evidence of fragmented or bizarre thought content. And although there is no clear evidence of delusions of reference—in which events, objects, or other people are given consistently particular and unusual significance—nevertheless, there is some clear evidence of delusional thinking. I would like to use an approach that would lead to better insight into the content of Ken's thought.

It is essential to gain insight into the sense of self that this young man presents, into the nature of his ego boundaries and the losses that may have been suffered in relation to his confused identity, into the meaning of his extraterrestrial delusion with regard to his sense of personal existence, and into his feelings and attitudes of self involving control by an outside force.

Ken manifests some disturbance in self-initiated goal-directed activity that at times may grossly impair work or other role functioning. This may take the form of inadequate drive, inability to follow the course of action to its conclusion, or regression to more primitive, primary-process cognitive associations.

I feel that this case is still in its early diagnostic phase and that a great deal has to be done to evaluate the degree to which familial patterns have played a role, particularly with reference to Ken's attitudes toward the mother, the grandmother, and his view of his grandmother's family as Nazis. A thorough assessment of familial influence is necessary. Earlier indications of Ken's paranoid attitudes or projections, particularly those typical of schizophreniform disorders, might then be assessed.

The thought process in this young man needs to be carefully evaluated. With sufficient additional information gained from one or two further consultations, I would suggest a hypnotic interview in which it would be possible to distinguish among (1) a disorder in the content of thought, (2) a dissociative disorder, or (3) a regression in cognitive functioning more typical of schizophrenic illness. I would like to use hypnosis to explore the nature of the perception and the affect connected with the original extraterrestrial reference and thoughts.

Contraindications to the use of hypnosis must be assessed during initial interviews. However, earlier misconceptions that use of hypnosis with borderline or schizophrenic patients would lead to dissociation or deterioration have not been borne out. Within the framework of rapid and positive transference that occurs in a good hypnotic relationship, there are safeguards that permit assessment of unconscious material, both ideationally and affectively, without jeopardizing the patient's equilibrium. This assessment requires considerable experience in using hypnosis as a diagnostic and therapeutic modality, and it requires awareness of the parameters of hypnotic responsiveness and the characteristics of the positive transference that may emerge.

In this instance, let us assume that after taking a comprehensive psychodynamic history, conducting a careful evaluation, and establishing a hypnotic relationship, the therapist decides to proceed to assess Ken's thought content and the extent of his dissociation and regression. All three assessments can be accomplished in a unified consideration of the patient's productivity and responsiveness within the hypnotic interview.

Spontaneity of verbalization, and of images evoked and suggested, give the therapist a rapid, clear insight into the degree of regression, whether it is in the service of the ego or whether it holds potential for acting out and for fragmentation. In one part of the diagnostic procedure, the therapist seeks to elucidate images of subjects Ken has mentioned, such as Nazis in his family and extraterrestrials.

One might say to Ken when he is under hypnosis, "I would like you to think about what an extraterrestrial looks like. You will be able to visualize an extraterrestrial. Tell me, in any way that you wish, what it is that you see." After Ken has related what he has visualized, the therapist might say, "Tell what you feel, what feelings the images stimulated." The clinical process consists of evoking images, asking direct questions about the associated feelings, and establishing some link between these feelings and the presenting symptoms. Although still within the assessment period, one might make tentative interpretations and monitor both the patient's interpretations of the emerging material and his response to the therapist's interpretations, and then compare the two.

For example, if an image or association to that image suggests a familial significance, the therapist might interpret it in a subdued but direct way. For example, "That seems, perhaps, to be related to some of the feelings you described about your grandmother." The response to the interpretation could be critically important. Part of this assessment would be to determine the degree to which alexothymia may be present—the degree of separation, detachment, or blocking of feelings, particularly unconscious feelings, that may hinder the structuring and attachment of words to describe these feelings. In patients of this kind, one often finds a special type of alexothymia; the words needed to relate unconscious feelings are so potentially conflicting that the intermediary process is one of establishing fantasies, hallucinations, or dissociative reactions as a defense.

It has been established that a disturbance of the kind Ken presents is the result of unconscious conflict. To plan a meaningful and effective therapy, it is necessary to understand the nature of Ken's inner conflict, its associations, and particularly the resistances and defenses that he has erected against it.

At various points in the hypnotic exploration, based on body posture, shifts, ideation, or verbal comments, the therapist should ask, "How do you feel, right at this moment?" According to the patient's response, the therapist might add a comment, perhaps an interpretative one, about the meaning of those feelings as they relate to the presenting symptoms. Based on the findings that would emerge, one might decide that this patient could better be treated either by a psychopharmacological approach with supportive psychotherapy or by a more intensive dynamic psychotherapy. The latter puts a good deal of pressure on the patient to feel, to come into contact with unconscious feelings, and eventually to be able to experience an intensification of resistance and its meaning, which would lead to some clarification of defenses. In this form of therapy, direct challenges to the resistances may be used to confront the patient with the need to remember and, particularly, with the selective nature of his inability to remember important things.

One could also use the hypnotic relationship, which brings about a spontaneous transference, to intensify the transference and to use it to mobilize the unconscious therapeutic alliance.

When this is possible, the effect is dramatic. There is often an immediate drop in tension, a feeling of relief, a rise in true motivation, and the emergence of strong positive feelings for the therapist. The patient's unconscious frequently becomes unlocked, and some major communication that reveals the nature of the patient's disturbance may appear.

This young man may be in a partial remission due to the Thorazine and the support given in the initial therapeutic context. Therefore, my sole conviction about Ken is the need to explore the parameters, both of cognitive functioning and affect, with particular reference to fantasies and delusions. This approach is designed to lead to a differential diagnosis involving the possible contributions of schizophrenic disorder, characterological problems, and conflicts that might make major use of dissociative mechanisms as defenses. I would consider using hypnotic procedures for such diagnostic exploration, and I would attempt to formulate a treatment plan based on the forthcoming information.

Because of the regressive components in the case of Ken, the clinical properties of hypnosis, particularly in relation to the analogues of multiple personality in psychotic states (Gruenwald, 1974), open avenues to rapid and comprehensive treatment in a case like this. In this case, regression must be considered a process that can generate and intensify the dynamic mechanisms of the patient's psychopathology and mobilize the development for the therapeutic transference. It is in this respect that Loewald (1979) has clarified the dual significance of the regressive experience for a patient—both as an expression of pathology and as a process of symptom formation—while simultaneously providing a state within which "restoration" may be achieved and from which a resumption of development may again proceed.

In Ken's case, the development of a classic transference neurosis would offer the matrix within which his pathognomonic regression would establish itself spontaneously under treatment circumstances. Such a transference crystallizes around certain core issues such as Oedipus conflicts, grandiose exhibitionistic or idealizing needs or wishes, or fantasies that belong to different developmental periods. It is this issue of different developmental periods that becomes magnified during the hypnotic process through transferences to help deal with the fragmented ego states that constitute the core of borderline disorders (Kline, 1984).

Thus, within this process of regression, self-cohesion is lost and regained a number of times due to interactional effects of the regressive nature of hypnosis and the reintegrating effects of therapeutic transference. It is within such a sequence of events that reality testing continues to undergo change and, in effect, becomes the target of the therapeutic intervention (Balint, 1968).

This process is a reflection of the importance of positive anticipation in the recovery of patients in the grip of serious emotional disorders. Within the total integration of the past, the present, and the anticipation of the future, it is crucial that the patient be able to foresee the possibility of escape from the bind of his own dilemma and, as a consequence, to attain potential satisfaction and happiness. Just as primitive thinking in normal sleep and in a remembered dream solves many a problem, so do these primitive processes in hypnotic regression. Particularly with sensory and motor involvement, these processes offer a field for direct therapeutic activity and the successful reintegration of masses of life experience that had failed to integrate as a functional unity in the past (Sullivan, 1962).

Points of Contention and Convergence*

Judd Marmor

In general, I am more impressed by the areas of agreement among Ellis, Frances, Kline, and me than I am by the disagreements. We all recognize that Ken has a major personality disorder, possibly a borderline personality disorder, with evi-

*Allen Frances was unable to contribute to this section due to a serious illness in his family.

dence of psychotic ideation. Frances and Kline focused somewhat more strongly on the psychotic features than did Ellis or I, but we all recognize the need to get more information from and about Ken before arriving at a definitive diagnosis. Both Kline and I feel that, if possible, getting a report from the university psychiatrist who prescribed Thorazine for Ken would be worthwhile. Frances placed greater emphasis on Ken's paranoid features and the risk of violence than the rest of us did, and his therapeutic approach is therefore a more cautious one. Otherwise, however, it is not essentially different from the rest of ours in recognizing the need for establishing a meaningful and trusting therapeutic relationship with Ken and for trying gradually to uncover the experiential sources and nature of his psychopathology. Both Frances and I recognize that some adjunctive pharmacotherapy may be indicated; Ellis and Kline do not refer to that as a possible contingency.

The only recommendation about which I have serious reservations is Kline's rather strong emphasis on the value of attempting one or more hypnotic interviews with Ken after a number of preliminary sessions. I believe that the risk of attempting hypnotherapy in a patient with Ken's unstable and paranoid personality would not be justified. The results that Kline hopes to achieve from such an interview or interviews can be equally well accomplished, and more safely, by the techniques the rest of us recommended. I say this without negative prejudice toward hypnotherapy. I have used it myself. But I believe the fragility of the transference relationship in this kind of patient is a contraindication for such therapy—certainly for the early use of it—until a genuine and strong patient-therapist relationship has been firmly established.

What I would emphasize about my own approach is its strong systems orientation (Marmor, 1982, 1983) and the flexibility (Marmor, 1974b, 1974c) that flows from it. I try to be alert not only to the intrapsychic mechanisms at play in Ken's psychopathology but also to the possibility of genetic and neurophysiologic factors that may be involved. I am interested in a historical reconstruction of his personality development, not because I consider it to be therapeutic per se, but because a better understanding of such past influences will help me interact more intelligently and meaningfully in the here-and-now therapeutic setting and during the corrective emotional experiences that I believe (as does Frances) are central to effective therapy (cf. Marmor, 1974a, 1975).

Finally, because I believe that his current life relationships are also of cardinal importance in the life-space system in which he operates, I am also prepared to explore and deal with the family system via family therapy sessions, if and when my understanding of the dynamics of that system indicates that approach would be helpful.

Albert Ellis

Regarding Judd Marmor's response, I agree that a psychotherapist could use much more information about Ken before arriving at a definitive diagnosis and treatment, but I personally would require much less developmental and early family history than he would. While I agree that Ken has an impaired self-image and feelings of masculine inadequacy, I would assume that these largely stemmed from his own constructs rather than from the standards and criticisms imposed by his family. His family and culture may well have taught him that masculinity is desirable, but his own commanding *must*abatory cognitions turned these learned preferences into rigid demands, and he thereby made himself disturbed.

Furthermore, I agree with Marmor that some family sessions might be useful—not mainly for diagnostic purposes, but for showing the family members that they only contributed to Ken's disturbance and that they did not really cause it. I would particularly try to relieve them of the guilt they very likely have about Ken's condition. I would educate them about his irrational thinking and its partial biological causes, and I would try to enlist their help for Ken in using several RET methods.

I would be much more likely than Marmor to have Ken consult with a psychopharmacologist; to check for psychosis, possible endogenous depression, and violence proneness; and to see if psychotropic medication would be recommended. I agree with Marmor that Ken is suffering from a borderline personality disorder.

I would, of course, never recommend psychodynamic or psychoanalytic therapy for Ken, because I consider it (after practicing it for several years before I originated RET) woefully inefficient for almost all clients and harmful for most borderline personalities.

Like Marmor, and like other cognitive-behavioral therapists, I would try to help Ken see how his perceptions of himself and significant others may have been distorted. But I would go further than this and show him his own underlying rigid musts that tend to bring on his misperceptions. Thus, his view of his grandmother and her whole family as Nazis is probably a gross exaggeration that follows not only from his perception (which may be accurate) of their bigoted behavior but also from his Jehovian command, "They absolutely must not be the way they are!"

Because Ken seems to be so seriously disturbed, I agree with Marmor that psychotherapy with him would probably extend over a longer period of time than is usual with RET. Clients like Ken tend forcefully and rigidly to hold onto their irrational beliefs, disturbed feelings, and behavior, so they had better be guided to change them by a forceful, directive therapist.

Turning to Allen Frances, I agree with his opinion that Ken may well have a paranoid personality. While I would carefully explore his propensity for violence, I would guess that he probably is not dangerous. I also agree that in his case, it is particularly desirable to win his trust, as we do in RET with unconditional acceptance of people like Ken in spite of their bizarre and sometimes hateful behaviors.

I agree with Frances that a psychoeducational approach is indicated with Ken, particularly regarding the dangers of his being violent, the difficulties he may encounter in therapy, and the disadvantages of cultism. Mostly, however, I would teach him the ABCs of RET: show him how Activating events

(A's), such as his family's presumed Nazism, do not directly create emotional and behavioral Consequences (C's), such as his hostility and his inability to study. Rather, I would teach him that his Beliefs (B's) about the Activating events (A's) more directly and more crucially upset him. I would show him how to Dispute (D) his irrational Beliefs (iB's) such as "I absolutely must be macho and act vengefully like Rambo, else I am a worthless wimp" (Ellis, 1962; Ellis & Dryden, 1987; Ellis & Grieger, 1986).

Psychoeducationally, I would also try to get Ken to use some of the RET self-help materials, including pamphlets and books. Those especially indicated would be *A new guide to rational living* (Ellis & Harper, 1975) and *How to stubbornly refuse to make yourself miserable about anything—Yes, anything!* (Ellis, 1988a). I would also recommend his listening to some of our effective RET cassettes, such as *Unconditionally accepting yourself and others* (Ellis, 1988b). I would encourage Ken to do the homework assignment of filling out several of our RET self-help reports (Sichel & Ellis, 1984), and I would review them with him.

I would risk much more closeness and directness than Allen would with Ken because I find that with borderline personalities, who tend to be vague and namby-pamby in confronting and disputing their irrational beliefs, my being very direct and forceful is often far more effective than keeping my distance. I would particularly experiment with vigorously challenging his ideas that he must be supermacho and that he immediately has to follow his impulsive desires. I would try to show him that underneath his feelings of great masculinity probably lie woeful feelings of inadequacy, and I would very powerfully show him that he—and any human— can fully accept himself whether or not he performs well and whether or not he is adored by others.

I would use, as would Frances, ventilation of feelings with Ken, but only in conjunction with several RET techniques to help him change his hostile and disruptive emotions. Thus, I would use rational-emotive imagery (Maultsby, 1971; Maultsby & Ellis, 1974) to show him how to imagine some of the worst situations occurring (such as people despising him for being too weak), to let him get fully in touch with his inappropriate feelings (such as intense hostility and vengefulness) as he did so, and to get him to change these to appropriate feelings (such as keen disappointment and frustration). I would also use other RET emotive techniques, such as getting him forcefully to make rational self-statements—statements such as "My grandmother's behavior is too rigid and Nazi-like, but she is a fallible, screwed-up person who has a right to be wrong."

I also agree with Frances that behavioral exposure to anxiety-provoking situations would probably be useful with Ken. But I would experiment with implosive as well as gradual in vivo desensitization, if Ken were willing to try it. Thus, I would try to help him perform a series of RET shame-attacking exercises (Ellis, 1969, 1988a; Ellis & Dryden, 1987). These might consist of his deliberately letting himself lose several karate matches to weak opponents and working on himself not to feel ashamed when he publicly lost them.

I would not only explore Ken's defenses, as Frances would, but also show him the grandiose commands that underlie these defenses. Thus, if he masks his feelings of weakness by pretending to be an extraterrestrial, I would try to show him that he is probably demanding that he must be superhuman and that he is a weakling if he is only human. I would then try to help him to dispute and surrender this godlike demand and thereby have no need to continue to create the cover-up defense.

I quite disagree with Frances that "Perhaps the most important agent of change in the treatment of patients like Ken is the corrective emotional experience that occurs in the interpersonal relationship with the therapists, so the choice of techniques should always be influenced by the effects they will have on that relationship." Hogwash! For several reasons:

First, as I noted above, the therapist's giving Ken unconditional acceptance is one important aspect of teaching him how to accept himself fully. But merely giving him this kind of relationship—as Carl Rogers (1961) used to do—may well motivate him to accept himself because the therapist likes him. This is highly conditional self-acceptance and will likely disappear when significant others later dislike him.

Second, Frances implies that the corrective emotional experience that occurs in the client-therapist relationship occurs because of the emotional aspect of the relationship itself. This may or may not be true. Thus, a number of my borderline clients have said that they disliked or did not particularly care for me. But they said I helped them considerably by teaching them how to look at themselves differently and how to become more effective; and they said their previous warmer therapists had hardly helped them at all.

Third, I discovered many years ago, when experimenting with Ferenczi's (1952) technique of being nice and warm to my clients, that they loved their therapy session and me. However, many of them, especially the borderline personalities, became more dependent and sicker. That was one important reason why I abandoned psychoanalysis and created RET.

Fourth, as several studies have shown, severe depressives and borderlines can significantly improve and stay improved when using cognitive and behavioral self-help materials, without the assistance of any therapist (Scoggin, Jamison, & Gochneaur, 1989).

Moving on to Milton Kline, I agree that Ken's low self-acceptance and weakened sense of identity underlie his extraterrestrial delusion and other symptoms. Ken and his therapist had better not only see this, as Kline indicates, but also actively do something to change it.

Kline asks for a thorough assessment of family influence on Ken's attitudes. But to ascertain possible genetic influences, I would also want to know how seriously disturbed the close members of both his parents' families were.

Kline recommends a hypnotic interview with Ken to explore dissociative and schizophrenic disorders. Although I wrote a paper many years ago favoring the use of hypnosis with borderline personalities (Ellis, 1958), and although I have recently shown that hypnosis can be used effectively in conjunction with RET (Ellis, 1986), I would not risk using it in Ken's case. I say this because it could encourage dissociation, could help Ken believe that it is some kind of magical cure, could contribute to his dependency on me, and could sidetrack us from the main theme of helping him unconditionally to accept himself.

Kline states that, "It has been established that a disturbance of the kind Ken presents is the result of unconscious conflict." This is a superficial psychoanalytic interpretation that has not been empirically established. Humans continually have conflicting desires, such as to have sex with a neighbor's wife and to act friendly toward the neighbor, without making themselves either neurotically or psychotically disturbed. They also add musts to their conflicts (and to their nonconflicts!) by which they disturb themselves—conflicts such as "I must have my neighbor's wife and not antagonize my neighbor!" or "I must not even think about having sex with my neighbor's wife!" By seeking Ken's unconscious conflicts and ignoring his unconscious and conscious commands, Kline and other psychoanalytic therapists will, I predict, futilely prolong his therapy and most likely will do him much more harm than good. Want to bet?

I agree with Kline that Ken will probably resist therapy and that direct challenges to his resistance may be usefully offered. But the challenges I would give would be radically different from Kline's, since I would mainly challenge Ken's low frustration tolerance that often would be the main cause of his resistance. Thus, if he refused to remember important things, he would usually be motivated by the irrational beliefs—"I can't stand remembering them! It's too uncomfortable!"

On the whole, although I agree with many of the points made by Marmor, Frances, and Kline, I believe that they are all much too psychoanalytic and too little cognitive-behavioral. Therefore, I believe they all tend to encourage Ken to spend excessive time in therapy while obtaining relatively poor results. RET might well not work with Ken, but I think it at least has a good fighting chance!

Milton V. Kline

I can only state my rather complete concurrence with all that Judd Marmor has expressed from his point of view in the evaluation of the case of Ken. The questions he raises as well as the recommendations he offers are consistent with my feeling that dynamic psychotherapy, on an intensive level within a strong supportive therapeutic alliance, is essential in the treatment of Ken.

I am in essential agreement with the point that Albert Ellis clearly makes—that therapy is in itself the most effective diagnostic procedure. I have, however, some reservations about the therapeutic value of looking for core masturbatory philosophies and of very direct confrontation with major irrational beliefs in this case. I fear this approach may tend to impair the development of a strong working alliance and to dilute the transference—results that could prove to be counterproductive therapeutically. I am less than enthusiastic about direct behavioral approaches as the core treatment plan in this case.

Allen Frances makes a good case for establishing a strong transference. I am in agreement with the desire for a firm, positive therapeutic relationship that also gives the patient space and distance to avoid being threatened. And I agree with the psychoeducational approach suggested by Frances, particularly with the avoidance of direct challenges to the patient. Perhaps the use of indirect rather than direct advice might be more consistent with my overall approach, but my views on this case are essentially in convergence with those of Frances.

While I have emphasized the selection of intensive dynamic psychotherapy using hypnosis in Ken's case, I do not feel that other therapeutic modalities would not be effective. Seemingly different therapeutic approaches may incorporate similar dynamic mechanisms that, in the final sense, contribute to recovery.

3

The Diplomat

🔳

Alvin R. Mahrer
George Stricker
Douglas H. Powell
Laura N. Rice

Case Presentation

The anxious young man calls to inquire about joining a therapy group. At the consultation, Michael wears a black cord sports jacket, white shirt and a narrow black knit tie, and black jeans. His wild hair, sparse beard, and feverish eyes give him the look of a nineteenth-century anarchist. All he lacks is a round black bomb with a smoking fuse.

"I'm a little hyper," Michael says. "Sorry I'm late. Everything went wrong"—he gasps for breath—"when I was trying to leave for here. I haven't slept for two nights."

He touches his beard nervously as he speaks, and I see there is something wrong with his hands. They are puffy and stiff and bluish. I examine one of his hands. It is cool and leathery to the touch, a corpse's hand!

"I can't hold a pencil most of the time," Michael says. "That's really a pain, because I have to write in the field, where there's no typewriter for twenty blocks."

"You have poor circulation in your hands, Mike," I say. "How long has it been like this? What do the doctors say?"

"I've had it since puberty," he says. "It wasn't so bad at

first, but it gets worse as time goes on. I've had a million tests. I've got a letter from the head of vascular disease to the head of endocrinology. It says, 'We have to watch this young man closely,' and it gives positive indications for four serious diseases it might be, and also why none of these can be diagnosed at this point. It might turn out to be any of them."

"I'd like to see the letter," I say. "I wonder, does the doctor who wrote the letter say anything about fear? Has anyone related these symptoms to your emotions?"

"Yes, one of the internists at the hospital sent me to a shrink, who put me on Valium, and aminophylline and ephedrine for my breathing. I don't feel that afraid, but I'd like to believe it's only fear instead of some terrible disease."

"Are you aware when it's better or worse?" I ask.

"It's a little better when I'm having a good time. Sometimes my fingers get almost pink. When I'm anxious, like when I think about going into group therapy, it gets worse, and my hands hurt."

"Do they hurt now?" I ask.

"Yes," he says.

"How about when you go out on a date with a new girl?"

"About like now."

"What are you afraid of in group therapy?" I ask. "Let your imagination go. What do you see happening?"

"I'm afraid of how I might come off in the group," he says. "I can see myself feeling above it and making clever remarks, and then everybody'd jump on me and crush my body and tear me limb from limb."

"You really see the group tearing you apart," I say. "Tell me, where am I meanwhile?"

"You're leading them. You start off," he says. "You hit me in the face and then the others rush by you and jump on me."

Michael knows that this scenario is unlikely. He expects my next question, about relationships in his family. "I'm the only one the others get along with," he says. "I have an older brother and sister and a younger brother and sister. My father and mother are separated now. Everyone in the family hates everybody else most of the time, but the alliances shift now and then. It's like power diplomacy among nations with armies along their borders."

"And you're the diplomat, the peacemaker?" I ask.

"Peace is out of the question," he says. "I don't even know what I'm supposed to be negotiating."

"Just that they'll keep liking you and not jump your borders?" I ask. "How did your parents treat you when you were little? What's the earliest you can remember?"

"Something I thought of before," Michael says, "when I said about you hitting me in the face. My father used to hit my older sister Cathy in the face. It terrified me." His eyes, the pale, taut appearance of his face, his posture, and his husky voice all suggest that he lives constantly in fear.

"Did he ever hit you?" I ask.

"No," Michael says, "hardly ever. I was considered too sickly to hit. Also, I was supposed to be the intelligent one, and he didn't want to bash in my brains. He used to chase Jack all over the house, hitting him wherever he could. That didn't bother me, because I figured Jack could take it. But when he hit Cathy, I went to pieces."

"You loved Cathy," I say. "What did you do when your father hit her?"

"I wanted to cry, 'Stop!' but I couldn't. I could hardly breathe. I couldn't go over to her afterward. I stayed away from her for days."

"You were afraid it was contagious," I say.

"That's it!" he cries. He is winded, takes long breaths to catch up.

"How did your father feel toward you, Michael?" I ask.

Michael closes his eyes and sinks into himself. "I don't know," he says at last. "He worked long hours. He was an intelligent man trapped by the depression into running a candy store. He always thought he should have been something more. He was remote from me, guarded, as though I might do something to disgrace him."

"Such as?"

"Something effeminate, maybe. I don't know. I can see

him grinning at me from behind the counter." Michael shivers.

"Not a smile of being glad to see you," I say. "What did the grin say?"

"It was mean, almost scornful," Michael says. "How could you be scornful of a little kid, your own son?"

"How could you hit your own daughter in the face?" I ask. "Would you do that, Mike?"

"God, no," he says. "But you're getting a one-sided view of my father. He can be gentle sometimes. Both my parents are big on charity. They adopted an asthmatic kid off the streets and raised him. Bobby slept in my room with me and my younger brother, and I remember waking up a lot with both my parents standing over him, trying to make him comfortable and keep him breathing."

"How did you feel about that?" I ask.

"It hurt that my father was affectionate with him," Michael says. "Really, he was a kind man, but I couldn't get any. I always had trouble breathing myself, especially breathing out, like I have a weight on my chest. My mother took me to the doctor. He said there was nothing there. My father believed I would stop complaining if I saw someone with a real problem."

"So, he turned your bedroom into a clinic," I say. "How do you feel toward your father now?"

"It's funny," Michael says. "I still want him to look at me the way he looked at Bobby, the asthmatic kid. Another thing, he always sent me money, supported me when I was at CCNY and floating around until I became a social worker."

"How do you like social work?" I ask.

"Great, I love it," he says. "I have too many cases, like everybody. Can you imagine all that can go wrong between visits to seventy-four desperate ghetto families? I can't physically get around to see some of them for weeks. I don't know who's going to get into trouble or die before I get back to them."

"How about your mother, Mike?" I ask. "What kind of a person is she?"

"What kind of person? She's who she is, very powerful behind the scenes, always gets her way, manipulative. She used to keep us in line by saying, 'You'll upset your father.' He's supposed to have a heart condition, which I think will finally kill him off in another thirty or forty years. My mother decided I should be a priest, so I spent three years in the seminary."

"Do you still consider yourself a Catholic?" I ask.

"Hell, no," he says. "I hate that stuff now. I can't tell you how I hate it. Every time I see a nun or priest on the street! Someday I'm going to kill one, and they'll put me away for good."

Michael is not going to kill anyone, but plainly he is afflicted by images of killing. He leans forward, eyes blazing, mouth taut with anger. His arms bow tensely, as though he were holding himself back from attacking someone. "You have no idea," he says. "I see myself taking an ice pick and smashing it through some goddamned priest's forehead."

"Then what happens?" I ask. "How do you feel after you imagine that?"

"I never think. . . . I just thought of something," he says. "Showing my mother the priest's head with the ice pick in it and his skull's cracked like a pot and the brains running out. And I'm screaming! 'Ma! Look! I killed the phony Jesus!' "

"And she responds by . . . ?"

"By crossing herself and giving me a look."

"What does the look say, Mike?"

"I don't know. Wait, it says two things. 'I don't want you,' and 'If nobody else wants you, if you're really *loathsome*, I have to take you.' "

"What did your mother want from you when you were a little boy?" I ask.

"She had some idea of a gentleman in her head. She wanted her children to be ladies and gentlemen. Whenever I heard those words I felt like puking. Throwing up."

"You just did it for her," I say.

"Did what?" he asks.

"Cleaned up your act for mother," I say. "Substituted a nicer phrase. Doesn't it make you want to regurgitate?"

"I actually remember her saying, 'Puke is common,' "
Michael says. "I thought 'common' sounded terrific. It's what
I always wanted to be, but I could never make it."

"Was she affectionate?" I ask. "Did she hug you?"

"All the time," he says.

"What was the quality of your mother's hugs?"

"She was smothering. It seemed to me there was something
sexual about the odor of her body when she hugged me—
she's a big woman—but it was hard to think that because
she's so religious."

"You felt she was sexual toward you?" I ask.

"Not exactly," he says. "I could be reading that in. She
used to call me 'darling' a lot, and that made me feel sick. It
was like I was her way of getting back at Dad."

"For what?" I ask.

"I don't know," Michael says. "Just that I was the means."

"How old were you when you first felt this?" I ask.

"As early as I can remember," Michael says. "I don't want
to sound precocious, but in the second grade, I got a valentine
card from her, and I hated it because I already knew valen-
tines were for real lovers."

"How about now? How's your love life?" I sense a defeated
quality about him.

"I have a girlfriend, Heather," he says. "But I don't think
she wants to go out with me anymore."

"What went wrong, Mike?" I ask.

"She's very shy," he says, "lives at home. I don't know if
she's ready for a real relationship."

"How old is Heather?"

"She's old enough, my age, twenty-eight."

"I don't understand, Mike," I say. "What do you want with
a twenty-eight year old who lives at home, isn't ready for a
relationship, and doesn't want to go out with you?"

"I love her," Michael says. "These things don't always
make sense. I'm very romantic."

"I'm beginning to see that," I say.

"Tell me, how was sex with Heather? Or, let me ask something first. Have you had sex with Heather?"

"We're platonic," Michael says.

"I haven't heard anyone use *platonic* that way in twenty-five years," I say. "I bet your fourteen-year-old clients aren't platonic."

"They're not," he says. "The girls get pregnant and I'm supposed to sort out their lives."

I cut him off before he can escape into his social work.

"And you're not seeing anyone since Heather won't go out with you."

"I see lots of women," Michael mutters.

"Yes," I say, "and how's the sex with them?"

"I'm not having much sex," he says. His eyelids blink rapidly. He is frightened and alternately pleading and hostile.

"You're not having any sex with women, Mike," I say. "That's not a sin, you know. It's just that you're missing something."

"I can't," he moans, looking away. "I get soft. I even tried with men, in the seminary, to find out what I was. I don't think I'm homosexual. I really am attracted to women."

"I agree with you," I say. "You just haven't been allowed to enjoy a sense of yourself as a sexual man. But you can still learn to be proud of your sexuality." He looks at me as though I had advised him to fly to the moon.

"How am I supposed to do that?" he asks.

A *DSM-III* diagnosis suggested by Stricker is as follows:

Axis I: Anxiety Disorder
Axis II: Passive-Aggressive Personality
Axis III: Impaired respiration, circulation, and potency

Formulations and Treatments

Alvin R. Mahrer (Experiential)

I have two main reactions to the account of the initial consultation. First, I am impressed by the useful experiential material elicited by the good therapist and the good patient. Second, I am struck by how differently I might have worked with Michael.

In the beginning of the initial session, when Michael lets all of his attention go to whatever it goes to, and when he allows himself to feel and to experience, what is the nature of the immediate experiencing? That is where we start. He may begin by attending to his hand and issuing a series of complaints about the hand as he experiences being a captivating new patient. Or, if he began by sinking into recollections of recent incidents with women as he blurts out that he is certainly no homosexual, his experiencing might be of distancing himself charmingly from the ladies.

Where we go from there depends on what happens in the ongoing experiencing. Does it deepen and intensify? Does it give way to some other experiencing? What happens as we work with the experiencings that come forward? Over the entire session, I need to know the nature of the experiencing and the context in which the experiencing is occurring. I find out by working with whatever good experiential material Michael presents.

The useful material comes from Michael's letting his attention go to whatever is front and center and from his allowing experiencing to occur. It does not come from my framing clinical inferences about Michael or from my leading him into providing information on topics that I select as important. Accordingly, I do not examine his hands, inquire into the history of their condition, inspect letters from physicians, or delve into his heterosexual relationships. Because the information I need is experiential, the methods I would use are those that produce a high yield of experiencing.

I will start from the very beginning. However, from the opening statement, I will have to invent what Michael might perhaps say and do, based on how he seemed to be in the interesting actual session. Because of space limitation, I will proceed only a little way.

P1: I'm a little hyper. Sorry I'm late. Everything went wrong [gasping for breath] when I was trying to leave for here. I haven't slept for two nights.

T1: [Our eyes are open. We are standing up. Therapy has not begun. So, I am the person I am, being whatever I am.] That's something! You started to leave for here two nights ago? [I motion him to the chair.]

P2: No, I just meant I feel a little hyper, and I know I'm a little late.

T2: [I am ready to begin.] OK, are you ready to start? [He nods.] Just lean back. Me, too, I will. No glasses. No smoking. Feet up. There. Now, close your eyes. I'm closing mine, too. There. And keep them closed the whole time. We'll open them when we are all done. OK? Good. Ready.

I now give standard instructions. In the initial session, if there is already something front and center on Michael's mind, if he is already in a state of experiencing, I want the instructions to give him a chance to attend to whatever is here right now. If there is no special focal center at present, no strong experiencing starting in him now, then there are additional instructions to show him how to locate something to attend to and how to allow himself to experience what is there, waiting.

P3: Uh-huh.

T3: There may be something on your mind right now, something you are aware of and thinking about, something front and center on your mind. It may be something you see, right now, or it may be something coming over you right now, that you can sense and feel in your body. There is something here already.

P4: Hmmm.

T4: Talk out loud. Talk out loud with feelings, any kinds of feelings that are here. Now you can let yourself start to have tears, or you can let yourself get mad, or you can have feelings of being scared or feelings of being gloomy and unhappy, or feelings of smirking, being secret, doing wicked things, laughing, feeling great. Let the feelings happen as you talk about whatever is front and center in your mind right now. . . . Now, I am going to stop, and it is your turn, if you are ready and if you are willing.

These instructions may be enough. They are for most patients in the very beginning.

P5:   Well, I called 'cause I was thinking about group therapy.

As soon as I had finished giving instructions, I got ready to let Michael's words come through me, as if they were my words, spoken in and from me. Nothing. The words are dead. No feeling. So, I am once again the instruction giver.

T5:   We can start here, with, "I called 'cause I was thinking about group therapy." We can begin with these words. Now, let yourself say them with feelings, with strong feelings, with any strong feelings that come as you let yourself say those words, and then you will be letting the strong feelings come into you.

P6:   I can see myself feeling above it and making clever remarks! And then everybody'd jump on me [rising feeling] . . . and crush my body and tear me limb from limb! [a rush of strong feeling]

When these words, said in this way, are as if they were coming through me, suddenly I am in a scene in which six or eight people are at me, pulling my arms and legs. Yet, the most compelling feature is the feeling in me. Actually, it is kind of sexy, vibrant, deliciously out of control. My words express this:

T6:   Oh, God! I think I like this!

P7:   [He laughs.] But wait'll I tell them the other things.

When these words come through me, there is a sense of wicked exhilaration at the bizarre things I can say, things that will shock them into even more whipped-up craziness.

T7:   [Excitedly] Yeah! OK! Here it comes!

P8:   I sometimes think about nuns and priests! Someday I'm going to kill one, kill the phony Jesus, stick an ice pick in his skull. It'll crack like a pot and the brains run out!

There is an almost giddy excitement with these words, and a freedom to explode with such delightfully bizarre statements. As these words come through me, I am charged with these feelings, and I can sense a freewheeling kicking off of all restrictions.

T8:   Right! Squishy brains, like just pouring out of the damned skull! This is fun!

P9:   They'll lock me up! [He is laughing, and there is a wicked sort of devilishness here. As the therapist has these words come resonating through, there is an experiencing of companionship here. It is as if we were buddies being openly bizarre, almost inviting them to lock us up.]

T9:   [Buoyantly, like a fellow conspirator] Well, they should! You're a first-class loony!

P10:   Boy, do I feel sexy!

These are merely the opening exchanges in an experiential session that may take about one and a half or two hours. We have only begun the first of the four steps of each session (Mahrer, 1989c; cf. Mahrer, 1985, 1986, 1989a, 1989b, 1989d, 1990). To give a fair picture of the four steps, here is a brief summary of what happens in the rest of this session:

The purpose of the first step is to attain a level of strong feeling. We are not there yet. When we reach this level, there is a genuinely strong degree of charge, force, energy, arousal, saturation, and fullness of any kind of feeling whatsoever. We proceed at Michael's own readiness, pace, and pattern, always in the direction of attaining a level of strong feeling.

Once we attain that level of strong feeling, an *inner experiencing* is accessed, sensed, felt, brought closer to the surface by means of the crucible of strong feeling. This inner experiencing is the jewel. We listen for what it is. It may be something that has been here all along, or it may be something new. Let us suppose that in Michael it is an inner experiencing of wicked, tabooed, devilish, risky, exciting sexuality.

The purpose of the second step is to appreciate this inner experiencing. We let it stay here for a while, we welcome and accept its presence, we enjoy it and let it feel good in us, and we lift up and carry forward its form and shape.

The purpose of the third step is to give Michael an opportunity to be the inner experiencing. The therapist shows him how to move out of the ordinary, continuing personality that he is and how to undergo the radical, massive transformation into fully being this inner experiencing. To accomplish this, Michael and I search for an appropriate scene or moment from earlier in his life. This is the context within which he can be the inner experiencing. We enter into this context. Michael can now enter wholly into being (living, feeling, behaving) as a new person who experiences wicked, tabooed, devilish, risky, exciting sexuality.

The fourth and final step offers Michael the opportunity for being and behaving as this inner experiencing in the imminent future world. Within the context of scenes and situations from tomorrow and next week and beyond, Michael lives out this newfound experiencing and acts and behaves as this significantly new person. Out of all these new ways of being and behaving, a few are selected, rehearsed, and—providing both Michael and therapist are ready and willing—can be carried out by Michael when he leaves the session. The change in his way of being and behaving may be large or small, significant or insignificant; it may last only a few minutes or from now on, but he has had a sample of what he and his life can be like as this new person.

Now I can complete the answers to the central questions.

With regard to diagnosis and characterization, the sole and critical information is the nature of the inner experiencing accessed in this session. The first step accesses the inner experiencing, and the ensuing three steps enable personality-behavioral change in relation to this inner experiencing. We have no working use for any sort of psychodiagnosis nor for identification of some problem as presented by Michael, as formulated by a therapist, or as conjointly arrived at by the two of them.

With regard to therapeutic relationship, Michael relates to his own immediate personal world. Both Michael and I attend to this personal world, live and exist in it, experience in it, and relate within it and to it. Michael's words are as if they were also coming in and through me, and all of this is helped by our eyes being closed throughout the session. We do not engage in eyes-open, back-and-forth conversation, attending to each other in the establishment and development of any sort of relationship between the therapist in one role and Michael in some complementary role. In place of our attending to each other in a relationship, I join with Michael in his relationships to and with and in his own immediate personal world.

With regard to treatment methods, I rely on the four steps as the very best way to enable personality-behavioral change in relation to whatever inner experiencing is accessed in this session. This approach leaves aside any so-called treatment of choice for supposed problems or conditions that are maintained from session to session. It also means that Michael is quite free, by taking advantage of any other kinds of treatment programs, to complement whatever experiential sessions offer.

With regard to therapy process, the frame of reference is this session by itself, and not an extended series of sessions. Experiential is a single-session psychotherapy in that each session goes through the same four steps, and each session starts with whatever feeling-related attentional center the patient is ready to start with. There is no presumption of an extended series of sessions, no set of stages of therapy over months or years, no counting on a gradually developing and evolving therapist-patient relationship, no treatment plan for what is to be done in future sessions, and no anticipated future themes of which the therapist should be wary. The term *therapy process* makes sense for the four steps in this session; it does not make sense for an extended series of sessions.

George Stricker (Psychoanalytic)

My approach in psychotherapy is one of continuous hypothesis formation, confirmation, and rejection. Much like the process involved in construct validity, a nomological net is constructed, elaborated, and revised. My framework is psychodynamic, but this same process can be used with any orientation. My approach to the task of understanding Michael and arriving at a treatment plan will follow this same procedure. I will go through the material provided, indicate the thoughts that I have, the confirmatory or nonconfirmatory evidence that later develops, and finally describe a treatment plan based on this initial contact.

Psychotherapy begins with the first contact, before the patient sets foot into the office. The first question I ask myself, and one the patient answers in both direct and indirect ways, is "Why is he here?" On the telephone, Michael asked for group therapy. Unless the therapist is particularly known for group, and I am not, this is an unusual request. In fact, many patients in public facilities make a point of asking for reassurance that they will not be placed in a group, preferring the attention they will get in individual sessions. Thus, the question from Michael would alert me to the possibility that he wishes to avoid such attention and that he has some difficulties in areas such as trust, closeness, and intimacy.

The information provided in the first paragraph gives an immediate indication that Michael has ambivalence about his relations with authorities and probably adopts a compliant but passive-aggressive stance toward them. Two clues lead to this formulation. The first is combining a rebellious personal presentation ("nineteenth-century anarchist") with a jacket, white shirt, and tie, but offsetting these by also wearing jeans. The second clue is coming late to the meeting but then feeling the need to be apologetic about doing so.

Michael begins by indicating that he has not been sleeping and generally presents himself as being quite anxious. I would have responded to that aspect of the communication, asking him to speak further about it. Under no circumstances would my initial contact with a patient be the performance of a physical examination, no matter how superficial the contact. The physical symptoms on Axis III certainly deserve medical attention, and I would want to consult with Michael's physician about them. But I see them as manifestations of the problems outlined above, and I would prefer to address those more directly.

Interestingly, the inquiry into the physical leads to the central role of anxiety, with Michael referring to some doctors in exalted terms (heads of departments) but referring to a mental health practitioner as a "shrink," thus continuing his passive-aggressive mode of relating. I would not have asked about his relationships with women so early in the session, not because I would not want to know, but because I prefer that the patient establish priorities.

The question on the fantasies about group therapy allows Michael to describe his extreme anxieties about being with people. The fantasies are extraordinarily vivid and filled with terror, suggesting the level of anxiety he endures and the extent of the rage he harbors. The next question I would have raised is why he specifically asked to be placed in such a frightening situation. His stated distrust of the therapist, who would lead the assault, may suggest why he would prefer the protection of a group—even though it might turn against him—to an unbuffered exposure to an authority figure.

I, too, would have gone from these fantasies to his early experiences, in which he learned how dangerous and untrustworthy his surroundings were and because of which he developed his coping tactics. It is clear that these tactics involved

passive and avoidance mechanisms, which were only temporarily successful, leaving Michael in a constant state of anticipating harm. Michael's identification with his sister Cathy,
combined with his passivity and the power and danger represented by his father, would raise some concern about his gender identity. The hypothesis of a gender identity problem is
supported by Michael's apparently self-generated impression
that his father may have thought him effeminate. I would
further note that, on being invited to express dissatisfaction
with his father, he responds by excusing his father and describing his good and charitable acts, all of which were to
Michael's detriment. His anger at his father is apparent, but
so is his fear of expressing that feeling.

Michael's choice of social work as a career gives him the
opportunity to use his considerable intelligence and to provide the care and assistance that he saw his father as providing
to others but not to him. At the same time, social work is a
profession that is stereotypically regarded as feminine, and
one he describes as great (with sarcasm?) before elaborating
all the frustrations and impotence he experiences in it. Career
for Michael is a way of identifying with the loved aspects of
his father without challenging the feared parts.

Michael's rage against his mother is more manifest. She is
less fearsome than his father, so there is less reason to veil his
feelings. Further, his feminine identification and self-loathing
combine to allow him to direct his fury at her as an external
representation of himself. Michael initially chose the priest-
hood, also a nurturing profession, at the behest of his mother,
but he later rejected it. Here, as in his earlier reference to a
group experience, his fantasies are vivid and lurid. His mur-
derous anger is directed at a disappointing father figure, the
anonymous priest he does in with an ice pick, which he
then presents to his mother. She, in turn, rejects this "gift,"
Michael's way of acting out her anger at his father, so he is
left with a sense of being impotent and unable to satisfy her,
whatever he does. The same fantasy also expresses his anger
at her by murdering her dream. But here, too, the anger is
ineffectual in that she will have to "take him" because it is

her duty to do so. This second expression of very primitive rage, to a virtual stranger in a first session, would rouse my concern about the adequacy of his defenses. Nothing presented here suggests that Michael acts out violently, but I would be alert for trouble signs.

As a boy, Michael was expected to behave himself like a gentleman and, as much as he did not wish to do so, he found himself complying. The interviewer is quite accurate in pointing out how Michael continues to "clean up his act" for his mother. Michael then goes on to describe his sense of being smothered, and the oedipal relationship with her is manifest. The combination of a smothering, seductive mother and a distant, rejecting, and punitive father makes the appearance of an anxious, passive-aggressive, sexually inadequate young man quite understandable. Michael's failure with women is predictable, and his concerns about homosexuality should not be dismissed as easily as they were. I suspect that the theme of insecure gender would be recurrent throughout the course of treatment, and reassurance from the therapist may only serve to block further communication about this sensitive area.

Despite Michael's initial request for group psychotherapy, I would prefer to see him in individual therapy, and he might come to share that preference. The very idea that a male authority would think enough of him to give him individual attention would be reassuring, albeit somewhat frightening, and potentially therapeutically valuable for him. The initial focus in treatment would be on the building of a safe and trusting relationship. I would be continuously aware of his anger but would not press for its expression. I would expect his feelings toward me to be, in turn, angry, idealizing, and homosexual, and I would like him to experience each of these as safe so that he could then go beyond them and begin to form a sense of his own identity. Observing that I can be comfortable with his anger, he might learn that it is less ferocious than he fears, and this realization might reduce his projection of it onto others and might allow him to function with less anxiety. Finally, as his anger becomes less frightening, his comfort with people should increase, and his physical symptoms might decrease. He might then begin to experiment with more direct expressions of his feelings, which would contribute to his sense of himself as an effective agent in his own life.

Douglas H. Powell (Behavioral and Integrative)

Michael seems to be an ideal candidate for integrative therapy. Impairment occurs across physical, familial, interpersonal, and sexual domains. He is beset by high levels of anxiety and anger, and the anxiety probably contributes significantly to his circulatory and respiratory problems, and to his insomnia. That he reminds the therapist of an anarchist suggests Michael's hostility is not far beneath the surface—an impression supported by his fantasies of being torn apart by a group or of killing a clergyman.

Family issues still trouble Michael. Father's violence toward his siblings and attentiveness to the asthmatic Bobby probably have an effect on Michael's physical symptoms, especially his breathing difficulties. Michael's relationship with his mother seems more opaque. We know that he sees her as manipulative, controlling, and religious and that she was affectionate to him during childhood; whether she was seductive is not clear.

Michael has pronounced sexual inhibitions. Impotence is one manifestation; avoidance of women with whom sexual intimacy might arise is another. Nothing is heard of a best friend, a group of people with whom he spends time regularly, or even activity-oriented acquaintances. This is a lonely, isolated fellow.

In spite of these difficulties, Michael has a number of resources that are positive for his prognosis. He is bright, and he has used his intelligence to charm his parents, to sublimate aggressive impulses, to pursue a college career, and to enter a field he enjoys and at which he seems quite competent. Michael is able to generate insights and articulate them pleasingly to the therapist, and he evinces a plasticity of ego structure. He can access primitive instincts and experience them without being overwhelmed; this characteristic could lead to more rapid progress than might otherwise be possible. Finally, Michael wants help and has resolved to work with someone who can help him. He appears able to form a therapeutic alliance quickly, perhaps because he has had treatment in the past or has learned from his own studies.

What else would I want to know about Michael? I would like to know more about Michael's mother and their relationship. How close were they when he was a child? Did they sleep together? Did things change when they took in Bobby? What else did she want from him, other than to be a gentleman and a priest?

More about the origin of the breathing problems would be useful. I suspect these symptoms may be an internalization of Bobby's problems, or they may be associated in some other way—although there is also certainly much more to it.

Because Michael's relationships seem so immature, I would like to hear something about his interpersonal development. Did he have a best friend? Was his same-sex attempt at physical intimacy with a chum? Was he part of a group in junior high school? How about his first experiences with women? What have his twenties been like in terms of his contacts with men and women?

Finally, what does he do fun? What gives him pleasure? Does he go to movies or concerts? Does he like to swim or play with a dog? Is he a New York Mets fan?

In terms of how I would proceed, I would prefer to treat Michael first in individual therapy; group therapy could certainly be useful later. The question of sequencing in the treatment process may be crucial. After a thorough history has been taken and an initial relationship established—and presuming no clear-cut etiology of the physical complaints—symptom-oriented interventions seem a promising way to begin. I would use autogenic training for the cold hands and hypnosis with guided imagery to try to reduce the severity of Michael's breathing problems. These behavioral techniques have a high probability of also reducing his tension. I would give Michael charts wherein he would rate his discomforts on these symptomatic dimensions. In learning to administer these behavioral techniques himself and following his own progress on his charts, Michael would enhance his self-confidence and would feel less helpless and dependent. The result would be a more collaborative, though perhaps less intense, therapeutic alliance.

During the process of behavior therapy, I would watch for spontaneous insights into repressed affects or cognitions associated with these symptoms. A woman we treated for cold hands broke down sobbing during autogenic training when she recognized how much she resented the attention paid to a crippled younger sister not unlike Bobby. Michael might recognize that his breathing problems are partially related to an internalization of Bobby's symptoms. Such spontaneous recognitions can give insight-oriented treatment a solid beginning.

Michael's psychological-mindedness and his ability to bring up primitive feelings may enable him rapidly to trace the psychodynamic forces influencing his thoughts or behavior; but keeping him focused on issues, resisting being drawn into interesting cul-de-sacs, and separating central from superficial issues will be a challenge.

I would proceed by asking him to talk about what it is like to be Michael, where he is happy and unhappy with himself, and how he would like to change with the help of the therapy.

I would listen for feelings about his family, especially his mother, because their relationship is crucial to understanding Michael as he is today. Paying attention to the quality of Michael's bonding with friends could lead into his anxieties about sexual identity. He seems heterosexually oriented, but he will have to find his own way. The therapist can help Michael clarify his sexual feelings by encouraging him to verbalize them and reflect on them.

Strong transference, especially with aggressive and sexual themes, might be anticipated. I would expect cascades of anger toward the therapist and others and would want Michael to be prepared early on to recognize and examine the historical origins of the anger. I imagine his anger terrifies him because he has had little opportunity to test it in reality. After he finds that his aggressive thoughts are not lethal, I would help him find ways to express the underlying feelings more adaptively. Perhaps assertiveness training would be in order.

It is not obvious what form his sexual feelings toward the therapist, if any, might take, although I would look for a sadomasochistic element. Helping him understand any such sexual material and generating insights into their antecedents might be an important element of the treatment.

These understandings could pave the way for a so-called growth-group experience from which Michael might learn to be more comfortable with peers. Such an experience could help him in thinking about what he wants from this phase of his life and motivate him to begin. Group work might begin while the one-on-one therapy is proceeding and then continue as the individual treatment tapers off.

Somewhere along the line, I would encourage Michael to involve himself in recreational activities that would bring him pleasure. This kind of activity could provide some balance in his life as well as introduce him to age-appropriate play.

The therapeutic relationship might go through several transformations. At first, the contact might be more matter-of-fact, as I helped Michael gain control of his symptoms through behavior therapy. Then, I imagine the relationship would heat up as intrapsychic conflicts about self-image, aggression, and sexuality are explored. I would expect positive transference and transference-based improvement. In the first year, Michael might bring in dreams that would bear on repressed material. Flurries of aggression toward the therapist and others may come out when Michael begins to feel safe in treatment. The primitive nature of these behaviors would be upsetting to Michael, partly because he might fear they would drive the therapist away.

Therapy could be stopped and restarted at various points or supplemented by group or other modalities. But the primary relationship over the years is going to be with a single therapist. Later on, when symptomatic treatment has ended and some of the neurotic conflicts relieved, there will be the more lengthy process of helping Michael cope with normal developmental endeavors, such as establishing an intimate bond, and, if he makes a heterosexual choice, having children. Continuing in therapy could greatly help Michael through the apprehension and ambivalence he might feel about these undertakings.

Michael's therapist should consider whether he or she has the time and is able to commit to working with Michael for several years. Michael would be exquisitely sensitive to the therapist's resistance or to other countertransference feelings about making this commitment. Michael seems to me a highly worthwhile young man; but each of us can have only a few clients like him in our professional lifetimes.

Laura N. Rice (Person-Centered)

I would try, even in the first interview, to begin to establish the Rogerian primary relationship conditions of therapist empathy, unconditional positive regard (which I prefer to call *prizing*), and congruence. I would assume that under the right conditions, he would be able to get in touch with his own crucial inner experience and begin to express it, explore it, and reprocess it.

I would probably not ask many direct questions, especially those involving a change of topic, even in the first interview— except for a few necessary factual questions toward the end. In my experience, a good open-ended reflection can lead to more differentiated information than would a direct question, and such reflection will not sidetrack the person. In other words, the purpose of a good open-ended reflection is to have the client feel really "received" but also to feel free to correct the reflection or to carry it further.

I would respond mainly with empathic reflections. These would not involve the kind of parroting or summarizing that is often attributed to client-centered therapists, but would be a real effort to understand. Unlike many client-centered therapists, I tend to differentiate between two different kinds of reflections (Rice, 1983, 1984). One kind I think of as *empathic prizing* at times when the client seems very vulnerable, and this kind of primary relationship response seems more important than a response intended to stimulate further exploration. At other times, the prizing is in the background, and the open-ended reflections have the quality of differentiation (Rice & Greenberg, in press).

I try to respond to the part of the client's statement that seems most poignant but not yet fully articulated. Without hearing the quality of the voice, it is hard to tell which aspects feel most significant or puzzling to the client, but in the real interview, one can hear them (Rice & Kerr, 1986). For instance, when Michael talks about his horror at his father's hitting his sister Cathy, I would have reflected briefly his terror when his father hit her, but I would have left the focus on Michael's not being able to go to Cathy for days afterwards. I might say, "It was just awful to see him striking Cathy. But then almost the worst part was later—you couldn't even go near her." This was what seemed most vivid and poignant for Michael but was not fully articulated. My hunch is that he would then explore his feeling of isolation from her, leading into some new path—possibly a feeling that he had failed her.

Michael is obviously extremely emotional, expressing anger, fear, and anxiety that are truly felt. But many of his comments and answers to questions have a dramatized, prepackaged quality. He is deliberately expressing his most extreme feelings and images. But I sense that his real, differentiated feelings are much more complex and involve aspects that he has never felt he could share with anyone. For instance, when he said, "It's funny, I still want him to look at me the way he looked at Bobby, the asthmatic kid," it had a "right-now" flavor, with an open-ended, considering quality, that might turn into something very powerful.

Toward the end of the first interview, I would suggest to Michael that we consider future plans. I would express my own doubts that group therapy would be the most profitable for him at this point and would explain these doubts if he seemed to want me to. I would suggest that individual therapy would be more productive, though a group might be considered later. I think it is particularly important in the early stage of therapy, and from time to time afterwards, to have clients feel free to ask questions about what we are doing and about why I am doing or not doing certain things. If he decided to embark on therapy with me, I would get his permission to talk with his physician.

Early in therapy, I would want him to become aware, either implicitly or explicitly, that we were embarking on a journey of exploration and that I would stay right with him, trying to get a real feel of what he was experiencing and exploring. But I would want him to realize that he was the leader of the search, moving into new territory and developing new awareness and understanding. This might not always be easy with Michael. I would guess that at times, he would want me to be the expert, even though, at the same time, he would resent it. But I think an honest discussion at such times not only can straighten out the working relationship but also can be therapeutic in itself.

I would expect that the quality of the primary relationship would be extremely important for Michael. From his discussion of his family, it seems probable that he has never felt truly cared about and respected by anyone. He might have some difficulty in working with a woman therapist, but I would not make any interpretations of transference reactions or focus on his relationship with his mother unless he chose to explore it. Rather than making interpretative connections, I think it would be more powerful to disconfirm his negative expectations through the consistency and genuineness of my respect for him and for his ability to discover his own insights and to set his own goals.

I do not think that all this would be easy; I think that it would require a great deal of energy on my part. But I also have the impression that he is an interesting, creative person, and that I could genuinely trust and respect him.

Points of Contention and Convergence

Alvin R. Mahrer

There were a few points of convergence with Laura Rice. On all other points, I seem to differ with all three of the other respondents.

In accord with Rice, I use the initial session as a more-or-less standard session of psychotherapy. We proceed through the same four steps as in every other session. Accordingly, it is not an intake or evaluation session. There is no interviewing about presenting problems, reason for seeking therapy, or case history. There is no assessment of prognosis, state of defenses, psychopathology, ability to form a therapeutic alliance, treatment plan, psychodiagnosis, or treatment of choice.

The patient lives in and relates to his immediately ongoing personal world. So do I. We both interact and relate to it; we live and exist and feel and experience in this personal world. This is made easier because our eyes are closed. What the patient says and does are in and to this personal world. When the patient talks, it is as if the words were coming in and through me. Even while I show the patient what to do as we proceed through the four steps, I am in the patient's immediate personal world, seeing what he sees, undergoing what he is undergoing, relating to what he is relating. Accordingly, we do not engage in the face-to-face conversation of most other therapies, in which attention is largely on one another. This, in turn, means there is essentially no basis for, nor does the experiential therapist try to establish, any sort of relationship, therapeutic alliance, transference, or person-centered relationship.

In experiential therapy, it is the patient—not the therapist—who is the active change agent, the one who undertakes and undergoes the work of therapeutic change. While the patient is the active therapeutic change agent, I am the one who shows him what to do and how to do it, and I go through the four steps along with him. Accordingly, what I do and say is not an intervention because I do not intervene. I do not administer therapy or do so-called treatment. I do not have private thoughts or make clinical inferences about him. I do not have clever ways of overcoming or disenfranchising or circumventing his so-called resistances to my treatment.

The only important data are Michael's immediate feelings and inner experiencing and the immediate personal world in which he is living and being. That is all. Every time Michael says and does something, I listen for and have the feeling or inner experiencing, and I see and exist in his immediate personal world.

Like Rice, I listen for the feeling. But it is almost certainly not the client-centered feeling. Instead, it is the feeling that occurs in me when Michael's words come in and through me, and as Michael is living and being in his own personal world, I am too. Also, I listen for and see Michael's personal world; once we complete the first step, the key is the accessed inner experiencing and not the feeling.

Experiential is a single-session psychotherapy. Whether Michael has one or one hundred sessions, each session starts with whatever attentional centers associated with feelings are here right now. And we proceed through the four steps that enable as much personality-behavioral change as Michael is ready and willing to undertake in relation to whatever inner experiencing is accessed in the session. Accordingly, no formulation of a treatment plan is supposed to hold in place over an extended series of future sessions. There is no problem that is supposed to be a stable and continuing treatment target over the series of future sessions. We do not anticipate topics to be explored, nor do we have themes that are expected to occur sometime later.

Our target of therapy, our direction of change, and our criterion of successful change all revolve around the inner experiencing that is accessed in this given session. It is in this very session that Michael has the opportunity to taste what he and his life can be and what the world of tomorrow and perhaps from now on can be. He is being and behaving as this new inner experiencing in the personal world that he constructs. Accordingly, therapy is not a process that is supposed to lead later to some outcome following treatment. There is no formulated treatment plan that is to be achieved later as the direction of successful change. There is no goal of trying to reduce so-called symptoms or alleviate problems.

Change occurs by using methods that enable the patient to attain a level of strong feeling, to appreciate the accessed inner experiencing, to be the inner experiencing in the context of earlier scenes, and to be and behave as this inner experiencing in the context of imminent future scenes.

It is here that I converge with the other respondents, because I use many of their methods (techniques, procedures) in one or more of the four steps.

George Stricker

I agree with Mahrer as to the desirability of following the patient's lead and amplifying those areas that are most salient to the patient. I would arrive at some clinical inferences and use these as a guide to my understanding, but I, too, would try not to impose these on the patient.

The relationship described by Mahrer is a highly empathic one, and I agree with the desirability of achieving this. My purpose in seeking to establish such an empathic alliance would be to heal past wounds as well as to have the here-and-now impact that Mahrer describes. However, I do not agree with some of the technical approaches taken by Mahrer. The relationship that he seems to be establishing is not simply empathic; he places demands on the patient for certain kinds of material, and that material is filtered through the therapist's unique set of responses. This use of countertransference (certainly not the theoretical formulation that Mahrer would adopt) requires much more attention to what the therapist is contributing than is described, and it requires a less certain and blanket assumption that it will be helpful to the patient.

There are a number of techniques described by Mahrer that I find problematic with this specific patient:

1. Asking the patient to close his eyes before you know him very well can be counterproductive. With Michael, fearful of authority as he is, and possibly concerned with homosexual attack, I think this approach would be a grave error, and possibly one that could shatter the potential for an alliance.

2. Demanding the expression of frightening feelings, again before trust has been established, may tend to confirm Michael's fear that he will be assaulted.

3. The sadistic fantasies seem correctly perceived as sexualized, but their encouragement might not lead to the response from Michael that is hypothesized. He might amplify them rather than exult in them, and surely he would be terrified by them (or perhaps it is I who would be terrified, but that is why I would like the patient to be the source of the feelings).

I agree with Powell's formulation of the case. I, too, would want the additional information that he would seek, along with a number of other things. However, I would assume that I would learn them all in due course. I do not do a thorough intake interview during the first session, but I ask for amplification of issues as the patient raises them. Occasionally I comment about issues that the patient has not mentioned. Both Powell's behavioral and dynamic interventions are as I would approach them, but I would order them differently. I would not begin with techniques directed toward individual symptoms, but would prefer to develop a more thorough understanding of the patient first. If, in the course of the exploration of general patterns, any symptoms remained troublesome and recalcitrant, I would consider the use of targeted behavioral interventions.

My choosing whether or not to keep Michael focused on the presenting issues, as Powell does, would depend on the time span projected for the treatment. Powell suggests long-term treatment. I agree, and if this were to be undertaken, I would be less concerned with focus than I would be for short-term treatment. Finally, I definitely would begin with individual therapy and would also consider the introduction of group therapy at a later point in treatment.

I agree with Rice's initial emphasis on empathic responding. I also agree with her observation that some of the more understated material may prove to be more important than the more flamboyant fantasies. The purpose of these fantasies may be to test the therapist and his or her capacity to accept, tolerate, and like the patient. I also feel that individual therapy is the better choice for Michael and that the relationship would be crucial regardless of the approach taken by the therapist.

I share Rice's feeling that Michael is appealing and that I could trust and respect him. More to the point, could he trust and respect me? There will be many tests, I will need to pass most of them, and he will have to learn to tolerate those that I fail.

Douglas H. Powell

What is so striking to me from reading the discussion by Mahrer, Stricker, and Rice is how many ways there are to conceptualize a complex case such as this and how many ways there are to do right by Michael. In my view, significant benefit would accrue to him from working with any of these individuals. Each brings to the treatment process ingredients associated with positive outcomes: compassion and respect for the client; an inclination to commitment, support, and empathy; a disinclination to go for the quick fix; the value of sharing poorly understood, conflicting, and inchoate feelings; and nurturing the hope in such an alliance.

As for points of convergence with my fellow panelists, I agree with the presumption that Michael's symptoms are related to his inadequate understanding of his inner experience. In spite of his psychological sophistication, intelligence, and previous therapy, he remains a mystery to himself. As Rice points out, his insights have a prepackaged quality. Stricker notes his avoidance defensive mechanisms, which leave him in a constant state of anxiety. Mahrer assumes from the beginning that Michael's initial thoughts and affects will give way to other feelings and to so-called inner experiencing closer to the center of Michael's conflicts.

We also are in agreement on three other major points. The first is the pivotal role of Michael's conflicts about aggressive instincts, which should be a central focus of treatment. The second is the agreement that group therapy is not indicated in the early going, or perhaps ever. Third, we concur that it is crucial for Michael to achieve a clear understanding of his experiential life, his past conflicts, the reality distortions arising out of defenses against anxiety, and his tendency to engage in self-handicapping endeavors. The growth of his capacity for self-understanding will be a necessary condition for maintaining the improvement that should occur in any of the therapies.

I now turn to areas of contention. Nearly seven years have passed since the Society for the Exploration of Psychotherapy Integration (SEPI) was founded, marking the "official" beginning of the integrative therapy movement. I am struck by how little impact this thinking apparently has had on my three prominent and skilled colleagues, whom I both respect and like personally. Reading their accounts of how they would imagine helping Michael, I have the impression that they would plan to follow a single theoretical perspective—experiential, psychodynamic, or Rogerian—unadulterated by the addition of other ways of conceptualizing the problem or other avenues of intervention. I found myself reminded of the *Four Psychotherapies* (Hersher, 1970) in which leading practitioners of two decades ago described how they would treat the same patient. It distresses me to think that so little has changed in twenty years.

A major point of divergence from my colleagues in the proposed treatment of Michael would be my conviction that multiple forms of therapy would yield more positive and enduring results than would a unitary approach. Moreover, there may be potentiating value in particular pairings or sequences of interventions (Millon, 1988; Powell, 1988). My choice of focusing on the cold hands and the breathing problems is an example and is at odds with the other clinicians. My experience, however, has been that this approach provides at least four benefits: (1) possible symptom reduction, (2) a greater sense of agency, (3) alleviating the distress of symptoms so that their function might be explored, and (4) the possibility of spontaneous insights into the nature of repressed conflicts surrounding the symptoms. Any of these effects could lead naturally into psychodynamic exploration of the origins of the difficulties.

Another major point of divergence is the likelihood of my being more directive in terms of suggesting things Michael could do outside the therapy to enhance his development. These might include encouraging him to develop his playful side or join a growth group. The dangers in this directiveness need to be appreciated, especially in terms of his conflicts with authority and passive-aggressive style. Should these conflicts emerge, they could be explored by insight-oriented therapy.

Laura N. Rice

I fully agree with Mahrer that the useful material would emerge if one encouraged and really heard Michael's own experiencing. The basic difference between us is in the working relationship. I would want to establish and maintain a relationship in which I was not the instructor and in which I would never totally merge myself with and speak from Michael's emotions. I would try to respond with evocative and truly empathic reflections, but I would consider it very important to maintain my own identity and the quality of the real relationship throughout.

Regarding George Stricker, I think I would feel very comfortable with many aspects of his approach, such as the importance of building a safe and trusting relationship. Clearly, the quality of this relationship is central for him. For instance, he states that he would not try to encourage Michael to express his anger; but when it is expressed, Michael's recognition that Stricker is not put off or disturbed by the anger would be curative in itself.

On the other hand, I would not want to follow Stricker's emphasis on forming and testing a series of hypotheses. Clearly, with a background knowledge concerning personality and psychopathology, one could not help having some ideas about the effects of Michael's developmental background and the conflicts with which he is struggling. I would not focus my energy and attention on these ideas, however. I would try to hear Michael as freshly as possible and to be aware of the feelings and other inner experiences that are salient for him at the moment. I would try, by means of empathic, open-ended reflections, to facilitate his expression and exploration of these inner experiences. I have often found that my expectations and assumptions may be in the right general area but that the actual feelings and perceptions that can emerge in a really good exploration are idiosyncratic and have a unique flavor. If I can really hear and respond to this special quality, it will turn out to be the most important part of the therapy. My assumption is that if Michael can make his own discoveries, and if I can hear and respect them, he will become more and more able to use his own organismic experience as a guide to satisfying relationships and functioning in the world.

I share some of Powell's enthusiasm for an integrated therapy, but I feel strongly that the combination of approaches used must be internally consistent with one another, and especially with the nature of the basic therapeutic relationship. This consistency is one of the challenges for psychotherapy integration.

I would probably not use behavioral techniques early in therapy because my primary goal would be to establish a process of experiential search in which Michael was the leader of the search. At some point, however, I might suggest a behavioral self-help strategy as something that he might find useful. If he seemed interested, I would help him to design such a program, but I would not push it.

I would not try to have Michael recognize the so-called "historical origins" of his anger, although they might emerge spontaneously. I would see it as more important that he make his own discovery of the unique quality of his own anger. It was interesting that Powell said he would listen for Michael's "spontaneous recognition" of relationships between intense feelings and the physical symptoms. Here again the issue in combining approaches seems to me to be whether one can contribute therapist-generated causal connections without losing the impact of the discoveries emerging from experiential search.

4

The Wallflower

◻

Arnold A. Lazarus
John D. Davis
Paul L. Wachtel

Case Presentation

"Know what my father said to me at breakfast this morning?"
Ellen begins. Her face is broad, she is moderately tall, and she
carries her excess weight well. Her large brown eyes are moist.
She sounds as though she is about to cry. "I was looking
through the fashion section of the *Times,* and he asked me
what would be in fashion next spring for wallflowers."

"Oh," I say. "What did you say to that?"

"I can never think of anything to say back. Later, I
thought, 'Same as last year.' "

In psychology class, the students who look over Ellen's
shoulder as she sketches are visibly impressed. Ellen previously asked me if I minded her sketching in class. She says
she cannot stand sitting for an hour without sketching, and
she has always been too nervous to take notes. However,
she jots down topics and references in the margins of her
drawings.

Ellen has painfully low self-esteem. She lives at home but
would like to find a husband nearly as much as her parents
want her to. According to Ellen, her major symptom is binge

eating. She can eat a whole chocolate cake in minutes, even if, especially if, the last five forkfuls taste revolting. Ellen admits she eats past enjoying it, wallowing in the knowledge that she is hurting herself with every mouthful.

"How would you feel about being at your most attractive weight?" I ask. [She knows what it is to the pound.]

"I've been there a couple of times," Ellen says. "I had a sexy bod. I attracted single men with a lot to offer. Nothing ever worked out. I couldn't go through it all again."

"How did you feel when you went out with men who had something to offer you?" I ask.

"I was nervous a lot of the time. I don't know why. Just being involved with someone who was . . . sure of himself made me jittery."

"And you would feel that way today if you met someone who was available, had something to offer, and was sure of himself?"

"Mr. Right," Ellen says, "yes, I would be nervous. I have this feeling; I don't deserve a good man all to myself."

"Tell me about your mother," I say. I have spoken to Ellen's mother on the phone. Her voice was concerned, but sugary and manipulative. She described her daughter as "a confused young person."

"What's there to say?" Ellen asks, but her eyes react.

"What did you think of just now?"

"Nothing. Oh, all right. I thought, 'Mother—that's where I'm heading.' "

"That's depressing, isn't it?"

"Only I had an even more depressing thought: 'There I go alone.' "

"You're thirty, right? I understand you feel that way, but you're too young to decide that. You're basically an attractive woman."

"But overweight and with no personality," Ellen says. "One reason I feel so down is that everyone puts everything in terms of looks, even you. You sound like my mother, always saying, 'Keep going, you're pretty, you'll get someone!' "

"Let's go back to your mother, Ellen," I say. "What's it like living with her?"

"She's supportive so far as she understands what I'm doing, pained a lot, anxious all the time. She makes guilt a way of life. She thinks it's all right to get you to do what she wants by making you feel guilty. You can't imagine how bad it gets."

"Then, may I ask, why are you living at home?"

"Everyone asks. Why not you? I gave up my apartment and moved in with my boyfriend. Once he got his law degree, he didn't want me around anymore. Since then, I've lived at home and specialized in married men. I can't take the bar scene, one-night stands and all. I know my pattern of seeing married men is hopeless, but at least I can tell myself someone wants me. I've had four lovers in three years, all married. Also, I was seeing a psychiatrist who said I was suicidal and shouldn't live alone."

"Did you attempt suicide?" I ask.

"No," she says, "just that I think about it."

"Are you taking antidepressants? Did the psychiatrist . . ."

"Yes, he gave me something that worked for a while. I felt OK, like everything was the same, but it was just the way it was. Then, the pills didn't work so well, and I started feeling crummy. He increased the dosage, but there were awful side effects. My mouth completely dried out. I stopped taking the pills, and I actually felt better. I don't want to go back to him because nothing changed for me. I'm just as overweight as when I went to him, and I'm two years older."

"When did your thoughts of suicide begin?" I ask. "When the law student dumped you? Or have you had them all along?"

"After him," Ellen says. "The lowest I got was a couple of months later, over a complete stranger. I was in the Modern looking at Rousseau's *Sleeping Gypsy*. A couple walked by, and the man said something, actually wise-guy humor—what the lion is saying to the gypsy, as though the painting is a big cartoon—and they kept walking. I thought, 'Why can't I ever say things like that?' Then, two minutes later, a great-looking man came by, about six foot three, and the best thing is, paint on his jeans. He was a painter, too. He stood next to me for a while, looking at the Rousseau. Then I came out with the quip."

"The one you had just heard."

"Yes. I wanted for once in my life to be spontaneous and witty. Well, he glared at me for two seconds and moved on. I drifted around the museum for an hour feeling sicker and sicker. I was hoping I would run into him so I could say, 'That wasn't me.' Then I went back to my apartment and stayed there. I called in sick to the private school where I was teaching art. I felt horrible, as though the children would pick up something contagious from me. I spent a couple of days and nights in the same clothes. All the dishes were dirty and I ate standing up in front of the refrigerator until all the food was gone. That's where my mother found me."

She continues, "I remember now, the worst part was feeling I had done myself in with that remark. People were always putting me down, but I could fight back. But I couldn't fight back this time because I did it to myself."

"How did you fight back when people put you down, Ellen?"

"I would say to myself they were ignoramuses, they weren't able to appreciate me, and so on."

"I'm not sure you ever fought back, Ellen," I say. "You took refuge in your own mind, in your feelings and attitudes about art. Then, when you embarrassed yourself, there was nowhere to hide. Did you ever consider there might be something in you worth fighting for entirely apart from your art, or even your knowing the difference between a fresco and a pizza?"

"I don't believe that," she says.

Ellen was an only child. Her mother encouraged her in her schoolwork and art. She recalls her father adoring her as a child, but "he was fussy and inhibited, always worried about me seeing him undressed or something." She felt her mother stood between them and didn't like her father to be too affectionate to her. Her mother was dominant in the home. Ellen remembers neither her mother hugging her nor wanting her mother to hug her.

Ellen's father withdrew into his paperwork and his newspapers. Ellen says that her mother made her father "beg for sex like a dog," but she doesn't recall any actual exchange that this impression might have been based on and admits it is unlikely they would have negotiated sex in front of her. It occurs to her that she may have derived the notion from her father's sarcastic morning-after remarks to her mother.

In recent years, Ellen has been hurt by her girlfriends, who, she says, dropped her when they got married. She has no close friends now, and perhaps as a consequence, she confides in her mother. Ellen seems much too involved with her mother, even as she rejects her ways and values.

She has not asked for her job back, since she never earned enough teaching art to support herself. She says she is "marking time," taking one course at a time toward her B.A. Her academic record is marred by many courses that she dropped or failed to complete. Ellen states that she does not want to work as a secretary or commercial artist; it is likely she thinks she would fail in an office environment. She does not want to go on living at her parents' home, but she has not been able to formulate a plan for entering the working world.

Formulations and Treatments

Arnold A. Lazarus (Multimodal-Eclectic)

The details supplied about the initial interview with Ellen give rise to the following modality profile:

> *Behavior:* Binge eating; unassertive; not working gainfully; poor study habits; tends to withdraw and isolate herself; defensive
>
> *Affect:* Anxious (especially in company of eligible males); fears rejection and criticism; guilt; depression; underlying anger; periodic feelings of hopelessness

Sensation: Restless; nervous; jittery

Imagery: Poor self-image; picturing herself alone

Cognition: Suicidal ideation; "I don't deserve a good man all to myself"; "There's no point in losing weight"; self-put-down ("I have no personality."); categorical thinking; buys into cultural nonfeminist roles

Interpersonal Relationships: No close friends; lives with parents; eager to find a husband; poor social skills; seeing only married men; problematic parent-child relationships; especially nervous around competent men

Drugs/Biology: Overweight; received antidepressants ("worked for a while")

Here are my answers to the questions posed to me. What else would I need to know about Ellen, and how would I find out? In treating adult outpatients, I use the Multimodal Life History Questionnaire (LHQ) (Lazarus, 1989b) extensively (obtainable from Research Press, Box 3177, Champaign, IL 61821). I would ask Ellen to fill out this twelve-page printed booklet and to mail it before, or bring it to, her second session. (For present purposes, let us bypass discussing those clients who "forget" or refuse to complete the LHQ.) The questionnaire would supply many details pertaining to her background and development—details that had not emerged during the initial interview. Since the LHQ also focuses on excesses and deficits in behavior, affect, sensation, imagery, cognition, interpersonal relationships, and drugs/biology (BASIC ID), items could readily be added to the preliminary modality profile to ensure a more comprehensive treatment trajectory. Ellen's specific treatment objectives and expectations would also be tapped by the questionnaire.

During the second interview, in addition to deepening our rapport and establishing a working alliance, I would dwell mainly on her sensory, image-forming, and cognitive modalities, since these three areas elicited the least amount of information during the initial interview. Inquiries into her sensual pleasures and pains; her main images, fantasies, dreams, and wishes; and her basic values, attitudes, and beliefs would enable me to comprehend more of Ellen's psychic and interpersonal functioning. All this information would round out the modality profile into a more complete blueprint for therapy meeting her specific requirements (see Lazarus, 1986a, 1986b, 1989a, 1989b).

Some questions that need to be answered early in the therapy are the following: What keeps her tied to her parents? What is she asking for? Do we have a fairly healthy person who is depressed? Does Ellen have a character problem? What gives her pleasure? What is the full extent of Ellen's drug and alcohol use?

With respect to the therapeutic relationship I would try for, I would ask Ellen whether she would be more at ease with a woman therapist. I would also consider (1) the value of a female therapist as a role model for her and (2) the relative advantages for Ellen in forming a healthy same-sex or opposite-sex relationship with a female or male therapist.

In keeping with the model proposed by Howard, Nance, and Myers (1986) on adaptive counseling and therapy, multimodal therapists endeavor to match the relationship style to the client's needs and expectancies. In essence, one tries to determine when the client is likely to respond best to a supportive relationship instead of one that is more directive and to determine when teaching and instructing rather than listening and interpreting are called for. The application of the wrong treatment plan and therapist style often results in premature, unsuccessful termination of therapy.

My clinical experience indicates that people who lack assertiveness and social skills usually derive the most benefit from a therapeutic style that offers high direction/high support. In this relationship style, treatment decisions are made in tandem with input and suggestions from the client, but the therapist makes the final decision. I would offer Ellen a good deal of encouragement and support.

When disputing Ellen's dysfunctional beliefs, however, the desired relationship style would probably be one of high direction/low support. In this situation, she would learn that people largely create their own emotional problems by the ways they interpret their environments. Ellen's excessive approval seeking, misplaced attributions, and catastrophic non sequiturs would be underscored. As is common—depending on the client's needs and progress—I might move from a position of considerable control to one of little control.

Turning to therapeutic interventions with which I would proceed, for clients with clear-cut problems of lack of entitlement ("I don't deserve a good man all to myself") and poor self-esteem, I usually target these areas for initial attention and administer the rational disputations of Albert Ellis (1989). Would we simultaneously address the binge-eating and excess weight problems and the particular steps Ellen might take to move out of her parent's home? Or would we examine her male-female relationships and treat her general lack of social skills? Howard et al. (1986, p. 414) stress the importance of task readiness: "What is the client's level of readiness with respect to the tasks that it is necessary for him or her to perform?" Perhaps Ellen's general anxieties, nervousness, and restlessness might take precedence and call for methods of deep muscle relaxation, meditation, restful imagery, and biofeedback as the initial treatments. The need for flexibility and a broad range of therapeutic skills and techniques cannot be overstated; it is the essence of the multimodal orientation.

Treatment for Ellen's problems in separation and individuation would include asking her to practice images several times a day—vivid images of informing her parents of her wish to move into her own abode, of countering their (presumed) objections, and of coping with the day-to-day activities in her new home. I would use role-playing to bolster her confidence.

While working on Ellen's poor self-esteem and deficient sense of entitlement, I would present the options of also addressing other problems. Clues from the first two or three sessions and the LHQ would alert me to contraindications—for example, that weight loss and the attenuation of binge eating might not ensue before Ellen developed more self-confidence.

By joining a self-help group in addition to her individual therapy, Ellen might be able to make up for some of the deficiencies of her social network, thus rendering herself less vulnerable.

I would be wary of Ellen's unexpressed anger. In the initial interview, when the therapist made supportive statements or offered encouragement, Ellen tended to become more negative and to attack: "Everyone puts everything in terms of looks, even you. You sound like my mother." The therapist as cheerleader—"Come on, you're attractive!"—would seem contraindicated in this case. I would be wary that Ellen's tendency to criticize herself could readily be transferred to the therapist, especially if she became afraid that she was not a "good enough patient" and that she might be rejected. Many clients derive benefit from learning to acknowledge and express their anger before acquiring more adaptive benefits of assertive (nonaggressive) responses.

John D. Davis (Integrative)

I should like to share my thoughts as they unfolded in reading the account of Ellen's initial consultation.

The beginning generally offers clues about the heart of the patient's distress. The psychotherapist who conducted the initial consultation notices Ellen's hurt at her father's comment implying that he wants her off his hands and that she is a failure and a disappointment to him. The therapist seeks information about her behavior—"What did you say to that?" I do not see this as the way to begin building a therapeutic alliance nor to approach what for me is a central therapeutic objective: enabling the client to open herself increasingly to her own affective experience. I might have commented that I had the feeling she could easily cry at the hurt she felt thinking of his remarks.

The helplessness in Ellen's reply suggests that she cannot accept the anger that must go with the hurt, a sure predictor that she will join in the attack on herself. We can anticipate her "painfully low self-esteem" and self-destructive behavior;

in due course, we hear of the self-punitive aspects of her binge eating and of her suicidal thoughts.

Meanwhile we learn of her artistic talents, but also of her anxious agitation in class. It is not clear what this is about, and the psychotherapist seems not to have pursued it. Coincidentally, it is implied that she is the therapist's student as well as client, a dual role that I would find unsatisfactory as therapist.

Ellen is living at home and shares her parents' wish that she get married. Although I do not yet know her age, I am alerted to what may be a failure to separate and individuate. I begin to wonder if she is developmentally ready for marriage and whether the wish for marriage may represent both an internalization of her parents' demands and a desire to "pass" as a normal, mature adult doing the conventional thing. I also begin to question from a systemic viewpoint whether her parents may subtly undermine her efforts to separate—as in her father's "old maid" comment.

Learning of the binge eating, I am reminded of a bulimic client who binges whenever her suppressed rage begins to rise; the food seems to force the rage back down. I would be interested in the affective contexts in which her binges occur, but the therapist follows a different line of thought—that she is avoiding looking attractive. This proves productive in that we learn that her relationships with eligible men have never worked out. I should have liked to know more about these failed relationships, but the therapist goes off on another tack. I am becoming increasingly irritated at the way the therapist moves from where the client is instead of staying with her. He or she totally ignores the client's statement that she could not risk trying such relationships again. Nonetheless, the questions elicit interesting material. Ellen is not deserving of a good man "all to herself." The overtones of female rivalry alert me to oedipal issues in the nuclear triad. The psychotherapist's directive to talk about mother seems to be an intuitive response to this implication, although I find its dictatorial flavor uncongenial. I wonder why the therapist has spoken to mother on the phone, and issues of confidentiality and ethics come to mind. At the same time, I am concerned at the affective tone of the therapist's description; it will not aid the client to separate and individuate if the therapist carries her anger for her. Mother's description of her daughter ("a confused young person") supports my hunch that both parents may be undermining Ellen's efforts to move away.

I like the psychotherapist's attempt to pick up on Ellen's here-and-now experience and the disjunction between her words and looks, though I might simply have shared my experience of her ("Your eyes seem to be telling me there is something to say"). I would like to know of the aspects of mother that she sees in herself, which depress her.

I now learn that Ellen is thirty. I had imagined her to be younger (a college kid), and I immediately see her problems as more severe and intractable. The therapist attempts to tell her she is not on the shelf. I feel this to be a mistake, both because it comes too close to the parental injunction to get married and because it suggests that the therapist cannot tolerate her despairing loneliness. Ellen confronts the therapist on donning her mother's mantle, and my prognostic meter immediately rises again; there is a real strength in the confrontation. The risk taken in sharing unvoiced thoughts about mother also betokens a strength in her. She may be sensing here a duplicity like her mother's in the therapist's comment: what does "basically" attractive mean? Is Ellen attractive or not? I wonder whether the therapist is a man or a woman.

I find the therapist's avoidance of the confrontation very worrying. There is no acknowledgment of Ellen's achievement in this direct act of assertion, and worse, the avoidance may suggest to her that such behavior is unwelcome to the therapist. As it is, we get a graphic account of Ellen's ambivalent experience of mother. Ellen, on the one hand, attributes supportive intentions to her, but, on the other hand, seems to experience herself guiltily as the cause of mother's pain and anxiety. Ellen is healthy enough to see mother as persecuting her with her martyrdom, but this does not stop the guilt.

Now the prognosis improves again. We learn that Ellen had lived away from home and that following her failed relationship with her boyfriend, she has played safe by having affairs with married men. The question of why she returned home is not answered. Could she really have been complying with her psychiatrist's recommendation? Why did she not then or later move in with a girlfriend? My hunch here would be that having taken her courage in both hands by moving out, she has run for cover after her bad experience in the big, wide world. I would like to know more about the transactions with mother and father during her period away from home with a view to assessing the systemic forces drawing her back into the fold.

The word *suicide* sounds a red alert for the therapist, who suddenly becomes preoccupied with assessing suicidal risk. However, the inquiry uncovers Ellen's self-disgust and self-hatred in more depth, along with the self-punitive quality of her eating binges. The part of herself she wants to destroy is the clinging Ellen who prostitutes herself and sacrifices the chance to be a separate, autonomous person. Missing the point of her comment that the crisis came when she could no longer avoid confronting this aspect of herself, the therapist suggests a more positive construction. This at least implies the therapist's belief in her, but Ellen simply rejects it as unfounded, again showing her strength. It might have been helpful to point to her confronting the therapist as evidence of her separate autonomous self.

There is no further information about the interview, just additional content. The oedipal theme is supported through Ellen's sense of her cold, powerful mother having kept her at a distance from father, whose adoration was tinged with sexual overtones. It seems that Ellen's sense of unworthiness may have its roots in her role of hated rival, which is reenacted as her girlfriends keep her away from the men they marry and as she engages in a succession of affairs with married men. I would imagine that she feels responsible for the marital friction between her parents and deserving of her rejections by women. I would also guess that she is denying a powerful wish for her mother's love and affection. The therapist's hunch that Ellen's binge eating is designed to make her sexually unattractive takes on greater meaning now: that effect may be understood as a way of avoiding appearing to be a sexual rival, thereby opening an avenue to maternal love and female friendship.

The final information on Ellen's "marking time" conveys her ambivalence about separating. She expresses a wish to move away, but her actions do not seem consistent with that goal. I come back at this point to wanting to understand the consequences for the family system if Ellen takes her leave.

With problems of separation-individuation, and there are several indications that we are dealing with such a problem here, I attach great importance to alliance with the growth-seeking part of the client. This alliance means acting to validate the client's autonomy and contraindicates any directiveness in my interventions. I would not impose expectations of what Ellen should achieve, nor would I pressure her toward goals; paradoxically, it is by challenging her assumptions that she has to lose weight, has to leave home, has to marry, and has to formulate a career plan that she will become freer to establish these or other goals for herself.

By providing a safe environment in which Ellen can explore herself, I would enable her to get in touch with aspects of her experience that she cannot currently acknowledge and that give rise to her symptomatic behaviors. (I would not be optimistic about a direct behavioral approach to her binge eating, except as an alternative route to the feelings the binges serve to avoid.) My approach would be basically client centered, and my ability to accept these unacknowledged aspects would play a critical role in enhancing her self-acceptance, sense of identity, and autonomy.

At the same time, I would be quite prepared to accelerate the process by holding doors open and inviting her to step through if she wishes. In this role, drawing on my understanding of what is involved in the issues Ellen avoids, I might at times be more interpretative, and I might make use of techniques borrowed from Gestalt and other therapies to facilitate the experiencing and expression of emergent feelings. I would anticipate the oedipal theme and her warded-off anger, hate, and denied wish for her mother's love coming into focus for her. I would hope that in this process, Ellen would grasp the systemic meanings of her ongoing transactions outside the family. Often, the initial pain and anxiety of separation is made bearable by the sense that becoming independent of the parents will please the therapist and cement the therapeutic attachment—in my experience, an appropriate step on the way to autonomy.

One of my main concerns in this approach to intervention is the effect on the family system. I have a strong preference for working with the enmeshed client individually—to symbolize the client's separateness and autonomy. (Very often, too, the client is simply unwilling for the family to be involved.) In rigid systems, however, it is possible for each therapeutic movement to produce a matching countermovement within the system. The client is then stymied in a tug-of-war between therapist and family. Were such a situation to develop in my work with Ellen, I should be inclined to explore the possibility of meeting with the family. In family sessions, I would seek to give a positive connotation, in terms of the family dynamic, to what the family (including Ellen) views negatively as symptoms or life failures—for example, by reconstruing her behavior as self-sacrificing efforts to protect her parents from what she sees as their inability to function harmoniously without her. Such intervention might help to free her individual work by removing her from the hot seat of "identified patient" in the family and shifting the family's attention to her parents' difficulties. A useful outcome of such intervention might be a referral of the parents for couple therapy.

Paul L. Wachtel (Cyclical Psychodynamics-Integrative)

Ellen appears to be a woman for whom conflict over anger is a central feature of the difficulties. Notwithstanding the cogent critiques regarding the general formulation that depression is anger turned against the self, in this particular case, such a view seems to make a good deal of sense. Ellen's behavior and attitude toward herself is such that one would have no difficulty describing it as hostile were it directed toward anyone else. Indeed, she can be downright sadistic toward herself, as when she wallows in the knowledge that she is hurting herself with every mouthful of the cake, and revels even more as the bites become more revolting to her. This brief description has enough self-loathing to satisfy the most discerning moral masochist.

There is also ample indication of anger toward others and of difficulty in knowing how to handle that anger or in accepting it without feeling considerable guilt. Ellen's experiential world is populated almost exclusively with people who let her down or hurt or disappoint her. Her view of others is terribly jaundiced, either explicitly (as in her tendency to view other people as "ignoramuses") or implicitly (as in her view of the men who use and mistreat her, of her psychiatrist, and of her girlfriends). She is capable to some degree of telling herself angry things about others. (That's how she fights back, though the wounds are always more apparent on her than on the other guy.) But she seems to have great difficulty expressing anger to others in a way that is even moderately effective or assertive. "I can never think of anything to say back," she says.

Putting the two sides of her conflict over anger together, we see a picture of a woman who is caught in a painful vicious circle of neurosis. Her way of life is extremely frustrating, self-depriving, and unsatisfying. Yet she feels she does not deserve anything better. The anger she feels toward others makes her feel guilty, bad, and disgusting. As her anger builds, she is frightened by it and therefore inhibited in expressing it. Instead, she is speechless and frozen and feels that she has "no personality." It is likely that her disparaging, basically hostile view of others is also a prime cause of her feeling undeserving; and since she is undeserving, she dare not assert herself, either to defend against attacks or to get her fair share.

Her penitence, however, is to no avail; its effect, ironically, is to keep her in the very state for which she is atoning. Her self-depriving, self-abnegating way of life means that she is frequently frustrated and is likely to lead others to ignore her needs. This, at some level of awareness, would tend to stimulate further feelings that other people are no good and that she is no good for feeling that way. Then, in turn, she will atone once more by being self-depriving and self-punitive, starting the same cycle one more time.

Therapy must center on helping Ellen to extricate herself from this vicious circle. A focus of my work with her would be helping her to see the dilemma in which she is caught and to find ways out of it. So long as she feels (albeit mostly unconsciously) that she is hiding how bad and angry she is, she is likely to feel that another person's compassionate or encouraging attitude toward her is based on the other not knowing the terrible truth. Thus, it seems to me important to communicate my understanding of just how angry she is (indeed, that she is considerably angrier than she herself consciously realizes). But it is also important to communicate this not in the manner of all too many psychoanalytic interpretations—with a tone of so-called unmasking and of forcing the patient to face "bad" things about herself (see Wachtel, 1987)—but rather with a sense of shared exploration: "Let's look at this together and understand what you're really feeling and where those feelings come from." In this vein, examining the vicious circle would be very useful, for it would enable Ellen to understand just how angry she is without having to be so self-blaming about it. She could see how her anger is an understandable response to the frustrations of her life and how it is ironically fueled by the efforts she makes to keep her "badness" in check.

Deriving from this circular conception of Ellen's difficulties, the therapeutic strategy would point beyond mere understanding of the bind she is in and of the feelings she has been unable to accept; it would point toward things she can do about her situation (cf. Wachtel, 1977; Wachtel & Wachtel, 1986). Assertiveness training seems a likely important feature of the therapeutic work. As in all applications of assertiveness training, it would be critical to assess just which situations Ellen is capable of handling effectively at any point and to help her choose where she will begin to expand the range of her options—in particular, to focus with her on where she felt justified in being more assertive and on how she can do so strongly and effectively, without inadvertently expressing her "bad self" image.

Finding situations in which the other person would also benefit from Ellen's being more direct and less self-abnegating would be especially useful. People like Ellen see life as a zero-sum game and fear that for them to get more, others must get less. Although this is certainly true in some instances, it is not nearly so prevalent as it may seem through the lens of her guilt and resentment.

I would expect that in the course of the work, some attention would have to be addressed to what psychoanalysts call *oedipal* issues. Ellen's description of her father as always worried about her seeing him undressed suggests that there was more than the usual amount of seductiveness to their interaction. Oedipal concerns are suggested as well by Ellen's thoughts regarding her parents' attitudes toward sex with each other—thoughts for which the basis is unclear even to her. Ellen's feelings that mother did not like her father's affection toward her (Ellen) and that her mother tried to get between them is also consistent with this theme. It is likely that Ellen's difficulties with men are at least partly related to conflicts in this realm. She is aware that a major determinant of her binge eating may be the avoidance of being too sexy and all that might mean.

Karen Horney's (1945) description of the "Moving Toward" orientation to life seems to me to fit the given material. Ellen seeks security by presenting herself as helpless and in need of others' attention. But because her efforts to attain security are exaggerated and driven by anxiety rather than expressions of a natural and spontaneous wish for a mutually caring relationship, they never lead to real satisfaction; and they are constantly threatened by the evocation of feelings and inclinations incompatible with her brittle defensive stance. Unlike Horney and many of her followers, however, I am skeptical that insight alone is likely to be enough in most cases like this. For that reason, I see the job of Ellen's therapist not only as fostering a better understanding of her feelings and of the dilemma in which she finds herself, but also as actively aiding the patient in taking on new patterns of interaction with others—interaction that can initiate a benign circle of change in the place of the destructive cycle in which she is now trapped. Further details of how I would work with Ellen are difficult to provide without the experience of interacting with her and her interpersonal force field. However, I would expect that at least in general outline, my approach would be consistent with what I have depicted here.

Points of Contention and Convergence*

Arnold A. Lazarus

Davis asserts that the therapist erred by inquiring how the client had responded to her father's critical remark vis-à-vis her marital status and that it would have been better had he or she commented that Ellen could easily cry at the perceived hurt. This is debatable. By focusing on the subjective pain rather than on overt action, one may reinforce an introspective penchant to wallow in unproductive feelings rather than to deal with them. I won't argue strongly for this position, but I do feel that it merits some consideration.

I would not share Davis's discomfort about playing a dual role as Ellen's teacher and therapist. A major drawback is that therapists typically see their clients within the confines of their offices and seldom gain firsthand information about their behaviors in other settings. It depends on the patient, of course, but I have frequently found it clinically expedient to play dual roles in my clients' lives. On occasion, I have

*Paul Wachtel was unable to contribute to this section due to pressing time commitments.

obtained cogent information on a tennis court, or at a dinner party, that would probably never have come to light in my consulting room.

I do not follow why the father's "wallflower" comment "may subtly undermine her efforts to separate." It did not strike me as a sabotaging maneuver, and I am curious to know what Davis read into it. Similarly, the mother's description of Ellen as "a confused young person" seems to be succinct and accurate rather than further evidence "that both parents may be undermining Ellen's efforts to move away." I also saw insufficient data to justify the "oedipal theme" or the notion that Ellen's greater physical attractiveness would undermine her mother's love, which seems wildly speculative to me.

I do not feel that directiveness is an all-or-none entity. To avoid all directiveness, as Davis proposes, would fail to offer Ellen the very guidance and encouragement that she seems to require in certain areas. As I stated in my own treatment outline, the important consideration is not whether to be directive or nondirective, but when to occupy one stance or the other.

It seemed to me that the therapist who interviewed Ellen was trying to obtain a general overview of her main problems. Had he or she not irritated Davis by following several leads and taking several different tacks, we would have gleaned far too little overall information to warrant a clinical exchange. Even so, it is rather fatuous to speculate how one would employ the scanty information provided to go about treating a person whom we have never met. Nevertheless, one can but hope that the reader will derive some stimulating and possibly some helpful notions from these expositions and interchanges.

The other contributor, Wachtel, makes a compelling case for viewing anger as the central feature of Ellen's difficulties. He argues that her other affective states, such as depression, fear, guilt, and anxiety, are derived from, or are secondary to, her major conflicts about feeling and expressing her anger. I remain skeptical about unifying themes in people's lives, especially when they hang together very neatly and allow us to make cogent arguments that bolster our positions. Clinically, whenever I unearth a so-called basic dynamic or discover some particular element or theme that seems to tie almost everything together, I invariably discover so many exceptions and contradictions over time that I have long ago abandoned the search for a master key, and I look instead for many different keys that fit specific locks (hence, my multimodal outlook). I feel that one could argue equally well that Ellen's problems emanate from an underlying anxiety, a pervasive sense of underentitlement, or various other "central features."

Whereas Davis and I both called for extensive additional information (albeit different types of information to be used for different purposes) before confidently proceeding along a particular clinical path, Wachtel zeroed in on the client's basic anger and formulated an entire treatment regimen based on this single diagnosis (hypothesis).

I gathered from the initial description of Ellen's case that her father was a rather inhibited individual, reluctant to be seen by her in a state of undress. On what pragmatic grounds does Wachtel assume that the father's reticence "suggests that there was more than the usual amount of seductiveness to their interaction"? It seems to be a catch-22. Had Ellen complained that her father sat around in his underwear, analysts would undoubtedly conclude that seductive overtones were present. If the father vigilantly avoids such behaviors, the same criticism applies.

Although Wachtel's final treatment trajectory overlaps in several respects with my own, I sense that he would not directly address certain cognitive, imagery, and sensory elements that I would consider essential for a comprehensive and durable treatment outcome.

John D. Davis

In considering the views put forward by my fellow commentators, I am going to say much more about Lazarus than about Wachtel. This is because I am comfortable with Wachtel's views and therapeutic plans, which occupy familiar territory for me, whereas with Lazarus, I am traveling in a foreign land and struggle with the strangeness of the culture.

I sense a basic difference between Lazarus's approach and my own, which is probably conceptual, ideological, and personal and has little to do with Ellen. For me, psychotherapy is at root an encounter between two people in a helping relationship. For Lazarus, I suspect, psychotherapy is at root a technical enterprise. My experience in reading his account is one of Ellen disappearing, partitioned into segments by the BASIC ID, viewed as a useful source of information for the planning of operations, and having the impaired segments repaired with careful surgery. Nowhere do I have a sense of Ellen, the person, of how her segments fit together, or of what sort of functioning whole they constitute. Where Lazarus touches on the issue of his possible involvement in a relationship with her, it is to tell us of his wariness of her unexpressed anger, especially that her self-critical tendencies could "readily be transferred to [criticize] the therapist." In line with the technical enterprise, it is Lazarus, not Ellen, who decides what to dwell on in the second interview, though to me, it seems he can scarcely know her; the purpose is to enable him, not Ellen, to comprehend. He tells us that following this initial prescriptive approach, he will decide on the basis of Ellen's needs whether to teach and instruct or to listen and interpret; yet, we know from the Sheffield Psychotherapy Project (Shapiro & Firth, 1987) that whereas clients found an exploratory-prescriptive therapy sequence quite comfortable, a prescriptive-exploratory sequence felt all wrong.

This caricature of Lazarus serves to express my discomfort with his basic approach, but it does not address the question of whether he will be able to help Ellen. How will she experience him? What emerges strongly for me is his confidence. He conveys that her problems are not insuperable, that they can be detailed and specified on a quite short list, and that he and Ellen are going to find ways to solve each one of them; he really does have answers. He also conveys a willingness to consult her about treatment decisions; he indicates that her views are worthy of attention, so Ellen will feel respected. Because he has clinical acumen and picks up her difficulties in separating and individuating, her underlying anger, and her lack of entitlement, she is likely to feel understood. These factors are likely, I think, to contribute to the initial establishment of a good therapeutic alliance and would perhaps see therapy off to a honeymoon start.

Though I would not go quite so far as Bordin (1979) in viewing the establishment and maintenance of a good alliance as the total work of therapy, I would certainly see these as necessary to a good outcome. With clients whose relationship capacities are severely impaired, Bordin's view becomes more accurate, and the therapist's skill in addressing alliance (relationship) issues becomes critical. With less impaired clients, the alliance is less fragile, and therapy can be approached more successfully as a technical enterprise. This is the point at which I become more skeptical about Lazarus's prospects with Ellen. For example, he suggests targeting her lack of entitlement and poor self-esteem for initial attention by rational disputation. But I would share Wachtel's view that this will merely confirm for her that Lazarus cannot know how bad she really is, and I doubt she is able to tell him at this early point in therapy wherein her badness really lies. Where interventions with positive therapeutic realizations can serve to strengthen the therapeutic bond (Orlinsky & Howard, 1986), interventions that misfire can only weaken the alliance. More generally, I fear that Lazarus's wariness of her anger, lest it be directed at him, will only confirm for her how bad she is and how she must protect others from the damage she will inflict. I doubt the honeymoon will last, and Lazarus has not convinced me that his conceptual frame would assist him in effecting repairs. Ultimately, I think Ellen's prospects with Lazarus will depend on the degree of her impairment. Borderline features are apparent in her presentation, but so-called borderline pathology covers a wide spectrum of functioning (e.g., Abend, Porder, & Willick, 1983), and I would not place Ellen at the severe end. Nonetheless, I would rather refer her to Wachtel.

I am generally very sympathetic to Wachtel's formulation of Ellen's problems and his proposals regarding treatment. I particularly like his portrayal of the cyclic interplay between her informal experience and her external transactions, which serves to maintain her stuck position, and I like his emphasis on helping her to understand the dilemma she is struggling with. I am reminded of Ryle's (1982) cognitive-analytic therapy, in which clients are presented with a written formulation along similar lines. I would also support his caveat about unmasking interpretations, which calls to mind the "persecutory therapist" described by Meares and Hobson (1977). Our research on therapist difficulties (Davis et al., 1989) suggests that therapists are more likely to use such technical interventions as coping strategies when feeling threatened than they are in other situations of difficulty, and I wonder again how Lazarus will deal with his wariness of Ellen's anger.

My only quibbles with Wachtel are minor ones. The first concerns his treatment of Ellen's difficulties with anger, the oedipal issues, and her anxious attachment as if they were separate issues; I would see them as closely interlinked. The second quibble concerns the process of actively aiding her in taking on new patterns of interaction. I fully agree that insight does not in itself necessarily produce behavioral change, and I do myself actively aid clients to varying degrees. However, I find that many clients are very proficient at identifying changes they want to make and at proceeding to make them, sometimes with minimal assistance and sometimes without any. In my experience, there is wide variation in the degree of active aid required. In Ellen's case, I am by no means convinced that she will require a formal program of assertiveness training, for example.

There is also an issue for me about choice. Clients are frequently quite frightened by what change will entail and by the costs they will incur through change. Ultimately, I see it as my responsibility to help clients become as clear as possible about the costs and benefits of change, and I would respect absolutely a client's decision to preserve the status quo. This is quite different from supporting clients in facing their fears about change or in assisting them actively in making changes if they wish to take that risk. Although it sounds unlikely in Ellen's case, some clients with problems of separation and individuation may only succeed in establishing their own autonomy, for example, if they are willing to sever all links with their parents, but it is not for the therapist to dictate clients' choices.

5

The Envious Lover

◙

Gerald C. Davison
Carlo C. DiClemente
Shridhar D. Sharma
James F. T. Bugental

Case Presentation

After nearly a year of psychotherapy, Ian comes to a session wearing a cutaway shoe and a cast on his toe. He looks as though he just lost a street fight. His face is puffy and shows recent cuts. His account of his weekend reveals a pattern of alcohol abuse and acting out under its influence that the therapist has been unaware of until this moment. When Ian first came into therapy, at age twenty-nine, he presented himself as an earnest, overly polite young stockbroker. His clothing was perfectly matched, the grays accented with burgundy and everything pressed and buttoned down. The therapist gathered that Ian's articulate sales pitches and solicitous voice had gained him a substantial clientele for his age. In his initial consultation, he admitted only to "drinking an occasional beer with friends," but after his wild weekend, he acknowledges "getting smashed" with his friends at irregular intervals about every six weeks. These binges often include some public rowdiness, especially on Ian's part, and sometimes visits to prostitutes.

Ian grew up on a farm, the eldest of three boys. His parents were unhappy with each other. His mother, regarded as the most attractive woman in the county, was vain and exhibitionistic. Her extramarital affairs, including one with her husband's brother, were major items of local gossip.

Mother tried (and partly succeeded) to keep Ian from growing up, indulging his immature ways and making fun of him when he rebelled. She insisted that he come directly home from school to look after his younger brothers while she was out and that he remain home to keep her company when she was home. Ian did not often get to join his classmates at play.

Ian felt (and to some extent still feels) responsible for her. As a young boy, he often asked her why she did not leave his father, since she was so unhappy with him.

Ian's first account of his father, a mechanic and inventor of farm equipment, made him out to be a macho brute. But in time, Ian himself realized he was describing a man who was merely a resigned weakling. The father seems to have given up approaching his wife sexually after he learned of her affairs. He appears to have lived an asexual life except when it amused his wife to invite him to bed. Infrequently, he beat the boys with a belt, but Ian does not seem to hold that against him. Ian does resent that his father not only never showed affection to him but also was typically scornful toward Ian and the prospect that he might ever amount to anything. His father forbade his sons from inviting their classmates home, which Ian feels wrecked whatever chance he might have had to develop socially.

By the time Ian reached adolescence, he was fifty pounds overweight, a hopelessly backward "blob" (Ian's word). He could not take part in sports, had no pals, and no hope of ever finding a girlfriend.

Ian was saved from despair by a talent for mathematics that enabled him to earn scholarships to college and business school. After sexual initiation by a woman professor fifteen years older, he was able to lose weight and "stop masturbating every six minutes." Their affair, which lasted five years until Ian left the university town to seek his fortune, was marked by his frequent hostility to her followed by his abject apologies. In most ways, she dominated the immature young man.

When Ian sought therapy, he mentioned that he was not following up on opportunities at work, was not doing his homework on the stocks he was selling, and was deliberately annoying his boss by pretending to be stupid. He had made friends with a few colleagues, but he noted a peculiar way he had of waiting for them to call him. "I want them to court me like a girl," he observed, "and I'm always afraid they'll figure that out."

Ian worked out in the gym every day, dieted, and became quite handsome. Nevertheless, he was still afraid to approach young women. Another affair with a much older woman followed the pattern of that with the professor. He came late for their dates and insulted her figure and everything about her— including her affection to him—and then, becoming terrified, he abased himself and promised to be good.

In the early months of therapy, following a hint by the therapist, Ian began to ask young women for dates. His good looks and emotional intensity made him highly attractive, and for a season or two he "fell in love" with another woman about every two weeks. He also went to prostitutes, to whom he felt superior, but they humiliated him. Because of the AIDS danger to Ian and his numerous sexual partners, the therapist adopted an unwontedly directive stance; he ordered Ian to cut out going to prostitutes entirely.

The pattern of Ian's love life at this stage was to have sex immediately with a new date, then to "move in" for three or four nights in a row of intense sex and emotional involvement, then a hysterical fight and breakup over the young woman's alleged attempt to possess and control him, and then a few days of recriminations, telephone calls, reconciliation, and final breakup—just in time for a sex-love binge with a new woman.

Probably again influenced by his therapist, who hinted that an ongoing relationship could be more rewarding, Ian decided that he wanted a long-term relationship with his current woman friend. Jill was a wealthy art dealer five years older than Ian. Soon after he moved into her apartment, Ian began to inquire about her previous relations with men. At first he acted as though knowing each other's past was a casual diversion, but then it became a test of her honesty to tell him everything. Ian imagined himself inferior sexually to all the men she had slept with, despite her assurances to the contrary. He envied her experience as more extensive than his, and he fantasized being a woman like her and sleeping with many men. He tried to get her to describe her sexual life in detail, but she declined. Notwithstanding his recent promiscuity, Ian accused Jill of having been too available to men. When she yelled at him in retaliation, he abused her physically, twisting her arm and pushing her about, and then stormed out.

After Ian roughed Jill up on Friday evening, she changed the locks the next morning. When Ian discovered that he was locked out, he kicked the door, breaking his big toe, as he later learned. He was already drunk and, limping from bar to bar, became much drunker. He went to Jill's art gallery, drank some complimentary champagne, shouted obscenities, terrified the patrons, and broke a tray of stem glasses. Jill began to dial the police, so Ian left, snapping off car antennas as he limped down the street. He wound up at a house of prostitution, where he was unable to get an erection because of his drunkenness and intermittent awareness of the pain in his toe. He offended the management by refusing to leave (at this point he had nowhere to go) and took a couple of punches in the face, after which he saw the management's point of view. He checked into a hotel, left an incoherent message on his therapist's answering device, and slept for twelve hours.

By the time Ian arrived at his therapist's office, his toe was in a cast and he was all sobered up, expressing more earnestly than ever his desire to change.

Formulations and Treatments

Gerald C. Davison (Cognitive-Behavioral)

Even for a cognitive-behavioral therapist cum humanist like me, who focuses primarily on the present and future, it is

impossible to overlook the importance of Ian's past relationship to his mother, who slept around, humiliated Ian's
father, and dominated Ian. It is conceivable that Ian may
have carried his fury at her into adulthood, generalizing it
to all women. Ian is described as having been hostile to the
woman professor who initiated him into sex (probably no
accident that she was fifteen years his senior), making snide
comments to another older woman he dated, going to prostitutes to whom he felt superior, and abusing his current
lover physically.

His seeming fear of women, then, I would construe as a
cover for his extreme anger at them. His problem in establishing intimate and honest relationships is consistent with a
deep-seated mistrust and dislike of women.

I would not see the allusion to his occasionally wondering
what it would be like to be a woman as a homosexual or
transsexual inclination, but as a kind of escape from the pain
that being a heterosexual male has been. After all, how enjoyable can his life be if he is raging at half the people around
him? What is not evident from the case report data is what
his male-to-male relationships have been. Has he had close
male friends? Or has his anger at his mother and other
women generalized to all people? That generalized anger is
suggested by his passive-aggressiveness, as in not doing his
homework on the stocks he sells and deliberately annoying
his boss by pretending to be stupid.

The alcohol abuse I regard as secondary to Ian's core anger
problem. As is often the case, alcohol is probably an anes-
thetic for his strong negative feelings about women and about
himself—feelings that arise in large measure from the stressful
situations he constructs for himself.

In the most general terms, I would set as the main agenda
item a change in his extreme hatred for women. What is less
clear is how I would go about the task. A principal choice
would entail whether to work on his current relationships with
women or to work on his earlier and maybe also current one
with his mother. If the mother is available, I might raise with
Ian the possibility of inviting her in for a few sessions to help

him express to her his hurt and anger at how she treated him and his father when Ian was a child. This encounter might also give her a chance to explain what life was like for her in a way that might enable Ian to forgive or at least to understand her from his current adult perspective. Children can seldom appreciate what emotional pain their parents endure but can often do so when they themselves are grown up. They may still not like very much what their parents did, but they may at least be able to empathize with them and forgive them for shortcomings. If I could help Ian and his mother in this way, perhaps his current anger at women would diminish.

Alternatively or in addition, I would work with Ian on his present relationships. Perhaps, as Ellis would say, some of his anger and remoteness could be construed as arising from the unrealistic, unproductive belief that others must be exactly as he wants them to be, that things absolutely must go as he wants them to. If such a belief is part of Ian's view of women, perhaps it can be detected in other parts of his life, such as work. His meticulous way of dressing may be part of the need to be perfect.

His being "overly polite" may be a defense against his rage and in turn may perpetuate that rage through cyclical psychodynamics (Wachtel, 1982). Ian's excessive politeness might be associated with lack of assertiveness and hence with being taken unfair advantage of, which could well lead to others abusing him or at least not taking his wants and needs adequately into account. Assertiveness training might be called for; it might help Ian to realize that he can express anger or hurt to others without injuring others or himself. Appropriate assertiveness can alter the kinds of interpersonal situations he finds himself in; if he is not taken advantage of, he will have less to rage against.

In addition to the usual behavioral what and when mode of interviewing, I might use a Gestalt empty chair technique to help him better discover and express his feelings. For example, I would have him imagine his mother in the chair—and probably also his father, at whom he might harbor anger for the childhood beatings and ridicule as well as anger for the father's failure as a man in accepting the emotional abuse and neglect by Ian's mother. Ian's attitudes toward and feelings about other important people in his life, past and present, might well be plumbed with this procedure. Also, if he were amenable, I might try to hypnotize him to help him express thoughts and feelings that he is reluctant to own up to. A person's merely believing that he or she is hypnotized can act as permission to think and say what is unthinkable and unutterable. In Ian's case, just allowing someone to hypnotize him might be beneficial as a model for trusting someone and not having that trust betrayed or abused.

There are social-skill deficits that I would approach via structured in-session behavior rehearsal, which (as part of the assertiveness training mentioned earlier) would also serve as an assessment instrument. Especially in initial sessions, it might help him and me see his hostility toward women, and toward all people as well. I might also assess his "self-talk" by a modification of my paradigm of articulated thought during simulated situations (Davison, Robins, & Johnson, 1983), a sort of stimulus-bound free association. I would construct a situation for him to imagine himself in, and then I would encourage him to think aloud. For example, I might have him imagine an attractive woman declining an overture from him: Does he verbalize only hurt, fear, and expressions of low self-esteem? Or does he, as I would expect, articulate thoughts and feelings of anger and rage?

There is much else in this richly textured, densely packaged case material, but these are the clinical hypotheses I would initially entertain and use as guides to further assessment and cognitive-behavioral treatment planning. In the midst of my directiveness and behavioral focus, I would try to remain sensitive to the subtle messages most patients send, particularly those signaling that sensitive areas are being touched.

Carlo C. DiClemente (Integrative)

Ian is an individual with multiple problems and a self-defeating cycle of relationships. Initially I would evaluate these problems along several levels of change. At the symptomatic level, his alcohol abuse, violent explosive episodes, and dysfunctional sexual relations would all be primary foci of concern. The self-statements about wanting to be courted like a girl and his fantasies about being a woman represent significant issues at the level of maladaptive cognitions. These symptoms would need greater elaboration. On the interpersonal level, Ian is experiencing interpersonal conflicts with women as well as with colleagues and seems unable to approach an intimacy of equals. Family of origin, social network, and employment systems are sources of conflict and confusion at the family-systems level. Finally, Ian seems to have problems with sexual identity, self-image, self-esteem, and individuation at the intrapersonal level.

Whenever I see a person with this variety and extent of problems at the various levels of change, a personality disorder diagnosis usually is most appropriate. Ian is best understood in terms of diagnostic classification as having a borderline personality disorder highlighted by intense anger, identity disturbance, impulsiveness, affective instability, and unstable interpersonal relationships. The levels of change, however, offer a more functional and practical perspective for intervention than does the *DSM-III-R* Axis II diagnosis of borderline personality.

The current crisis in Ian's life raises interesting questions and offers unique opportunities for the course of his therapy. We need to know more about the pattern of Ian's drinking— frequency, duration, precipitating factors, and consequences. Are there other drugs involved? What emotions, thoughts, and behavior does he express when he is under the influence? Alcohol's loosening of inhibitions supports the ancient phrase *in vino veritas* (in wine—truth). I would bet that some of the more destructive and dysfunctional parental behaviors were facilitated by alcohol; and I would like to know about parental and sibling drug and alcohol use.

Ian's ambivalence toward women, involving rage and idealization, would also lead to a whole line of questioning about sexual abuse, sexual identity, and sexual preference. Homosexual fears and activities would be another line of inquiry. In addition, an exploration of self-destructive or suicidal thoughts or behaviors as well as feelings of emptiness and abandonment would be of interest.

In working with this type of client, I have found that a firm, authoritative, empathic-but-not-overly-involved approach, which enables me to be open without being manipulated, works best (Prochaska & DiClemente, 1984). The process of developing a therapeutic relationship is a critical pathway to change for borderline individuals, so I would avoid being too directive with Ian, since he is likely to blame the therapist if things do not work out. Idealization and devaluation will be part of the picture as Ian attempts to get close to the therapist, and issues of trust and abandonment will emerge often. The therapist should be clear about expectations and should warn Ian well in advance of any shifts in schedule or absences.

I would expect the therapy with Ian to proceed from one personal crisis to another, indicating loss of control in one or more aspects of life. Problems at each of the levels would need to be examined and dealt with in a thoughtful and empathic manner. Training in problem-solving skills, assertiveness, and cognitive-behavioral anger control techniques, as well as employing rational-emotive strategies, would be useful to handle specific problems as they emerge—provided Ian is ready for action in these areas. The issue of what to do and when with Ian would depend on his stage of change with respect to the problems at each level. So far, he and his therapist appear to have focused on relationship issues. At this point in the therapy, Ian may be able to move toward contemplation or action regarding his drinking and anger control problems. I would certainly focus on the symptom-situational level at this time of crisis.

I would also consider a medication evaluation if Ian became depressed. Especially after the recent disruptive events, Ian might experience a serious depressive episode. Medication could help stabilize him and allow the work of psychotherapy to proceed.

Clearly, Ian would not be considered a short-term therapy case. That he has been able to remain in therapy for a year is a good sign. But given the multiplicity of his problems, he requires intensive and extensive therapy to accomplish characterological change. While dealing with current issues and problems, I would attempt to address underlying themes at the system and intrapersonal levels. In a nonconfrontational manner, I would encourage consciousness raising, self-reevaluation, and environmental reevaluation, and I would explore his individuation and differentiation from his dysfunctional family. In many ways, Ian is living out his family legacy. I would relate current issues to his roles as surrogate spouse, mother, and father in his family of origin. The current incidents provide a wonderful opportunity to explore Ian's dichotomous thinking; contrasting the dapper and polite Ian with the rebellious, angry, and acting-out aspects would help to address identity issues. Idealization and devaluation of self and others would be another critical theme that I would weave throughout our sessions as the therapy moved from crisis to crisis. If both Ian and his therapist can handle discouragement and disappointments, significant changes can be made at many of the problem levels. Maintaining these changes and integrating them into Ian's sense of self will be the long-term challenge.

Shridhar Sharma (Psychoanalytic)

Ian, a handsome, educated, and intelligent stockbroker, grew up in an atmosphere of prolonged parental conflict and inadequate opportunities to socialize. Before commencement of therapy, it would be necessary to determine whether Ian's problem is chiefly one of personality disorder causing difficulty in interpersonal relations and sexual relationships or whether his interpersonal difficulties and sexual problems are independent of each other.

More details are required about Ian's alcohol abuse—pattern and severity and use of other drugs concurrently with alcohol. Earlier reports of depressive symptoms and anxiety attacks need to be verified. These patterns would indicate whether any medication would be necessary.

Ian's case seems to fit into the passive-aggressive type of personality disorder. His background of disturbed childhood with parental conflicts, personality problems with both his parents, and his continued maladaptive behavior at work and in his personal life support this diagnosis.

Another diagnosis to be considered would be substance or alcohol abuse disorder. Ian's work performance seems mediocre. Substance abuse may account for his multiple difficulties ranging from street brawls to breakups in his relationships. But Ian's own perception is that he "deliberately acts stupid" to annoy his boss, suggesting a personality problem rather than substance abuse.

Therapy should concentrate on exploring the interpersonal difficulties and behavior patterns that are the cause of his recurrent difficulties.

A supportive, nondirective approach seems to be most suitable for Ian. From the case report, it appears that Ian uses the therapist's suggestions in a passive-aggressive manner. Clear, attainable therapeutic goals should be established to help Ian realize and accept responsibility for the self-defeating nature of his actions and to change his behavior to a more adaptive style.

Ian's long-term relationships with two older women and his temporary affairs with women of his age group have been superficial and unfulfilling. The interpersonal context of these relationships needs to be examined in light of his love-hate relationship with his mother. Ian must come to appreciate mutually satisfying and rewarding involvement and learn not to exploit his relationships.

Ian's alcohol problem has been discovered late in the therapy. This may indicate that Ian is poorly committed to the therapeutic contract. Group therapy is likely to be less threatening to Ian, and his self-defeating behavior patterns can be handled in a group; hence, group therapy also appears to be indicated.

James F. T. Bugental (Existential-Humanistic)

My approach to life-changing therapy rests on the belief that there is a fundamental division of responsibility between therapist and patient. Patients are the only ones who can know their own lives and are, therefore, the only ones who can guide their lives. The therapist is a coach who observes and comments on how patients use their capabilities for life direction. This position implies that I do not try to solve patients' problems, advise on courses of action, discover so-called causes of symptoms or problems, or work out psychodynamic formulations to teach them. I do pay close attention to the immediacy (in the hour) and genuineness of patients' concerns for how their lives are going. I observe and offer feedback on the many ways patients avoid immediacy and genuineness. I insist that patients are responsible for what they say and do, that there are always more alternatives available than those the patients describe as the only possibilities; that their route to better self-guidance and reduction of distress (pain, anxiety, repetitive failures) lies in intensive and extensive exploration of their perceptual worlds.

I am less interested in learning about Ian than I am in persuading him that he needs to learn a great deal more about himself. I do not make a formal diagnosis except as insurance forms may require. Long before this point, I would have satisfied myself that Ian had no major thought disorder, that his ego strength was sufficient to accommodate depth explorations, and that he could make a commitment to come at least two times a week and to hang in over a period of at least one and preferably two years. Since the case synopsis suggests the work with Ian has been going on for some time, I assume those desiderata have been satisfied.

The fact that Ian has these drinking and fighting episodes as often as at six-week intervals and that the therapist has never picked up at least some clue to this highly significant aspect of his life is important in itself. For this to be the case, it seems that either the therapist has been too much in charge of what was talked about or Ian is a remarkable actor (psychopath?).

The history of Ian is so totally focused on Ian that there is no cue to the relation with the therapist or to how the alliance was evolving. It is also evident that the personality, style, and emotional receptivity of the therapist are not deemed sufficiently important to be included.

I would insist on a therapeutic relation in which Ian discovered his responsibility for his own life. This relationship would come about from my refusal, for the most part, to enter into discussions of his motives or to offer interpretations of his dynamics and from my repeated identification of the ways in which Ian avoids taking responsibility.

I would depart to a limited extent from my position—somewhat as did Ian's therapist—to insist that his frequenting of prostitutes during the AIDS epidemic was resistance in that it put our work at risk. Whether I would say to Ian that it was also acting out with suicidal potential would depend on the state of our alliance.

Considerations in conducting this first interview when Ian arrives physically and emotionally battered are represented by the following questions: How ready is he to be present genuinely and to work to explore the meanings of the previous night's debacle? Is he reenacting with me the guilt-and-reconciliation script he has so often played out before? What are my reactions and impulses to the presentation he makes? Am I moved to sympathy, to anger, to take satisfaction, or to want to reassure? I would not likely act on any of these impulses, but I need to know the answers to these questions to recognize what Ian is pulling for and how my responses may be adulterated.

Assuming that Ian has some amount of (desirable) apprehension arising from the episode, I would attempt to bring it forward so that he truly and strongly experiences alarm at what is happening to his life. I would do this by spotlighting the ways in which he might seek to downplay or explain away the events of the night. Here are some examples: (1) You are trying to persuade yourself and me this is really not very serious. (2) It seems as though it would be overwhelming to you to recognize just how far out of control you can get. (3) You want to be the sad, repentant sinner here so that we won't get into what this episode really means for you. That way you can go out and pull another one when you need to.

All told, I would regard this situation as a window of opportunity to require Ian to renew his commitment to our work and to gain genuine direction in his life.

The foregoing is suppositional and brief. To carry it further, I would need more information about the previous course of the therapeutic alliance and Ian's sophistication about inward searching.

Points of Contention and Convergence

Gerald C. Davison

Beginning with DiClemente, I did not employ a *DSM-III* diagnosis and was interested to see his reference to borderline personality. I can see how Ian could be given this Axis II diagnosis, and yet I would not materially change my therapeutic approach to him if I too had labeled him in this way. DiClemente's approach raises in my own mind the interesting question of what benefits are achieved by employing the borderline personality diagnosis. Like the narcissistic personality a few years ago, the borderline seems to have become a popular rubric, in spite of a paucity of evidence on the validity or utility of the diagnosis.

DiClemente's allusion to the Latin aphorism *in vino veritas* assumes that what comes out from Ian when he is drunk is somehow more valid than what one sees of him in the sober state. I would caution against assuming this. Consider, for example, that sexual arousability generally declines when considerable alcohol (as Ian would ingest) is consumed. Would one then conclude that the person is sexually hypoactive? I doubt it.

I like DiClemente's comments about the general approach he would take with someone like Ian. Concern about being overly idealized and then damned by the client is well taken. Moreover, there are commonalities between us in the specific approaches that we might take—assertiveness training, for example—although my own focus would be more clearly on Ian's anger toward women.

It is noteworthy that Sharma uses an Axis II diagnosis different from that of DiClemente—passive-aggressive personality. His reasons make sense and are consistent with recent data pointing to considerable overlap among personality disorder diagnoses. There seem to be very few "clean" cases, and this paucity constitutes an argument against the typological *DSM* approach in general. Sharma's specific therapeutic suggestions are too vague for me to comment upon substantially; basically, I cannot tell what he would actually do with Ian, aside from being supportive and nondirective. However, the caution that Ian may use therapist suggestions in a passive-aggressive manner does suggest that a paradoxical approach may be needed. Such an approach would drastically change the cognitive-behavioral suggestions I made. I would want to watch for this potential conflict with my generally directive and prescriptive approach.

I am probably in clearest disagreement with Bugental's suggestions. My sense is that if Ian could operate as autonomously and responsibly as Bugental assumes he can, his clinical picture would be much different and less serious than it is. I would agree on such behavior as goals, of course. It is noteworthy that Bugental would directly insist that Ian not go to prostitutes because of the AIDS crisis. While I would do the same, I contend that this negates the ultranondirective approach he advocates. Ian's going to prostitutes is not "resistance" that puts the therapy at risk; it is behavior motivated by reasons the therapist should investigate, behavior which until recently was relatively common among men.

Carlo C. DiClemente

My training and background ally me with both the cognitive-behavioral and humanistic perspectives. The integrative transtheoretical approach that I currently use to direct my therapy allows me to integrate these perspectives with my experience to make clinical decisions. Reviewing the responses of my fellow panelists renews my commitment to developing an integrative approach. While I can resonate with the clinical recommendations of Davison and the philosophical stance of Bugental, I disagree with them and Sharma on several points.

Readiness for change and taking responsibility for one's life are similar. The model of the stages of change that I work from focuses on intentional change but does not assume that clients are ready for action on any one problem when they enter or remain in therapy. Bugental assumes Ian to be in action or close to action, and he assumes that focusing on Ian's experience of the night of chaos by offering genuine feedback about responsibility will be therapeutic. Although I agree that intentional, responsible activity is needed for change, there may be many times when Ian will be at earlier stages of change—times when he may be too unaware, unable, unconvinced, or unskilled to assume responsibility. Self-regulation involves not only commitment but also cognitive and behavioral processes applied or encouraged at specific stages of change.

Bugental also seems to concentrate on the interpersonal and intrapersonal levels. I concur that there are serious problems at both of these levels. However, the failure to address the alcohol abuse as a serious and separate (but not completely separable) issue is problematic from my perspective. Many aspects of Ian's life and problems significantly reduce his capacity for intentional, responsible action. These aspects must be addressed if we are going to be able to offer him a comprehensive treatment program.

Davison's plans for intervention are probably most similar to mine, but I am somewhat distressed by his brushing aside of the alcohol abuse as simply a medication for emotional pain. My focus on Ian's alcohol abuse represents a major difference in approach. Etiology of a problem behavior is often quite different from the maintenance of that behavior and from the issues to be addressed to change that behavior. Whether Ian began using alcohol to self-medicate, to mimic mother, or to release anger, current patterns of use, benefits, and consequences are much more relevant for change. Unless the therapist focuses on the alcohol problem, gains made in the sober state will not transfer to these binge drinking episodes. The alcohol-as-symptom perspective, a pet peeve of mine, is partially responsible for the current rift between psychotherapists who focus on emotional problems and alcohol treatment personnel who focus almost exclusively on the substance abuse (Prochaska & DiClemente, 1984). A truly integrative perspective would allow for the importance of each domain and also acknowledge the interrelatedness.

Davison would focus on the interpersonal level by prescribing assertiveness training. Again, I concur but feel that this would be the most difficult level at which to get substantial change quickly. The importance of the cognitions and their role in producing and maintaining the problem behavior are key points of convergence between Davison and me. Cognitions are alluded to by both Sharma and Bugental but are more directly and explicitly addressed by Davison and me. However, I would not use hypnosis or free association with Ian. It seems to me that those techniques would be counterproductive. Issues of trust, rebelliousness, and unclear personal boundaries would make hypnosis and free association difficult. To avoid such difficulties, I would offer a rather structured interpersonal approach and cognitive intervention.

Sharma seems to evaluate the case diagnostically in a manner similar to mine; however, he sees the diagnostic classification as giving more direction to his intervention than I do. Diagnostic levels are helpful for insurance reimbursement and have implications for treatment as they become more specific and specified. However, the current *DSM-III-R* system does not allow for a more functional and problem-oriented perspective like that of the levels of change. A more descriptive, functional diagnosis of problems seems most useful in this case. The personality diagnosis can help in deciding the characterological traits that will be encountered and that will influence the therapeutic relationship. However, simple Axis I and II labels do not often yield clear directives for treatment.

Sharma assumes that Ian's failure to disclose his alcohol problem is indicative of his lack of commitment to therapy. Since individuals can be at various stages with respect to problems at various levels of change, I do not think it is helpful to overgeneralize attributions of resistance (Miller, 1985). It seems to me that Ian has been ready to work on relationships with women during his year in therapy while being less willing to work on or admit an alcohol problem. This behavior does not indicate a lack of commitment, but a limited commitment.

It is not surprising that I would find my perspective more useful and compelling than those of the other authors. This case does point out that, as therapists, we are directed by our own theoretical frames, however broad or limited they are. While I see a good deal of consensus among the four of us in our approach to Ian, there are both major and minor points of divergence. The field of psychotherapy continues to elude formal consensus and integration while becoming more homogenous at the level of practice.

Shridhar Sharma

I will begin with the points of convergence. There is basic agreement in the diagnostic impression that Ian is experiencing a personality disorder that is causing both interpersonal problems and drug and alcohol abuse. It appears that Ian is the major source of available information, but his mother or girlfriend might also provide additional information helpful in forming a well-knit psychodynamic formulation.

A few indicators suggest the presence of parental conflict and an abnormal parent-child relationship. These have probably triggered Ian's problems, both in relation to his sexual conflict and his poor interpersonal relationships. Ian appears to be lonely, searching for a lasting and satisfying relationship with the opposite sex—a relationship he is unable to accomplish due to his psychopathology. Probing is needed regarding possible homosexual tendencies and early sexual traumas.

Despite general agreement on the diagnostic formulation, there are points of conflict on therapeutic interventions—conflict due to different perceptions and approaches to resolving the same problem. From the available history, it is difficult to suggest that Ian has any homosexual inclination, but to conclude that his behavior is an escape from the pain that a heterosexual male may suffer is also not clear and evident.

I believe that individual psychotherapy alone may not be sufficient. Ian would benefit from being placed in a therapy group involving his mother and, if possible, his girlfriend. The emotional support and understanding on the part of his girlfriend and his mother would enhance understanding of the problem and would help in establishing a more positive therapeutic process. I totally agree with the idea to involve Ian's mother in a few therapeutic sessions, which may also help in understanding some of his conflicts and in establishing positive emotional relationships. The results in such cases are usually difficult without adequate social and emotional support from the family.

James F. T. Bugental

The response of Gerald Davison is ingenious, multifaceted, and dynamic, but somehow it is almost totally therapist focused. He lists hypotheses about Ian and then proposes things he (the therapist) might do to and for Ian. Only the very last sentence mentions the possibility of being tuned in to Ian and to what is happening to Ian. It is as though Ian is to be regarded as an object, a puzzle box to be speculated about from the outside.

DiClemente's approach initially is diagnostic with much emphasis on identifying issues or symptoms and on acquiring information about Ian. Sensitive speculations about the likely therapeutic relation and how it should be modulated still retain the strong flavor of objectification of Ian. The mobilization of many possible therapeutic instrumentalities suggests the implicit question in the therapist's mind, "What shall I do to this person?" Again, the last sentence is revealing in that, for the first time, it shows some sharing with Ian—"If both Ian and his therapist can handle discouragement and disappointments . . ."

Sharma, not recognizing therapy has gone on for a year, begins by saying a diagnostic judgment must be made "before commencement of therapy." Again, the history is disregarded with the observation that "Ian's work performance seems mediocre," despite the report saying that Ian had gained "a substantial clientele for his age." These points are only important to show how the center of gravity is in the therapist, not in Ian.

The other three psychotherapists and I part company most markedly in terms of the stance from which we approach the work with Ian. Each of the others tends to look on Ian as an object to be diagnosed, explored, helped, treated, and impacted in a variety of ways. Information is to be collected, collated, and reduced to various diagnostic judgments and treatment strategies. This approach is very much in the current mainstream of American psychological therapy (cf. Zeig and Munion, 1990). I recognize, therefore, that mine is a radically contrasting point of view (Bugental, 1978, 1987, 1988).

My perspective can be most economically set forth in a set of beliefs that forty years and many disappointed efforts to work from other bases have brought home to me. I believe that Ian, and only Ian, is the possessor of whatever knowledge about himself is going to be needed for him to change his life. I believe that only if Ian genuinely and vividly experiences his present life as something he does not want to continue will he begin to go through the misery that lies between him and a changed life experience. I also believe that Ian is continuing this self-defeating pattern because of the way he has implicitly come to define himself and his world; and changing this self-defeating pattern means to Ian (at some level) a kind of death. Thus he does well to avoid it. And I believe that I, the therapist, can bring essential aid to Ian by doing three things—and, for the most part, by doing only these three things: (1) developing an alliance with Ian in which it is firmly established that he is in charge of the content of what we deal with but that I am insistently attending to and calling on him to attend to how he deals with whatever he does talk about, (2) focusing on how Ian avoids being totally, genuinely present in the therapeutic hour, and relentlessly confronting him with his evasions, and (3) standing steadily by Ian as he encounters the feared, agonizing, tragic, irrevocable, and heretofore suppressed and repressed elements within himself.

It appears to me that the other psychotherapists commenting on Ian's case manifest informed and, doubtlessly, caring concern. Still, our current implicit metaphysical foundation for therapy devalues and disregards the subjective in the client and, indeed, in the therapist as well. We are taught that objectivity is the highest virtue, so we often fail to consider that the core of psychotherapy is, and must be, the subjectivity of the client. Treating the client as an object only reinforces one of the pathogenic tendencies of our time.

I read into statements of Davison and DiClemente an underlying empathy for the client. In keeping with so much of our training, the greater parts of what they propose focus on objective aspects of Ian, his history, and what the therapists might do; however, each at the end of his statement suggests something not expressed earlier. Davison said, "In the midst of my directiveness and behavioral focus, I would try to remain sensitive to the subtle messages most patients send, particularly those signaling that sensitive areas are being touched." And DiClemente said, "If both Ian and his therapist can handle discouragement and disappointments, significant changes can be made at many of the problem levels." Is it too presumptuous to speculate that they felt it not quite proper to bring in such subjectivity but that their deeper feelings slipped out before they stopped writing?

Psychology, seeking to be a science on the model of nineteenth-century physics or early twentieth-century medicine, avoids subjectivity in both client and therapist as it would sepsis. The consequence is an overvaluing of detached diagnosis and overt technique and an underestimate of what clients can and must do if they are to make major life changes.

6

The Survivor

🔲

Larry E. Beutler
Spencer Eth
Saul I. Harrison
Nolan Saltzman

Case Presentation

Anne is twenty-eight, a nurse at a hospital in New York City. She is afflicted day and night by involuntary memories of childhood abuse. These flashbacks keep her from sleeping, and she is exhausted. She relives these memories in a trance-like state from which she can be brought out by gentle shaking and insistence on eye contact. The expression on her face at these moments reflects a disoriented horror and agony. The therapist surmises that she is especially vulnerable to these memories whenever she thinks that she has done something wrong or that she is imposing on anyone.

At the first consultation, Anne said she was finding it impossible to pursue her studies toward certification as a psychiatric nurse. She was afraid of flunking out, being unable to give oral reports, or losing control, although so far her work had always been acceptable. These usual-sounding student worries reflected a deeper anxiety that she might be unsuitable for mental health work because of what she had gone through and that if she failed, she would be exposed and subjected to punishment for attempting too much.

Anne was a victim of incest and torture by her father throughout her childhood. He construed both sex and torture as punishments for alleged misbehavior. When she was eleven, he threw her out of the house. She became associated with a drug gang, who used her to smuggle drugs. She describes herself as "up for grabs," meaning she had sex with members of the gang as necessary. Her father also picked her up from the streets for sex and then returned her to the streets. Twice, he showed the gang members how he "taught her a lesson." The gang allowed him to do whatever he wanted with her because she was on loan to them; he could have had her picked up (possibly carrying drugs) at any time by the police, as she was still a minor.

It appears that the father projected all of his self-loathing onto her. Her mother, a passive cripple, went along with whatever her husband wanted, at times collaborating with him. After Anne, they had three more children. The parents maintained what to Anne seemed normal relations with the other children. However, Anne was not included in the family; she was not allowed to eat at the table nor to sleep in her bed.

Anne was hospitalized sixteen times between the ages of four and eleven. The first time was at four, when her father threw her down the cellar steps. She was kept in the dark cellar, naked, subject to rape and sadistic abuse much of her childhood. She was forced to eat dog food from the family dog's bowl, without using her hands. She says that to this day she feels discomfort eating with other people at a table and that some nights she feels as though she has no right to sleep on a bed; to relieve this feeling, she gets off her bed and curls up on the floor.

Anne's manner and voice are honest, and her story is internally consistent. She suffers intensely in searching out and expressing each piece of her past. There is nothing at all about her to suggest that she would invent these atrocities. In spite of Anne's fears that she is "crazy," she seems to her therapist to be just the opposite. She is someone who has suffered a million times the trauma the human mind and body were meant to take, and yet she has always coped as well as she could. She has retained a remarkably balanced judgment about most real issues, she has learned and applied useful skills, and she shows considerable concern for others.

Throughout her childhood and adolescence, Anne denied her parents' fiendish natures and hoped for reconciliation with them. Concomitantly, she lacked the ability to become enraged at their crimes; it seems to have been tortured out of her. Anne said that she never thought of what her father did as torture; that was her therapist's word for it. "How did you think of it, then?" he asked. "It was just Dad doing his thing," she said. This form of denial was given up soon after therapy began. A second, more insidious form—"Since the other children were spared, I must have been bad as Dad said"—has not been wholly overcome.

When she was five, her father saw her "blowing bubbles" into her younger brother's belly, a common way of playing with babies. Accusing her of sexual interest in the baby, her father raped her as punishment. She told her mother what had happened and showed her the blood on the sheets, but her mother merely scolded her for going back to bed. Not long afterward, her father raped her again, this time adding an excruciating torture that was often present as an element thereafter. He heated metal objects and put them into her.

Anne spent much of her childhood hiding in a closet, delirious, rocking in pain, or locked in the cellar. After one severe burning, when she was "unable to go to the bathroom," she was taken to the hospital. Her father, a consummate dissembler, told the staff that she played with fire and burned herself. Thus, she eventually acquired a psychiatric record of sixteen occurrences of accidental or intentional self-injury that has put the parents beyond legal retribution.

On one occasion, a teacher told Anne to tell her what was troubling her. Anne told her, and the teacher slapped her face. No one in schools or hospitals believed Anne's stories.

On another, more recent occasion, her father trapped her alone, tied her up, raped her, and burned her. Afterward, she attempted suicide. Largely because this torture followed the pattern of her father's description of what Anne had done to herself in childhood, a grand jury did not find sufficient evidence to indict him. It was her word against his, and the jurors were swayed by the sixteen hospital records reflecting her parents' accounts that Anne had injured herself.

The father carried out a repertory of sadistic acts upon Anne, but she repressed these memories totally. That is, although she suffered from waves of horrible feelings, she did not connect them to events in her past. In time she decided to leave the streets and make something of herself, so she studied nursing and has worked as a nurse for six years. In sessions over the past three months (supportive psychodynamic exploration and elicitation of abreaction, mostly), the walls of repression have crumbled, and she remembers everything now, too well, in flashbacks that overwhelm her as often as minutes apart. She is rarely spared them for as long as an hour.

One of the worst memories, brought up in pieces through several sessions, was of Christmas Eve when she was twelve years old. She felt unusually tired and returned home to sit by the tree. Her father said, "You look terrible," and then observed that she was pregnant; she had not known. Anne says it was his child. He tied her to the kitchen table and aborted the fetus by punching her in the belly and inserting household implements. Her mother made her put the fetus into a garbage can and clean up the blood. Her father doused the fetus with gasoline and forced Anne to ignite it, saying, "Look what you did! You killed it!"

Later, Anne's father threw her out again, and she walked several miles back to Times Square, where she collapsed. When she came to in a clinic, she was told that the pregnancy had gone about six and a half months. It had been possible to determine this from examination of her tissues and the extent of the tearing of them.

Anne cries over and over, "I didn't want to burn my baby!" The therapist does all he can to persuade her that no guilt attaches to her, that it was her father's crime—against her.

Anne has had a love relationship for more than four years. For the past year, the lover has been on a study-work program in a distant city, but they write, telephone, and spend a weekend together about every three months. Anne's social life with her peers is circumscribed by the nearly total hearing loss she suffered in her early twenties. She has dinner occasionally with one or another coworker.

Anne's therapist asked her, when the image of her father coming at her occurs, to scream. The abreaction gives Anne relief that lasts for hours, but then she is exposed to new and more detailed memories, probably because her screaming and her therapist's acceptance has weakened the repression.

Anne is a determined patient. She sometimes rejects suggestions when they are too frightening to her, but at other times, as she is able to, she may attempt what is for her exceedingly painful and scary work. An example is the suggestion that she express rage toward her visualization of her father. For some time, she was unable even to begin, but now she will hit a bolster a few times while uttering a few harsh angry sounds.

Anne's psychotherapist would be interested in other therapists' experiences with victims of torture and in what psychological methods they have used to deal with patients' obtrusive memories. Hypnosis, an approach that suggests itself, is not readily applicable for two reasons. First, her deafness presents a problem. Anne is a skilled lip-reader, but lipreading is a demanding exercise even for the conscious mind. Second, as soon as she relaxes her defenses or gives up contact with reality, she is tormented by memories.

Formulations and Treatments

Larry E. Beutler (Eclectic)

I was overwhelmed by the degree of abuse and destructiveness wreaked upon a victim who appears to be a true survivor. I was also aware of my own rescue fantasies aroused by the intensity of Anne's neediness. The presentation of Anne's case leaves me with great respect for the therapist and even greater respect for the patient. I am impressed by the collaborative nature of the relationship, and I am optimistic that the process will take a natural course of resolution in time. The therapy relationship will allow Anne's fears to unfold naturally, slowed only by the fears that she constructs in her own cognitive-imaginal life. What I can add in the way of specific technical suggestions will surely have less power than the collaborative, supportive, and evidently caring nature of the relationship between therapist and patient.

Since much detail is missing, let me reconstruct the case of Anne as I imagine her to be. I must make certain assumptions about the patient based upon clues within the narrative and upon my experience with individuals who have been victimized. I imagine Anne as an individual who has not yet decided how to resolve and interpret the abusive events—sometimes questioning her own stability and worth, at other times expressing halting anger at her victimization. I see her memories and their expression as efforts to incorporate the therapist into her world as a supportive resource and as a sounding board. The simple trust that the patient reveals, the intensity of her struggle, and her efforts to involve other people in it provide the basis for a productive therapeutic alliance.

Beyond this general formulation, there are some other pertinent assumptions and inferences upon which my recommendations will be made: (1) The therapist observed that the patient adopts a trancelike state in response to intrusive, disruptive, self-generated thoughts. These qualities suggest that the flashbacks are dissociative but not hallucinatory. (2) The narrative portrays Anne as a survivor, now overwhelmed by her anxiety. I assume she is not currently a suicide risk. (3) I assume the patient's memories and reports of flashbacks are in part motivated and constructed to derive something from interpersonal relationships, including that with the therapist. (4) On the basis of the description, I must infer certain coping style characteristics for treatment planning. I assume that Anne does not maintain either the detached or rebellious stance that characterized her earlier efforts to cope.

Individuals with histories of severe victimization are often demanding and active nurturance seekers, and they often vacillate between intense attachment and withdrawal when their needs are not met. If Anne is like this, she may attempt to establish reassuring relationships and to invest herself in other people, and she may frequently feel abandoned, victimized, and rejected when these efforts are not reciprocated. Her efforts to involve herself as a helper, and to provide others with what she was deprived of, in part represent this externalizing and redirecting defensive strategy.

At the same time, Anne may be pushing herself to earn other people's approval, and she may deny or control her anger by translating it into feelings of interpersonal rejection. These internalizing patterns may lead to emotional lability, tearfulness, and crying spells. Together, the internalizing and externalizing patterns may suggest a cyclical and unstable coping style at the present time (Beutler & Clarkin, 1990).

The Anne I am reconstructing from her history also has a high need to maintain a sense of interpersonal control, is on guard against other people, and is excruciatingly sensitive to rejection and to the withdrawal of attachment objects. She alternates between feeling helplessly needy and, at other times, being resistant, suspicious, and feeling abandoned. Hence, I would expect her to react moderately against directive interventions.

Setting aside the question of the accuracy of the foregoing reconstruction, let me share some thoughts about treatment. After forming some understanding of the patient, the next step is the development of a bonding relationship. According to the case history, this has been successful, and the initial relationship has allowed the patient to recontact a painful history. Therapist and patient are now at a second stage in which neither the bonding with nor the caring support of the therapist is sufficient alone for the patient to derive a sense of safety to allow her fears to be extinguished.

In this stage of increased instability and sensed danger, issues of the patient's safety come to the fore. If the patient is presenting suicidal gestures and thoughts, the pattern of instability and the probability of few intimate sources of support would lead me to raise the possibility of a brief hospitalization.

My effort would be to move the patient from introjection to a more outward expression of anger, and to confront her urgency to make others love her in order to feel safe. I might use two-chair dialogues and role reversal (Daldrup, Beutler, Greenberg, & Engle, 1988) with her imagined father to help her express her rage, to integrate her view of her father, and to review her cognitive injunctions. The aim would be to help her disincorporate the negative image of self and to direct her resentment externally.

I would be mildly but gently directive, trusting Anne's ability to tolerate therapeutic interventions and to benefit from them. I would help her construct sentences to externalize the anger, and I would validate her rehearsal of those sentences to cope with the intrusive thoughts (Beutler, 1983). I would shy away from abreactive interventions since Anne's arousal level and vulnerability to deterioration are so high. The internal representations of her struggle, her guilt, and her anger also lead me to attempt to reduce her arousal level by providing structure, support, and safety. Anne's sense of security would be enhanced by reassurance and by some social support systems to help guide, monitor, and structure the expression of her struggle. Hence, I would favor group therapy as a modality of intervention. Within a victims group, she could learn to share secrets, reassuring herself that others are also victims. And she could gain vicariously through others' efforts to resolve feelings of defeat, victimization, and neediness.

Anne may be resistant to group work; she might point out that she has a number of "good friends" (who may turn out not to be intimates) and that she needs more individual attention. But the group can help defuse her needs to be treated as special, and in any event, group therapy does not preclude concurrent individual therapy.

The extensiveness and disruptiveness of the symptoms, and the fear attached to those symptoms, suggest that the therapist must attempt to go beyond symptom removal. I would focus on Anne's needs to attach to others, to find support in others, and to heal others as representing her needs to complete herself. Transference issues in our relationship would help us explore how she works ineffectively to gratify her needs.

Since my reconstruction is of a patient who exhibits both external defensive patterns and overactive ideation, I would look for therapeutic interventions that combine cognitive and behavioral strategies (e.g., Yost, Beutler, Corbishley, & Allender, 1986) and that are designed to reinforce the patient's sense of control, to resolve dependency conflicts, to reframe her stance as a victim, to reduce the amount of anxiety present, and to deemphasize the therapist's control. In analyzing her self-criticisms, I would try to provide her with skills for controlling her emotions through self-instruction and cognitive rehearsal.

An early task would be to reduce Anne's arousal level and increase her tolerance of being alone. I agree with the therapist that hypnosis might be terrifying. Given that her interpersonal boundary definition is weak, hypnosis might threaten her boundaries rather than strengthen them. The same would be true of any therapist-controlled procedure for which the patient is expected to be receptive. I would look, instead, to interventions that reinforce her individuality and provide structure in her environment.

Paradoxical interventions are particularly useful with patients who resist loss of interpersonal control—as reported in Anne's case—at least sometimes in psychotherapy sessions. With respect to Anne's intrusive thoughts, for example, I would encourage her to have them, rather than avoid them, and concomitantly to work to establish stimulus control for these thoughts. I would suggest that Anne establish locations at home and at work that she can use as "worry places." After a trial run in my office and then at her home, I would urge that she retreat to one of her worry places whenever the thoughts intrude upon her. I would suggest that when there she make herself anxious by recalling frightening memories. By reversing the patient's nonfunctional but natural tendency to try to reduce anxiety, I would expect the anxiety to lose both its intensity and the second-order fear associated with it. Additionally, I would endeavor to clarify the interpersonal anticipations that activate Anne's anxiety, and I would attempt to help her understand the relationship between her fear and the associated sense of dependency on others.

To the degree that Anne's intrusive thoughts increase or decrease under paradoxical instructions, I would reinforce her exercise of them. I would continue to ask her to monitor and even to exaggerate the frightening images, at her own pace, over the course of some weeks. As she acknowledged the change, I would begin a process of cognitive analysis and self-instruction.

We would try to define the demands and overgeneralizations associated with her anxiety and deprivation of love. Then, we would construct tests of these beliefs and more comforting alternatives that Anne could practice in times of stress. As the anxiety associated with her thoughts decreased, cognitive rehearsal, social support, and thought replacement would be used to redirect and refocus energy when the intrusions occurred. These replacements would be developed as consistent alternatives to the dependency themes that evoke her anxiety. The therapy relationship will supply other opportunities to reflect on and change thoughts associated with Anne's interpersonal neediness.

I would trust the strength of the collaborative and caring relationship to ride the process through. In the meantime, I would provide whatever assurance I could that her resolution process is a natural and workable one, and I would strive to avoid being intrusive in a natural process. This process would entail pointing out to her repeatedly that she is a survivor, one whose many internal resources have already allowed her to overcome obstacles far greater than oppressive memories. The reality is that she copes, that she can establish relationships, and that she can function as an unimpaired individual. At this point, she is a victim only of her remembrances, and as she learns to disown self-incrimination to establish her justified, outward anger, I would convey my faith that her therapeutic goals would be achieved.

Again, my compliments to the therapist and, particularly, to the patient.

Spencer Eth and Saul I. Harrison (Integrative)

Formulating a treatment plan begins with the process of differential diagnosis. The possibility of premature closure increases when we are confronted with a case history as horrifying as that of Anne. The historical events are so compelling that even reading about them elicits countertransference reactions, to phrase it euphemistically. Some clinicians might summarily dismiss Anne's story as a perverse fantasy, too terrible to be believed. It is painful indeed to contemplate the brutal torture of an innocent child, and disavowal has served to protect most of us in this culture from that awareness. On the other hand, we must guard against the temptation to accept uncritically everything a patient confides. It is incumbent on us to be empathic and caring, without suspending our judgment—the state that medical sociologist Rene Fox (1957) labeled *detached concern*. With these caveats in mind, what *DSM-III* (American Psychiatric Association, 1980) Axis I diagnostic considerations are relevant for this patient?

Anne's presenting complaint centers on her fears of failure, and such fears suggest the possibility of an anxiety disorder. The panoply of symptoms described suggests elements of *social phobia* (a persistent fear of one or more situations in which the person is exposed to possible scrutiny by others and fears that he or she may act in a way that will be humiliating or embarrassing), *generalized anxiety disorder* (unrealistic or excessive anxiety and worry about life circumstances), and *posttraumatic stress disorder* (experience of an event that is outside the range of usual human experience and that would be markedly distressing to almost anyone, followed by persistent reexperiencing of the event, persistent avoidance of stimuli associated with the trauma or numbing of general responsiveness, and persistent symptoms of increased arousal).

Anne's therapist describes repeated episodes of a "trancelike state" from which she can be brought out "by gentle shaking and insistence on eye contact." The essential feature of such *dissociative disorders* is a disturbance or alteration in the normally integrative functions of identity, memory, or consciousness. Included in this category, and perhaps relevant to Anne, are *depersonalization disorder* (persistent or recurring experiences of depersonalization during which reality testing remains intact) and *multiple personality disorder* (the existence within the person of two or more distinct personality states—each state with its own relatively enduring pattern of perceiving, relating to, and thinking about the environment—with at least two of these personality states recurrently taking full control of the person's behavior). Multiple personality is associated with histories of severe physical and sexual abuse in childhood (Kluft, 1985).

Some or all of Anne's symptoms could be a product of a *borderline personality disorder* (a pervasive pattern of instability of mood, interpersonal relationships, and self-image, beginning by early adulthood and present in a variety of contexts). Childhood cruelty and deprivation may figure prominently in the genesis of serious character pathology, and the diversity, severity, and chronicity of Anne's symptoms are not inconsistent with this condition.

The final entity, which should be mentioned for the sake of completeness, is *factitious disorder with psychological symptoms*, presupposing that Anne's symptoms and perhaps her history are not genuine. This diagnosis can be established only after other etiologic explanations of the problem have been excluded. In raising this possibility, it is vital to remember that although these patients' symptoms are self-induced, their suffering is real, and treatment, albeit of a different kind, is indicated.

With such an array of diagnostic possibilities, definitive treatment planning requires further assessment. The clinician should obtain all medical records: pediatric, gynecological, and psychiatric, along with available legal and social-service reports on Anne's family. Depending on what is found, further medical, neurological, audiological, and gynecological examinations and psychological testing may be needed. Interviews with family members and friends might provide valuable data, especially if Anne experiences dissociative memory gaps. Sequential sessions with Anne would add to the material gathered and would confer a needed longitudinal perspective on her mental status.

To formulate a treatment plan based only on the data at hand, let us assume, as a provisional principal diagnosis, posttraumatic stress disorder. What, then, can be offered to help this young woman?

Our treatment model is a biopsychosocial one. The therapeutic application would be integrative (Engel, 1980); however, for the purpose of exposition, each component will be considered in turn.

Although the term *posttraumatic stress disorder* (PTSD) is relatively new, the concept has received attention throughout this century. Biologically based treatments, alone or in conjunction with psychotherapy, date back at least to World War I, when it was found that sedation, nutrition, and exercise were therapeutic. In World War II, cathartic abreactive psychotherapy was promoted by the intravenous administration of barbiturates under the rubrics of narcosynthesis and narcoanalysis (Grinker & Spiegel, 1945).

The present-day application of biological psychopharmacology is more sophisticated. At least three different classes of drugs are in common use to ameliorate the distress of PTSD (Ettedgui & Bridges, 1985). Benzodiazepines (such as Valium or Xanax) are employed for the immediate, nonspecific relief of the symptoms of anxiety and insomnia. Two types of so-called antidepressants, the tricyclics, such as imipramine, and the monoamine oxidase inhibitors (MAOI), such as phenelzine, have been found to be beneficial in several small studies of PTSD in Vietnam veterans (Hogben & Cornfield, 1981). These medications typically require several weeks of treatment before symptoms are controlled and are accompanied by appreciable side effects at therapeutic dosage; some patients experience relapse when medication is withdrawn. The desired response to these agents does not appear to depend on the presence of an affective disorder. In this regard, the drugs are not acting as antidepressants, although the underlying neurochemical pathophysiology of PTSD may overlap with that of major depression. Both the tricyclics and MAOIs are also standard preventive treatments for endogenous panic attacks, another severe anxiety disorder. In the authors' experience, flashbacks and nightmares, comparable to those upsetting Anne, have been highly sensitive to the so-called antidepressant medications.

Psychological treatments for PTSD abound, ranging from traditional psychoanalysis to behavior modification (Horowitz, 1986). A catalog of available individual psychological treatments would include but would not be limited to supportive psychotherapy, open-ended exploratory psychodynamic psychotherapy, brief focal psychotherapy, cognitive therapy, hypnotherapy, systematic desensitization, biofeedback, and flooding. In addition, a variety of group therapies have been employed.

Individual therapy with PTSD patients should be flexible and should accommodate the incident-specific features of this condition. An interview protocol for use with traumatized children, applicable also with adults, has been elaborated (Pynoos & Eth, 1986). Mastery requires an affectively charged, thorough experiencing of the traumatic event. Although the sessions often may be exquisitely painful, sharing the terrible memories is fundamental to the process of overcoming the helplessness inherent in the traumatic state. With each reworking of the experience, greater confidence and enhanced coping are achieved. And the patient might have the opportunity to compensate in the transference for the deprivations and indignities suffered in childhood.

Anne's presenting fear of failure in the educational program could be dealt with in sessions wherein she was exposed to imagery or role-playing the anxiety-evoking situation, in combination with relaxation techniques. Such procedures in some cases have produced significant, lasting improvement. A relaxation technique often used is systematic desensitization augmented with biofeedback. The patient's overall sense of self-efficacy may be enhanced with the newly learned capacity to interrupt escalating anxiety and to perform in a stressful environment (Jansson & Ost, 1982).

The social dimension should be a major concern in Anne's

treatment. The proliferation of incest support groups affords Anne the chance to connect with other women in similar predicaments. Mutual support and friendship are powerful forces countering the alienation and despair with which the stigmatized survivors of sexual abuse are afflicted. Anne should be advised also to investigate whether there are legal avenues open to her. A civil suit against her father for damages arising from multiple assaults and rapes could take Anne from the role of victim and engage her in the role of competent adult seeking appropriate redress. Also, there may be an indication for vocational counseling to explore rationally the advantages and disadvantages of her chosen career, psychiatric nursing. To the extent that Anne may be nursing troubled patients to restore what she was deprived of and vicariously to cure herself, her efforts may be handicapped, and she risks remaining unfulfilled.

The biological, psychological, and social components of Anne's therapy are complementary. A complete treatment would encompass each of these dimensions and very likely would draw on the expertise of many specialists. Anne represents a therapeutic challenge, but given the availability of a full array of mental health services, her prognosis is not unfavorable.

Nolan Saltzman (Experiential)

What does it say about Anne that she survived a home like a private death camp, where solitary confinement, rape, and genital torture were routine, and then adolescence with a drug gang, to become a nurse working for psychiatric certification—despite deafness? My first principle would be to acknowledge that there is no body of knowledge that encompasses this case or delimits what this young woman may be capable of.

The history barely mentions the mother, beyond saying that she was a passive accomplice. Did she ever succor Anne? Did Anne hope her mother would rescue her? The dismantling of defenses as described should lead to more memories of mother's role.

While Anne's chosen career as a psychiatric nurse may be a self-fulfilling one, she has oriented herself to meet others' needs through a course that is arduous and presumably painful for her. In contrast, her therapist's account of her love affair at a distance sounds idyllic. I would accept Anne's report of it for now, and, when appropriate, try to learn more about the relationship. Is there a mutual exchange of nutrients, or is Anne relating primarily through meeting her lover's needs, as she (and her mother) had to meet her father's needs?

Anne came to therapy with adjustment problems, but she has evidently been induced to gamble for higher stakes. I suspect she has a fixed delusion that she is bad and deserved what was done to her. Such feelings protect a false self by keeping down any sign of rage, for which she was (further) tortured. The delusion of being bad also allows the hope that, by trying ever harder, she might become good, escape the torture, and be accepted as the other children were. To undermine this delusion, a perceptual coping scheme from childhood to the present, is risky. It ought to be undertaken only when a sufficiently strong bond with the therapist enables her to give up the false coping self. Anne may then be ready to leave the safe island, where she suppresses her rage and feels bad about herself, and to strike out through a terrifying void for the shore, where she would own her rage and a new sense of acceptability as a human being.

I would suggest to Anne that if she strives for characterological integration, her cognitive and behavioral patterns must change together in three ways: (1) She needs to accept that she is a good person, entitled to be loved, but, then, (2) she always was good, implying that her parents' treatment of her was wanton cruelty, and (3) she has the right to express killing rage toward them. Or, another sequence is possible: (1) She allows herself a killing rage at her parents, enabling her to stop turning her rage and loathing against herself, (2) that healthy reversal of the direction of the rage will also allow her to get angry at the obtrusive memories, the agents of her father's punishments in her own mind, and drive them out, and (3) she will then feel for the first time like a good person, entitled to receive others' love.

Assuming Anne develops trust in me, I would confront her on using the word *punishment* to describe her father's sexual abuse and tortures, pointing out that no one but her parents and she would use that word for what he did. I would ask Anne to use words the same way everyone else does. "Anne, suppose we were to go down to the street and ask the next fifty people, 'Was that *punishment* or *torture?'*—what would they say?"

In another session, I would ask Anne to say to me, with feeling, "I'm a good person," anticipating that she would dispute this or avoid it or that if she attempted it, the words would engender distress. Although I would be concerned about the risks of stripping away the delusions that enabled her to build a life separate from the agonies of her childhood, I would not hold Anne back if that was what she wanted to do. I would continue the approach of the presenting therapist. Since Anne is willing to engage in abreaction in a supportive environment, it affords her relief that lasts for hours, and it also brings up new and more detailed memories.

There are many entries to climactic expression besides the useful one mentioned by the therapist—that of visualizing the approach of the abusive father. A simple phrase such as "I'm a good person" or "I have a right to be loved" can also provide access to the depths of the emotions in a person who has never been allowed these feelings about himself or herself (Casriel, 1972). In my bio psychotherapy, I integrate psychodynamic, cognitive, and experiential methods with the techniques called EEVR—eliciting emotions in a setting where they meet with spontaneous validating responses. I elicit climactic expression (gut screams) as part of a learning experience, never for so-called ventilation (Saltzman, 1989).

More than fifty years ago, Ferenczi tried "loving his patients healthy," hugging and coddling them to restore what they had been deprived of in infancy. De Forest (1954) remembers a discussion in Budapest, not long before Ferenczi died, in which Ferenczi said, "Psychoanalytic 'cure' is in direct proportion to the cherishing love given by the psychoanalyst to the patient." Ferenczi's approach often did not work well. His patients had not exposed their deep emotions, so he was embracing all the layers of defense. However, Ferenczi had the right idea, and today we know how to let love fulfill its healing role when the patient casts aside his or her defenses in out-of-control expression.

In the present instance of a young woman sexually abused and tortured throughout childhood by psychotic parents, a therapy based on loving responses as initiated by Anne's therapist appears to be a good prescription. As always, one must respond lovingly to healthy expressions of the self, not to symptoms, which may be interpreted as defenses against expression. Further, the therapist had better not show sympathy or pity, because they muddle the expression of love. It is likely Anne would tend to reject love as pity, anyway, and it is incumbent on the therapist to respond cleanly and, as necessary, to help Anne discriminate responses.

As with all patients who enter intensely emotional work, but especially with survivors of incest and abuse, it would be necessary for Anne and the therapist to agree that the therapist's "love" means good feelings toward her essential nature, that a hug expresses these feelings, and that the therapist's touch is never motivated by lust or sadism. Unless Anne accepts these notions at least intellectually, holding is ruled out. If Anne accepted the initiation of a hug, but then became violently fearful, the embrace itself could become a passage to intense emotional expression.

Anne may already know how to lose control of her screams. If not, since she is deaf, I would ask her about working out a mode of communication such as squeezing her shoulder for "Louder!" and rubbing her upper arm for "Longer!"

One approach to EEVR would be to ask Anne to express parental attitudes she was forced to accept. When she says, "Since the other children were spared, I must have been bad as Dad said," I would say, "Yes, you must have been. Would you say to me, 'I'm bad!' " Then, I would urge her to say it louder and louder, longer, again and again, until she was screaming it out through loss of control. This approach does not reinforce the dysfunctional feeling. Instead, if Anne would scream "I'm bad!" until she was out of control, she would ultimately become enraged and reject it. I note that she is able to work up to a "few harsh angry sounds." If Anne were unable to go further, to express climactic rage, she would likely become depressed. I would anticipate the depression, but I would point out to her that in the session she had expressed some anger to her father and that there had been no consequent torture. And I would point out that she now has an ally who feels closer to her and heartened by her ripening rage and that she can choose to relate to these changes and perhaps get still angrier next time. In fact, it may take a long time, with much other material intervening, but, one hopes, growing trust will accompany the change.

The clinician will understand why I describe much of my work as *emotional conditioning,* by analogy to behavioral conditioning. Since expressing emotion is a primary mode of behavior in human beings and in primates generally, it is behavioral conditioning, too.

Another method of EEVR is referred to as *exorcism* (Saltzman, 1983). I would ask Anne to acknowledge at least intellectually that she had learned bad feelings about herself through bad treatment. If she acknowledged that, I would assert that anything learned can be unlearned. No patient has ever challenged that. It is the crux of the matter, but I am not at all certain that a psychological structure to which traumatic experience contributed can always later be undone— even by the greatest effort of the patient or the tenderest care by the therapist. If Anne raised the doubt, I would acknowledge my doubt, and ask her whether she wanted to back off because it may not work or to take the leap on the chance that it may. If she assents, I would ask her to lie on her back. (I have a mat in my office, but a couch or reclining chair away from walls is usable.) I would sit or recline on the mat by her. If she did not assume an open position, I would suggest she put her arms at her sides and uncross her legs. I would ask her if she were ready to cast out bad feelings and be rid of them. Her assent would help create a suggestible state. With my voice comforting but decisive, I would reiterate that underneath the imposed bad feelings are the natural, rooted, good feelings about herself that she was born with.

I would begin by resting a hand supportively on Anne's shoulder and saying, "When I say to, not just yet, make a sound, Ahhh. Let your body make the sound. The sound your body makes will be the bad feelings about yourself." The key word, *be,* is much better than *stands for* or *represents.* Anne might bring herself halfway out of her suggestible state by remarking, "I don't know how to do it." I would say, "Your body will know once you begin. If you wholly choose to, that will be enough."

The sound Anne would make might express pain, disgust, or the fear of retribution. Whatever it was, I would urge it louder and longer, using our special mode of communication, and through loss of control. When Anne was done, I would ask her to see that I accepted her, and I would offer a hug.

Sometimes victims of torture recapitulate counterpain maneuvers, such as slamming the head to the mat or rubbing together the fingers of a (formerly bound) hand. I would restrain any movements by which she might injure herself. I would also secure her permission to block counterpain efforts generally. Then, if, in reliving experiences of torture, she began to writhe in silent agony, withholding her screams by exercising a counterpain maneuver from her past—all out of vocal contact—I would interrupt the maneuver by holding her head or her hand, for example. This action would tend to trigger abreaction, but survivors attempting to relive traumatic experiences have told me they feel comforted by a firm handclasp or embrace, which they apprehend on some level as protective, not as abuse.

After months of individual work, I would bring Anne into one of my intensely emotional groups. Most group members would feel valuable in contributing to her recovery, and the one or two who might not be able to take her regressions to the torture scenes could be offered a transfer to another group or to individual work. The warmth and support of the group would help Anne eventually to feel accepted as a regular person rather than as a survivor or a psychiatric nurse.

Points of Contention and Convergence

Larry E. Beutler

I agree with Eth and Harrison when they assert that a clear and specific differential diagnosis is central to treatment planning. However, unlike them, when I make this statement, I am referring to a spectrum of observations broader than those required for the differentiation among traditional diagnostic labels. Elsewhere, I (Beutler, 1989) have outlined the problems with traditional diagnostic labels when planning comprehensive treatments that include psychosocial and psychotherapeutic interventions. Briefly, diagnostic labels are symptom descriptions that are founded in a level of abstraction that is better suited to psychopharmacology than to planning psychotherapy. Formal diagnostic criteria help in determining whether a person requires treatment and in selecting among broad classes of medication (anxiolytics versus neuroleptics versus antidepressants), but the *DSM-III-R* categories are of little use in the decisions that characterize psychotherapy.

Consistent with their emphasis on formal diagnosis, Eth and Harrison spend some time developing a case for and against various medications. The nonspecificity of diagnoses for even these decisions is observed in the poor relationship between the diagnosis and the drug selection. For example, if Anne is diagnosed with PTSD, any of the three classes of medication described by Eth and Harrison is likely to be used, but the effectiveness rates are unimpressive for all of them. Scrignar (1984) observes that benzodiazapines are likely to be effective only in the acute stage of PTSD. If the condition becomes chronic and resolves into a panic disorder, the selection of medication is quite unrelated to the diagnosis. Alprazolam (a benzodiazapine), tricyclic antidepressants (TCAs), or MAOIs all may have some value. Similarly, if PTSD resolves into a depressive constellation or if the patient develops recurrent panic attacks, either TCAs or MAOIs may be indicated. Hence, this diagnosis provides only a general contraindication for the use of benzodiazapines.

While antidepressants are probably the most prescribed medication for treating chronic PTSD, their uncertain efficacy further demonstrates the shaky value of diagnosis as a basis for treatment decisions. In what is still one of the best recognized studies of medication usage in PTSD following nonmilitary crises (war-related PTSD may be a very different condition), Burstein (1986) reports weak effects of antidepressant drug treatment, observing that nondiagnostic and environmental variables, more than diagnostic ones, seemed to account for patient response to treatment.

John Clarkin and I (Beutler & Clarkin, 1990) have emphasized that since specific psychotherapeutic procedures are useful for and adaptable to a variety of diagnostic conditions, a comprehensive treatment plan must rely upon an assessment of environmental demands and supports and upon a delineation of several nondiagnostic personality and attitudinal variables. By and large, these variables may be combined with information about the therapist's intervention style to aid in the selection of procedures that will both enhance the therapeutic relationship and result in resolution of the presenting problem.

A final point of disagreement between my own position and that of Eth and Harrison may represent only a matter of emphasis. Namely, I find the categorization of psychological treatments by brand names to be of little value. Like patient diagnoses, global categorizations of psychotherapies provides insufficient information about relevant variables to serve as a guide to treatment selection. Most brand-name psychotherapies have much in common as well as having some distinctive qualities. I prefer to describe psychotherapies in terms of long-term objectives, mediating goals or tasks, formal demand characteristics, and probable effects. Hence, I would select a cross-cutting menu of procedures that would aim at conflict resolution (as opposed to symptom change). Moreover, I would address the sequential mediating tasks of relationship maintenance, arousal reduction, cognitive change, and affective redirection, and I would select techniques and procedures at each stage that would be likely to accomplish these goals.

Specific therapeutic procedures are only tools to accomplish the specified goals and subgoals of treatment by directing and maintaining the patient's attentional focus, embuing the therapist with positive valence, managing the patient's level of arousal for optimal therapeutic effect, and selectively exposing the patient to avoided information or experience. As such, procedures are best discussed within the context in which they are implemented, and with a knowledge of the therapist's fit with the patient. Without attending to this context, identifying theoretical brand names has little value.

Turning to Saltzman, I find myself in agreement with his formulation of Anne's important dynamics. That is, I agree that the goal of treatment is to resolve conflicts about emotional expression and to reawaken and redirect suppressed and denied rage at parental figures. I also agree that redirecting and reconstructing language patterns may be useful for this patient because of her cyclical and somewhat unstable coping pattern. Relabeling her *punishment* as *torture* might help break down her denial and redirect her rage externally.

On the other hand, I disagree with the use of experiential, abreactive procedures with this patient. Ventilation procedures like those used in EEVR are potentially intrusive and, like most such procedures, are designed to raise arousal levels in the face of denied experience. The evidence is very poor for the therapeutic value of catharsis (ventilation) without redirection, and the evidence is relatively good that such emotional escalation can and does produce deterioration in individuals who are critically distressed (e.g., Beutler, Frank, Scheiber, Calvert, & Gaines, 1984; Lieberman, Yalom, & Miles, 1973). Anne's arousal and distress level is already critical, as implied by her dissociative states and the (apparently) recent flood of childhood associations.

Given the foregoing and the assumption that Anne is reactive to external direction, I would certainly want to encourage a slower and less therapist-controlled direction than that suggested by Saltzman. I consider healing to be a normal process, not one to be forced. Therapist direction is necessary when patients have constructed defenses to protect themselves from anxiety, and the natural presence of anxiety is an indication of unforced movement potential. Here, the therapist should work to keep anxiety from getting so high that it impairs reasoning and perceptual efficiency (indexed in Anne by derealization and dissociative states) rather than to raise it further. To use intrusive measures under these circumstances is very risky. By fostering (and forcing) the retrieval of painful memories at a speed that is faster than Anne can achieve with some degree of comfort, the therapist may inadvertently recapitulate the patient's victim status, now with the therapist as the victimizer who forces her to stand naked before him. This unfortunate recapitulation of victim status is all the more likely if, as suggested, the arousal potentiating effects of the interventions result in the therapist physically restraining Anne.

While I do not disagree with the value of using touch and other experiential procedures, I certainly do urge caution. There are certain things that a good therapeutic alliance does not automatically justify. Lying beside Anne as she reconstructs painful memories may be a stimulus whose power is too great and may arouse her anxiety to levels that seriously impede her ability to process information and that therefore actually prevent the desired extinction from taking place.

Spencer Eth and Saul I. Harrison

Beutler and Saltzman propose treatment plans that include some elements we endorse and others that generate discomfort. For centuries, the healing professions have assigned priority to the dictum *First Do No Harm*. It is vital, particularly with someone like Anne who has suffered so much, that the patient not be subjected to the risk of further victimization via therapeutic misadventure, however well intended.

Unhesitantly, we endorse Beutler's formulation that treatment has entered a middle phase in which the patient has bonded with her therapist. It is encouraging to consider the apparently constructive elements in the therapeutic alliance. The next challenge is to decide how most appropriately to proceed to assist Anne in expressing anger directed toward her sadistic father. We join Beutler in advising caution in mobilizing angry, aggressive affects in such a fragile and disturbed young woman, burdened with the potential for self-destructive acting out. Two-chair dialogue, role reversal, cognitive rehearsal, thought replacement, and paradoxical interventions are among the several potentially useful approaches to addressing Anne's problems and to facilitating her mastery of them. Although our therapeutic transactions very likely would appear markedly different than what would transpire in Saltzman's so-called emotional conditioning, there nevertheless are conceptual overlaps.

It is evident that we are concerned about the therapeutic approaches suggested by Saltzman. Characterizing Anne's self-appraisal as an erroneous belief, we would join Saltzman in confronting her with her use and apparent endorsement of the concept of punishment in lieu of describing her experiences more accurately as torture.

We cannot recommend the technique Saltzman describes as EEVR since we do not understand the rationale for so-called gut screams. Further, the suggestion that the therapist respond lovingly with physical embraces is, we believe, contraindicated. Although a hug may be intended and appear to be nurturing, it represents a potentially dangerous transgression of professional boundaries. Patients such as Anne, with histories of prior sexual victimization, are at greatest risk (Pope & Bouhautsous, 1986).

We are troubled also by the technique Saltzman referred to as "exorcism," whereby the patient lies on her back and the therapist sits or reclines next to her. The patient is then instructed to "cast out bad feelings and be rid of them." This abreactive approach has not been accepted generally and again poses the risk of unintended emotional and sexual exploitation (Eth, Randolph, & Brown, 1989).

Nolan Saltzman

I admire Larry Beutler's deep and encompassing reconstruction of Anne, but I disagree with some of his methods. Let me first list some suggestions with which I concur. Square brackets denote my variations from the given approach.

1. Considering a brief (voluntary) hospitalization
2. Working toward outward expression of anger helping Anne construct sentences to externalize anger [intensifying the work toward climactic expression of killing rage]
3. Setting up two-chair dialogues [intensifying expressions of terror, pain, and rage as they arise; while role reversal with the father would not arise in the usual sequence of my adaptation of this gestalt mode, I might try it here as an experiment but would quickly withdraw the suggestion if Anne resisted]
4. Helping counter self-criticism through cognitive rehearsal [although I would not couple this with provision of so-called skills for controlling her emotions, since I work toward emotional freedom rather than control]
5. Collaborative defining of demands and over-generalizations associated with Anne's anxiety and deprivation of love; testing of her beliefs and supplying of (reality-based) comforting perceptions
6. Clarifying the interpersonal anticipations that activate Anne's anxiety
7. Providing assurance that her resolution process is workable and that she is a survivor whose many internal resources have already allowed her to overcome obstacles greater than oppressive memories

Spencer Eth and Saul Harrison's "principal provisional diagnosis" of PTSD is reasonable. I would incline toward depersonalization disorder, which they also think may fit. I might offer Anne their discussion of the medicinal menu to prepare her for a visit to a psychopharmacologist; I concur with their prescriptions for friendship and a support group. Legal action appears not feasible here, unfortunately.

Eth and Harrison's prescription for Anne of "affectively charged, thorough reexperiencing of the traumatic event" converges with the intent (and perhaps, to some degree unclear to me, with the techniques) of the emotional work that I would use.

Methods I would not use involve encouraging Anne "to monitor and even exaggerate the frightening images," establishing of a "worry place" (Beutler), and teaching Anne relaxation techniques, conventional desensitization, or biofeedback (Eth and Harrison). Anne is overwhelmed with memories— so far as we know, not just images, but memories—of which it seems impossible to exaggerate the terror and anguish. Furthermore, memories overcome her "every few minutes," so that there would seem no chance of getting to a special place. Nor would I want to suggest, say, imagining a pleasant event or bucolic scene to someone struggling against memories of a father with sizzling implements of torture. In sum, I estimate that all these well-motivated prescriptions may be too weak in this case. They do not seem to me likely to allow the reconstruction of Anne's sense of self that can be accomplished by elicitation and validation of intense expression of the emotions associated with the traumatic memories. However, since I have not treated a single survivor of abuse and torture by relaxation, desensitization, or biofeedback methods, my preference is nothing more than my preference. I could be wrong.

On the other hand, the principles my fellow panelists advance as underpinnings for their approaches also provide a rationale for eliciting intense emotional expression and validating responses (EEVR). In Beutler's words, "By reversing the patient's natural tendency to try to reduce anxiety, I would expect the anxiety to lose both its intensity and the second-order fear associated with it." And, again, Eth and Harrison's prescription of "affectively charged, thorough reexperiencing of the traumatic event" sounds as though it is just what the therapist is achieving; he needs encouragement to stay the course.

When the patient relives the memories of abuse and torture,

utters climactic screams of pain and terror, and experiences the loving, comforting response of the therapist, then the primary terror (of the pain) and the secondary fear (of expression of pain and fear) will abate.

Recall that Anne experiences hours of relief after each session involving climactic expression with her supportive therapist. Given what she survived and what she has made of herself, despite deafness, she will only become more stable in the course of intensely emotional therapy with a caring, supportive therapist.

Editorial Comment on Therapist-Patient Boundaries

We feel compelled to respond to the imputation of sexual impropriety in eliciting and validating climactic emotional expression. Criticism in the "Points of Contention and Convergence" sections may cause many panelists to feel misunderstood, and perhaps they all deserve another round for rebuttal. However, the potential damage in these hottest of charges requires special consideration.

In reproving "catharsis (ventilation) without redirection," Beutler cites studies of therapy unrelated to Saltzman's in origin, theory, or practice. Beutler ignores Saltzman's explicit statement that he never elicits emotional expression for ventilation, but always as part of the learning experience afforded by a spontaneous, warm response. Eth and Spencer write that they do not understand the rationale for gut screams. Yet Saltzman proposes not simply eliciting screams, but a deep process: ". . . to let love fulfill its healing role when the patient has cast aside his or her defenses in out-of-control expression."

Referring to elicitation of emotional expression, Beutler introduces pejorative phrases such as "forcing" and "intrusive" and projects the therapist as "forcing [the patient] to stand naked before him." This may describe his own impulses or fantasies, since Saltzman prescribes collaboration and tender support. That climactic expression of emotion is achieved only through the patient's will and determination to become whole again (not under duress and not compromised to please parents or others) is a major condition of its efficacy.

Eth and Spencer's censure of a proposed offer of a hug after the most soul-wrenching work could be nearly as harmful to our profession as the "potentially dangerous transgression" they conjure up. A hug is a hug, not a touch on private parts. To suggest that these are the same—or that, because sexual congress between lovers sometimes begins with a hug, the offer of a hug must be tabooed as an invitation to sex— can have a chilling effect on a healing aspect of many therapeutic relationships. It would be as illogical to suggest that psychoanalysis or hypnosis or marriage counseling or dentistry leads to sexual violation of the patient. When exploitation occurs in any of these, it is not the profession or the method that is to blame, but a gravely dysfunctional mindset in the professional.

Similarly, Beutler cautions against lying next to the patient, although it is not uncommon in contemporary therapy for the therapist to recline on an elbow next to a patient regressing to an early childhood state. Clinicians who defend against impulses toward impropriety by maintaining vertical, noncontact attitudes can be respected. On the other hand, therapists capable of finding sexual and emotional fulfillment in their own personal lives are not tempted to exploit their patients, obliterate their therapeutic accomplishments, and ruin their reputations. Hence, they need not abstain from reclining next to a patient or imparting warmth to heal the wounds of early abuse and deprivation.

As Saltzman states, if transference causes the patient to perceive the therapist as lustful, extractive, or sadistic, then holding is ruled out. Eliciting memories of traumatic abuse and validating a patient's emotional responses through giving the tender affection deprived in infancy demand the utmost professional skill and delicacy. Exploitative intent or behavior is incompatible with the character of a therapist capable of performing this work.

7

The Don Juan

◙

Leslie S. Greenberg
Janet L. Bachant
Marvin R. Goldfried
Gertrud B. Ujhely

Case Presentation

Hal is forty-four, a successful entrepreneurial chemist. In his initial consultation, he doubts he can benefit from psychotherapy. His sole complaint at first is a dread of dying that comes over him several times a day. He wakes from sleep "chilled to the bone, paralyzed, heart pounding," thinking that nothing matters, for his life—in five years, ten, or twenty—will be over. He demands that his therapist, a male of almost the same age, tell him honestly whether he does not feel the same thing when he thinks of himself dead. The therapist acknowledges he shares the same existential concern but asserts a difference in frequency and degree. Within a few weeks, Hal is ready to talk about other problems, such as his choices in love relations.

Hal is short and aggressive. He has a bullet head, thick sinewy neck, and barrel chest. His suit looks custom-made. He says, in a blunt monotone, "My company grows, I am proud of that. I make money and I spend it, yet I don't enjoy myself much when I'm not working. Women like me, but it doesn't do me any good. Do you know what I mean?"

Hal is used to being in control. He admits feeling he has to be "the number-one man . . . to know everything, speak all languages, make all the beautiful women."

He says that he gets along well with his fifteen-year-old son, who lives with his ex-wife. One day he begins his session by saying, "I just learned from Sybil before I came here that my son Steve is smoking marijuana. I almost didn't come today."

"How do you feel about Steve smoking pot?" the therapist asks.

"How do I feel? I feel afraid! I'm afraid he's going to fail in school, or just get by and be a nobody!" Hall sounds exasperated, and he thrusts forward in his seat as he speaks. His eyes flash and his teeth are literally on edge. His face is crimson.

"You're not afraid, you're . . . what?" asks the therapist. When Hal looks blank, the therapist suggests he is angry.

"I'm angry? I'm angry?" Hal cries and shrinks back in his chair.

"No, now you're scared," the therapist says. "You're scared of how angry you are at Steve."

"What am I?" Hall asks in a tense, thin voice, looking around, wide-eyed.

"When you were angry at your son's pot smoking, you thought you were scared," the therapist says. "As soon as you became aware of how angry you are at Steve, you actually became afraid."

"Steve always says I am out of touch with my emotions," Hal says. "I don't know what that means, or if it means anything."

Hal describes his ex-wife as "neurotic as hell, a manipulating bitch." When the therapist asks him about his present love life, he responds, "Let's just say I like gorgeous women, and they often turn out to have emotional problems."

"You'll put up with these emotional problems if the women are gorgeous enough?" asks the therapist.

"As long as I don't have to get married again, yes, I'll put up with anything from a beautiful woman for a while," Hal says. "Then I say, what am I doing with this person? And I break up."

"It's always you who breaks it off?" the therapist asks.

"It looks as though they leave me," Hal says. "I give them enough hints so they can depart with dignity. These ladies are very much in demand. Every once in a while, there's one I think I'm going to have to call the sheriff to get out of my apartment."

"They fall in love with you."

"Some of these ladies are awfully ready to fall in love."

"But they fall in love with *you*. How do you feel about that?"

"Great," he says, but he looks somewhat pained.

The therapist points out that while he says, "Great," his mouth is turned down and his forehead lined.

Hal thinks that over. Then, he says, "I can't really enjoy that they love me."

The therapist asks Hal about his parents and his early life.

"My mother is a career woman who never had time for us," Hal says. "My kid brother and I were both unwelcome surprises. I understand she tried to abort me, which was no light thing in her time."

"How do you know she tried to abort you?"

"She told me."

"How do you feel about that?"

"It wasn't directed at me. She just didn't want to be tied down."

"Yes. And how do you feel about that, and about her telling you about it?"

"It's too bad my mother is such a cold person," Hal says.

"Did she ever hold you?"

"I don't remember it if she did. I don't think I would have wanted her to."

"How about your father? Is he living?"

"No. My father died at fifty-one, which I used to think was a full life, but it seems awfully young now. He was a physicist and a professor, in the lab at six every morning to get something done before his students came for the eight-thirty class.

He worked late every night, and I never saw him except at dinner. Saturday was a workday. Sunday was his day; he went off by himself. Walked in the woods, climbed mountains."

"He never took you?"

"No. Anyway, they sent us to boarding school."

"How do you feel toward your father now?" I ask.

"OK. I respect him. Or isn't respect a feeling?"

"It's a form of fear, associated with attitudes, values, and whatnot. But I'm having trouble getting an idea of how he treated you. What did he expect from you?"

"To think straight, work hard, get top grades. He used to quiz us every night at dinner."

"He wasn't physically affectionate, was he?"

"Not at all. We understood he cared about us, though teaching was the only way he could show it. He gave me a book on calculus for my twelfth birthday. I remember him saying that if he woke me in the middle of the night, I should be able to integrate the sine cubed of theta in my head."

After three months of therapy, Hal tells of a dream about his therapist: "I had a dream where we were going to bed. It was hazy and I'm not sure if you were supposed to be a woman or I was, or who was going to do what to whom."

The therapist says, "How does the thought of actually doing that appeal to you?"

"It's repulsive. What do you think it means that I dreamed it?"

Formulations and Treatments

Leslie S. Greenberg (Gestalt-Experiential)

My first general concern would be to establish a good initial working alliance with Hal. In the early sessions, I would want Hal to experience me as a safe, accepting person who is able to be genuine and make contact with him and his inner experience. This approach would reduce his anxiety and help promote inner exploration. Hal's initial goal, which I would accept, would be to explore his dread of dying. We would discuss what was going on in his life that led to this anxiety, and I would meet his directness with directness. Early in our work, I would enable Hal to feel more deeply his emotions in different situations. I would encourage him to focus on the pain and sense of inner emptiness that drive him, and I would attempt to get at the feelings and perceptions underlying his anger.

In my first meeting with Hal, feelings would arise in him, if only in a fleeting manner, and I would encourage him to stay with these feelings to develop them more fully. The process would then unfold, with perceptions, feelings, and thoughts leading one to another. I would continually help him to bring out his experience as it emerged. I would not like to have read a clinical description of Hal (such as the given one) even if it were available, since I would not want to have preconceptions that would prevent me from focusing on what was most alive for him in the moment. I would focus first and foremost on the ongoing experiential process.

Hal appears to be an ideal client for an awareness-oriented approach. After establishing a warm and accepting bond and enlisting his agreement in undertaking inner exploration, I would direct his attention as often as possible to his inner experience as he talks to me. I would guide Hal in reexperiencing feelings and perceptions that he does not usually process fully in his life, and I would use a variety of experiential techniques: Gestalt dialogues (Perls, 1969), focusing (Gendlin, 1981), and evocative unfolding, among others (Rice & Greenberg, 1984). Deeper access to his emotional experience would bring about discoveries and acknowledgments and would stimulate a host of complex meanings and beliefs. We would reinspect these "hot cognitions" (Greenberg & Safran, 1987) in the safety of the therapeutic situation. This reinspection would lead to emotional restructuring (Greenberg & Safran, 1989) and preparation to risk new ways of being and behaving in the world.

Hal's fears of his feelings and of intimacy would become the focus of treatment. I would set up a number of two-chair dialogue experiments (Greenberg, 1979) in which Hal would become aware first of how he controls his feelings and then of *what* it is he is controlling. In one chair, he would be his controlled feelings; in the other, he would experiment with how he interrupts or prevents his feelings. He would become aware of the cognitive aspects of control (Greenberg, Safran, & Rice, 1989) such as injunctions not to feel ("or else you'll get hurt, be criticized or not responded to"), beliefs ("weakness is unacceptable"), and muscular control (tightening the muscles of his jaw, neck, throat, chest, and stomach). If he got angry, I would ask him to intensify the bodily aspect of his experience to help him bring these processes and the controls into awareness. As Hal gained control of his controller, he would eventually become more able to relax at his discretion.

The combination of therapeutic safety, empathic understanding (Rogers, 1961), and awareness would be sufficient to allow him to begin to contact his inner experience of emptiness, his need for affection and comfort, and his anger. It appears that he would also benefit by dealing with unresolved feelings of loss and anger in relation to his mother, his father, and his ex-wife; we could employ empty-chair dialogues for resolving this unfinished business (Daldrup, Beutler, Greenberg, & Engle, 1988; Perls, Hefferline, & Goodman, 1951). Hal needs love and acceptance in his life as well as success, and I would stress the theme of need for balance in his life.

Therapy for Hal would involve a combination of awareness training, gestalt experiment, and empathically aided self-exploration to stimulate awareness and discovery of feeling and creation of new meaning. I would ask Hal to attend to his current momentary bodily sensations and experiences and to build from these to more complex meanings and experiences. I would encourage him to reexperience fully and concretely situations in which he reacted in ways that troubled him or in which he experienced his dread of dying or his lack of enjoyment of his women or anything other than work. Thus, we would evoke the idiosyncratic, automatic perceptions and meanings he attributes to people and events and the inner feelings and reactions he experiences. Certain core organizing beliefs such as "I can never trust anyone to be there for me" or "I'm unworthy or unlovable unless I excel" would be revealed through this process; needs and wants such as "I do need people" or "I want to love and I see it is possible" would also be revealed. Beliefs and needs both emerge from a fuller experience of his feelings and deeper emotions.

I would ask Hal to engage one of his beautiful women in a two-chair dialogue and to identify alternately with each side. This dialogue might help him access some of his own feelings of worthlessness and rejection as he identifies with the woman and as he experiences his scorn and imperviousness as himself. The role play of the other often leads to a "reowning" of the attributed feelings and might eventually expose Hal to hitherto avoided sadness and anger associated with being unloved or unvalued. The complex array of felt meanings would then be explored, and new meanings incorporating a new sense of self-esteem would emerge.

Contacting feelings leads to change both by a process of accepting previously avoided experience and by creating new meanings. What is needed in Hal's work is emotional restructuring whereby the complex emotional-cognitive structures governing his experience are activated in therapy and made accessible to new information from other elements of his experience (Greenberg & Safran, 1987, 1989). Thus, his tough, unfeeling aspects will be integrated with his needs for tenderness and caring.

Throughout the therapy, Hal's dreams would be welcomed. In response to the dream involving the therapist, I would invite Hal to play the different parts in the dream, owning the feelings that would be brought up and discovering for himself the meaning of the dream. Depending on what he experienced in this dreamwork, I would engage him in an I-Thou dialogue wherein we would talk genuinely about our feelings toward each other.

It would be helpful if Hal agreed to work with at least one of his relationships in therapy, preferably his relationship with his son. A moment of live contact and intimacy with his son would be worth hundreds of hours of therapeutic talk about his needs for contact or hours of reworking old scenes with his mother or father. I would attempt to promote an interaction between father and son that would direct Hal away from criticism or preaching and toward an expression of his underlying anxiety about life itself—and through this expression, to a demonstration of his concern for his son. The goal would be to have Hal express softer feelings to his son and to have the son see his father as vulnerable, thereby creating or reestablishing a bond between them (Greenberg & Johnson, 1988). From this bond would come better communication and interaction. Work on this relationship might then open up a discussion of how Hal and his ex-wife deal with Steve. More information about the family structure and interaction patterns would be required to guide this type of intervention. Clearly, any changes in Hal's relationship with Steve would affect the relationship between Steve and his mother, and this would have to be attended to in some manner.

Janet L. Bachant (Psychoanalytic)

Hal's presenting symptom, a dread of dying that comes over him several times a day, "chilling him to the bone," suggests that he may be struggling against a deadness both within himself and in forms he projects onto the world—as in his doubt that treatment can help him. On some level, he may experience his life now as over. The sense of urgency and near-panic accompanying this experience lead me to suspect that it is a childhood anxiety against which his defense is now breaking down. He looks for comfort from his therapist via a regression, a return to merging, demanding that the therapist acknowledge having the very fears he is struggling with.

If I were Hal's therapist, I would address these issues from the beginning of the treatment, but my immediate priority would be to engage Hal in establishing the basic psycho-analytic situation (Stone, 1961)—one that would foster my neutrality and his capacity for free association. Therefore, I would avoid overactivity and would try not to join the patient in a dialogue, aiming instead to allow more of the unconscious process to emerge. This approach seems especially important with Hal since he uses conscious control as a defense against his feelings (particularly his deadness).

Although Hal's desire for contact and comfort from merging can put his therapist under considerable pressure, I would use this demand to engage him in the development of the working alliance by empathically acknowledging his concern with feeling normal and his distress over the dead feeling inside him. I would add, however, that in the course of our work together, he would probably have a lot of questions about me and what I experience. I would explain that, in general, I would not be answering them so that we would be able to allow his feelings, fantasies, and associations to emerge more freely. At this point, I would ask him to tell me everything that came into his mind, even if it distressed or embarrassed him or seemed unimportant.

I would expect that my standing outside his attempt to engage me via his maladaptive solutions (desire for merging, control of the other) would facilitate the emergence of the transference, especially of feelings of being disconnected, abandoned, or vulnerable in relation to me. Although I would have to do this carefully with an eye to maintaining and developing a positive therapeutic alliance, it would enable us to work directly on feelings and mechanisms that, although rooted in his early childhood, are operative (largely unconsciously) in the current dynamics of our relationship.

I would try to structure the therapeutic situation to facilitate the emergence of specific unconscious detail and to develop contact with him through an alliance with his observing ego rather than his desire to merge. I would want to know more about the less conscious material deduced from his fantasies, the train of his associations, and the nature of his interaction with me. I would be particularly interested in the type of object relation Hal would attempt to construct with me, and I would alternate, therefore, between empathic involvement with him and observation of my own response to him. I would not try to develop any particular therapeutic relationship but would note the roles he was implicitly and explicitly asking me to play.

I would imagine that following the structuring of the analytic situation, work on Hal's narcissistic defenses would be a primary focus of the treatment. What is Hal looking for in his perpetual quest for gorgeous but neurotic women? One possibility that occurs to me is that he wants to incorporate the feeling of being desirable by possessing and merging with "ladies who are very much in demand." I wonder if in this way he is trying to compensate for feeling dead and undesirable inside (killed off by his mother's wish to abort him, by her insensitivity in telling him of her wish, by his father's absence and lack of affection?). His choice of women who are beautiful and neurotic suggests that the combination of the two is important in ways we do not yet understand.

My efforts in the beginning phase of treatment would be to explore this behavior in detail by trying to uncover what he is getting from this repetitive, apparently unsatisfying pattern of relating. The work during this phase would center on the establishment of a more secure sense of self and would focus on issues of the safety and preservation of the self. Hal's fear of dying, his sense that nothing matters, is a metaphor for a fragile and crumbling sense of self. Addressing his defensive need to use beautiful women as a way of protecting the vulnerability of the self might involve offering the following interpretation: "If you can possess and discard beautiful women, you can make yourself feel powerful, and then you don't have to look at how dead and lifeless you feel inside." The aim here is to help Hal express his anxiety, not by acting out in the world, but in the analytic situation, where he can reexperience it and work it through in the therapeutic relationship.

Concomitant with the analysis of his narcissistic defenses and the development of a firmer foundation for his self, Hal's ambivalence toward women ("Women like me, but it doesn't do me any good") would become manifest in the transference—in his feelings and fantasies about me. As our relationship developed, I would listen for a similar response to me—

how, although I might like him, I wasn't doing him any good, either. As with the gorgeous women he gets involved with and wants something from (only to find that he is inevitably disappointed), I expect he would fantasize that I have something that could fill him up and make him feel good, only to be disappointed in me or in the treatment or both. I would use this experience as an opportunity to explore and elaborate the specifics of his particular fantasies about me and women in his life. If I picked up signs that he was "putting up with anything" in relation to me—expressed, for example, in irritation about my fee or my ending of an hour—I would try to bring this pattern into the transference with an interpretation along this line: "So, I too disappoint you, maybe even to the point of wondering if you want to break off with me." He could then experience, explore, and work through directly with me his defense of breaking off relationships to maintain control and to keep himself safe from intimate involvement.

In the course of the therapy, we would reconstruct a narrative of Hal's development that makes sense of his particular choices, and we would work through his specific feelings and fantasies in the transference.

Marvin R. Goldfried (Cognitive-Behavioral)

Following the first consultation, I provide clients with a questionnaire to obtain basic demographic and historic information. I would want to learn more about Hal's educational background, religion, family composition, the nature of his relationship with his parents, work history, past therapy experiences, and some indication as to why he sought therapy at this point in his life.

I would be particularly interested in learning more about the onset of his symptoms. Did it at all coincide with the death of a friend, colleague, or relative? Given his concerns regarding death and his anxiety and depression, I would look into the possibility of a delayed grief reaction. What did his father die of? Did he mourn his father's death? Is he concerned that he will die similarly at an early age? Since Hal is hard driving and aggressive, he may well be at risk of a heart attack.

Hal shows many characteristics of the stereotypical male role, emphasizing achievement, power, competition, and sexual prowess. A consideration of the possibility that his son Steve may depart from this role is extremely threatening to him. Some of Hal's difficulties may be manifestations of a mid-life crisis. He has made it financially, he appears to be successful in his sexual conquests, and the question for him may be, What now?

Finally, I would want to know more about Hal's current social system, an increasingly important area of focus among many therapists (Goldfried, Greenberg, & Marmar, 1990). Who are the significant others in his life, if any? What is the nature of his current relationships? To what extent do they encourage a symptomatic behavior pattern?

Bordin (1979) describes the therapeutic alliance as comprising three separate factors: (1) a positive therapeutic bond, the so-called chemistry in the therapeutic relationship, (2) client-therapist agreement on goals, and (3) agreement on therapeutic interventions that will be used to reach these goals. A positive therapeutic alliance has been found to predict successful outcome, regardless of therapeutic orientation. But establishing and maintaining a positive therapeutic alliance with Hal may be difficult. Would he be willing to be influenced? He is a self-made man, accustomed to being in control, who begins by expressing doubts that therapy can benefit him. I would be mindful in working with Hal not to undermine his sense of being in control. As suggested by Brehm (1966), individuals who believe their sense of control is being threatened are likely to respond with "psychological reactance." One can anticipate that Hal would react to such a threat with resistance and noncompliance. Following strategies described elsewhere (Beutler, 1983; Goldfried & Davison, 1976), I would avoid being too directive in any suggestions I offered to him. As I have done in similar cases, I would explain to Hal the dilemma confronting me: that if I were too directive, he might dig in his heels and fight back, and if I were too passive and nondirective, I might not be helping him. I would then ask for his suggestions as to how I might best proceed. Thus, within the context of a caring and concerned relationship, I would attempt to have Hal give me permission to influence his life. It is likely that we would need to return to this issue at various points in the therapy.

The precise therapeutic intervention would greatly depend upon the case formulation that would follow from the additional information. From the information provided in the original description, however, certain issues are evident.

Hal's mode of functioning is task oriented at the expense of awareness of his own emotional state. Toward the goal of assisting Hal to become better able to identify his emotions, I would, as did the therapist in the case description, provide him with feedback on discrepancies between what he was saying and how he was saying it. I would encourage Hal to identify the bodily cues associated with the various emotional reactions, perhaps using written descriptions of emotional states as an aid. I would also guide Hal in differentiating between positive and negative emotional reactions in various situations and then in making finer distinctions within these categories.

Hal finds himself attracted to beautiful women, only to discover that they "have emotional problems." These relationships are clearly pursued within the context of his achievement-oriented style. By instigating the termination of these relationships with women who are "very much in demand," Hal is able to leave uncomfortable situations and continue to feel that he has successfully achieved something. In discussing specific past relationships, I would explore the possibility with Hal that he may have inaccurately attributed the causes of the women's behavior to *their* emotional problems. In the spirit of Pogo's conclusion, "We have met the enemy and it is us," I would encourage Hal to entertain the possibility that the behavior of the women he found unpleasant might have been the consequence of something *he* was doing—or not doing.

In an attempt to motivate Hal to acknowledge and work

on changing how he relates to others, I would discuss with
him the impact of his early childhood experiences. I would
try to have him become aware of the extent to which his
current interpersonal relations were modeled on his father's
and mother's behavior toward each other and toward him.
What he learned from them, in essence, was to work but not
to love. His father was a model of a striving, achievement-
oriented male who invested more in his career than in his
family. The primary contacts with him that Hal recalls were
on task-related issues (quizzing him every night). His mother
was similarly achievement oriented and probably aggressive
(as manifested in her telling Hal that she had wanted to abort
him). I would also draw a parallel between the way Hal was
treated as a child and how he relates currently to Steve.

Hal is clearly unable to deal with others on an intimate
level and is probably fearful and inept in doing so. My
general intervention strategy would be cognitive-behavioral,
with the goals of removing the inhibitions caused by anticipated, feared consequences and helping him learn interpersonal communication skills. His relationship with his son
would probably be a good place to start, particularly since
Hal is concerned about Steve's future. Consistent with an
anxiety-reduction and skills training model, we would focus
on graduated risk taking, perhaps using simulations within
the consultation.

Before closing, I would like to acknowledge the utility of
an exercise such as this, in which several clinicians are asked
to specify how they would handle the same case. However,
the limitations of such an approach must also be noted. Just
as our clients and patients may not always be accurate in
predicting their behavior, so may we be limited in outlining
how we will handle a given case. In the final analysis, a comparative analysis across therapists must be based on what we
do, not what we say we do (Wolfe & Goldfried, 1988).

Gertrud B. Ujhely (Psychoanalytic)

What else would I need to know about Hal, and how would I
find out? I don't know that I need to know anything; if the

patient wants to focus only on his own priorities, I could go along with what is given. I would prefer, though, having knowledge about Hal's ethnic background, where father, mother, and grandparents came from, their occupations, the sibling order of the patient (how many, oldest, youngest, and so on), and his chronological account of important events in his life as he sees it. I would ask Hal whether he would be willing to write his autobiography, of whatever length he wished, in installments if necessary. As I received these installments, I would read them between sessions and ask questions or comment on them. If Hal were unwilling to write his history down, I would ask whether he would be willing to recount it to me orally.

I would also want to know about recurrent dreams in Hal's childhood and later on, who his heroes in fiction were, and so forth.

Since Hal questions that psychotherapy can be of benefit to him, I might want to know what got him to come despite his doubts and whether he had ever been in psychotherapy before, and (if so) when, for how long, what it was like for him, what the difficulties were, and possibly, with whom.

Finally, I would not only want but also need to find out when he began to be plagued by his fear of dying, what the circumstances were then, and what precipitates these fears from day to day.

I would tentatively diagnose Hal's condition as a panic disorder on Axis I of the *DSM-III* and narcissistic personality disorder on Axis II.

In his midforties, Hal is undergoing a necessary mid-life crisis. In Jungian terms, he has been leading a one-sided life of extraverted adjustment, using mostly extraverted thinking, sensation, and intuition. His introverted feeling life is making claims on him, while the extraverted functions are getting tired, so to speak. His old way of life is "dying," and something in him is becoming aware that life does not go on forever. One might say that his symptoms have the function of calling him toward the hitherto neglected development of unconscious parts of his personality.

In terms of the therapeutic relationship, I would make sure Hal never felt that I was controlling our relationship. When I would suggest a course of action, I would elicit his feedback and agreement with it.

I would suggest that in the beginning we meet six times, once a week, and then reevaluate. I would not use "couch" therapy, but a face-to-face encounter. After a few weeks, his overall attitude might change. He might begin to become interested in his own psychological process. We could embark on a long-term analytic approach, then, meeting once or twice a week, still in face-to-face dialogue rather than on a regressive basis.

I would not talk about feelings per se, since these are his inferior function, not related sufficiently to his conscious ego. Going directly after something that is not conscious would only increase Hal's already present anxiety. Instead, I would use broader phrases, such as "Tell me about it" or "What was that like?" or "Would you enlarge on that?" I might also ask, "Where do you experience this in your body?" and "Are there thoughts associated with these images?"

I might also ask, "What about dying?" "What all comes to mind?" "Have you ever experienced the death of loved ones, or others?"

I would ask for clarification and enlargement of Hal's statements, but I would not make interpretations that are specific to him. If Hal seemed receptive to it, and when appropriate, I would talk in general about mid-life psychology and the overall process of coming to terms with as yet unused functions. I might also talk about the symbolic meaning of dying in contradistinction to the literal one. I might also ask him what provisions he has made for his actual death.

Given Hal's personality structure, I would be wary that he might suddenly terminate the therapy or set me up to terminate it. Therefore, I would keep tabs on his negative reactions and transference. I would encourage him to voice any dissatisfactions, and I would attempt to resolve them. And I would encourage Hal to state his reactions to the previous session at the beginning of each meeting with me.

As stated above, I would not at first go after feelings, but rather after thoughts. Deflecting Hal from the literal meaning of the dream, I would explain that sexual union in dreams can be taken symbolically to mean a coming close or connecting. I might ask myself, though, whether the erotic merging anticipated in the dream might not be Hal's compensation for an actual lack of contact with me as therapist. And I would explore with the patient how things are going between us (again, eliciting negative responses if they are there and making covert ones overt).

Hal has been very much deprived of human contact and mirroring in his childhood. Underneath his gruff, omnipotent exterior is a lost little boy. Gradually, as the data come up, I would ask him to describe what it was like. I would speak of the little boy in the third person and, perhaps, express my feelings for the little boy and later elicit his feelings for the boy. I would not identify him with the boy, though, since I believe this would be too threatening to his defended ego, and he would have to flee.

Points of Contention and Convergence

Leslie S. Greenberg

Convergence was evident around the importance of establishing an alliance and focusing on inner feelings of emptiness. I think we all regarded as important the establishment of a secure sense of self (Bachant), issues with love and intimacy (Goldfried), and the importance of the lost little boy (Ujhely). I was struck, too, by the agreement among Goldfried, Ujhely, and me on the goal of increasing the client's access to his feelings.

I differ with Ujhely's concern that the client would find it too threatening for a long time to contact his lost little boy and the feeling associated with this. However, I do agree that initially contacting the little boy through thinking would be necessary and that broader phrases such as "What was that like?" rather than "What do you feel?" would be good. It is true in general that one accesses feeling states better through the broader associative description evoked by "What's it like?" than through conscious intentional labeling evoked by "What do you feel?" I also would not actively pursue discrepancies between what the client was saying and how he was saying it (as Goldfried suggests) because I feel this creates anxiety in the client. Discrepancy feedback sets up a role relationship pattern with me as an expert observer and does not convey the kind of acceptance and safety I wish to provide. When an alliance is very strong, I might occasionally use discrepancy feedback to promote awareness, but only if I think it will be experienced as nonjudgmental.

I agree with Goldfried's and others' concern about a control issue with Hal, and I would be sensitive to sharing control in ways similar to Goldfried's and Ujhely's suggestions. My client's need for control may eventually become a focus of therapy, although I prefer to deal with this issue in his life rather than with his relationship to me. In this regard, I differ most strongly in my practice of short-term therapy from Bachant's intentional use of the relationship to look "with the therapist" for signs of therapist-formulated client problems. I would not actively look for signs of Hal "putting up with me" nor would I interpret that "I too disappoint you." I find these interventions place the therapist in the superior role of expert giving "news" to clients about themselves in a manner that does not enhance the process of deeper experiencing and self-discovery I am attempting to promote. In much longer-term therapies of mine (over two years), I find transference and interpersonal interpretations more acceptable as another aspect or way of dealing with a clearly established theme in the person's life—but only when it is already very clear to the client that the pattern is occurring between us, so when I comment on it, I am not giving my client news of something he or she does not know.

While focusing on my differences with Bachant, I might point out that I also would not interpret Hal's possessing of beautiful women as making him feel powerful in order to avoid his dead and lifeless feelings. The client may indeed discover this, but I do not know, and I am not sure I ever could know, that this is his true motivation. It is not that I believe certain things about my client to be true and then withhold them from my client. I do not, in general, think these things and, if I do, I do not take them too seriously, because I view them as speculative and as not having much validity unless the client begins to tell me that this is his or her experience. My criterion of truth lies ultimately in the client, and I do not put too much weight on my formulations.

My role, in contrast to that of interpreter, is process facilitator and coconstructor of a reality, one that fits the client's experience. I do not want to offer my clients interpretations of the meanings of their experiences in order to give them insight. I want to help them construct new views of themselves by helping them focus on hitherto neglected aspects of their experiences. I am directive in process, but I do not like to be directive in relation to content to define the meaning of a client's experience. I especially do not want to interpret what is occurring in our relationship, for those views are most susceptible to influence by power imbalances in the relationship—or to being perceived that way.

My primary goal is to provide a confirming relational experience rather than to provide an insight to my client about a specific aspect of content. My second goal is to promote awareness in my clients about the processes in which they are engaged—processes that produce their internal experiences. I direct clients to help them experiment and discover how they function, not why they do. I see this process orientation as central to my approach, and it presupposes that people are fundamentally processes and that awareness of how they create their realities and experiences will empower them.

Janet L. Bachant

Common to all contributors in the case of Don Juan is the need to establish a therapeutic alliance that will be able to bear the weight of more intense exploration. This need is fundamental, a point of convergence for each theoretical perspective. The importance of the relationship to the therapist, of which the therapeutic alliance is one component, was first recognized by Freud (1895) and has received increasing recognition across a broad range of therapeutic modalities. Currently, in psychoanalytic thinking, relationship factors in the analytic work are now seen by some as rivaling interpretation as the primary vehicle of change (Greenberg & Mitchell, 1983; Pine, 1985). Development and maintenance of a good therapeutic alliance are especially important in working with Hal in that feeling positively connected to others is so conflicted for him.

A striking point of divergence between the psychoanalytic orientation and the other theoretical perspectives is a focus on the development and emergence of unconscious material in the psychoanalytic approach. The psychoanalytic approach addresses itself to helping patients better understand themselves by uncovering those unconscious wishes, conflicts, and fantasies that interfere with their conscious needs and goals. The analyst takes care to follow the patients' associations rather than to direct them along a given path, whether it be a questionnaire, a dialogue experiment, or a question about what provisions they have made for their own deaths. While skill building and educative approaches may be helpful and supportive in some ways, they do not address the patients' unconscious dynamics on which their own skill building and educational approaches have already foundered. Although attempts are made in the other treatment modalities to deal with this issue, the structure of the therapeutic situation is not organized in a way that assures the emergence of unconscious material; nor does the structure assure that material can be brought into the transference to be worked through in the therapeutic relationship.

This brings me to a second point of divergence. A central difference between the psychoanalytic approach and the other therapeutic perspectives is paradoxical in that the psychoanalytic situation is structured to facilitate the emergence of unconscious dynamics by asking the analyst to sit back in some respects, but it alone is characterized by an intense, intimate involvement in the analysis of the transference. While the other therapists speak of developing a sound therapeutic alliance, the absence in their reports of how they would develop and deal with their relationships to the patients is significant. There is much discussion of getting Hal to talk about his feelings, his thoughts, and about his relationships with women, with his son, and with his inner little boy. However, the most powerful and immediate vehicle of change—the here-and-now relationship to the therapist as a container of the transference—is given priority only in the psychoanalytic approach. This lack of focus on the analysis of the transference, especially of the negative transference, puts the most powerful tool of the therapist out of reach. For example, Hal's need to control is dealt with largely by avoiding it rather than by using his fears, fantasies, and wishes to control the therapist as a means of analyzing and working through this issue.

> Transference analysis gives the psychoanalyst a second chance to understand the analysand. The need to repeat in transference the vulnerable points of fixation draws attention to these difficulties and highlights them in a way that could not be understood in the mere telling of the biography. In transference, the earlier battles that were fought and lost by the ego are now refought with the help of the psychoanalyst, with a better chance of favorable results [Bergmann, 1987, p. 162].

Being able to explore, develop, and work through the negative feelings toward intimate involvement with others in the context of a positive working alliance is essential in every treatment. But it is especially important in a case such as this, in which considerable hurt, anger, and frustrated longing have organized Hal's patterns of relating since early childhood. If these feelings are not addressed (and the psychoanalytic point of view contends that they are most effectively addressed in the transference where they can be directly experienced and dealt with in relation to the analyst), then the heart of the problem is missed, and the therapy itself risks recapitulating, on a deeper level, the earlier lack of parental involvement.

Marvin R. Goldfried

Bachant's emphasis on the importance of establishing an alliance with the patient's observing ego represents a very important guideline in my own clinical work. In many respects, this concept is quite consistent with a cognitive-behavioral approach to therapy, which focuses on assisting patients in learning to cope more effectively with their lives. It is precisely that more adultlike aspect of patient functioning that cognitive-behavior therapists attempt to strengthen— particularly as a way of reevaluating misconceptions, behavior patterns, and emotional reactions that may create problems for patients. We differ, however, in that I would not attempt to assume an analytic stance, but would feel free to self-disclose whenever appropriate—to serve as a model to help Hal normalize his thoughts, emotions, or behaviors that he may have difficulty in accepting or to point to ways in which he may more effectively handle these.

I would also find it important, as Ujhely would, to learn more about Hal's past therapeutic experiences and his reservations regarding therapy. This information would help uncover his implicit expectations as he approaches the treatment process and would be relevant in forming the therapeutic alliance. The importance of such a working alliance was underscored in my own comments, as well as in those by Greenberg. To the extent that a patient's problem is interpersonal in nature, a therapeutic alliance can provide corrective experiences in its own right. In other instances, it can serve to set an optimal therapeutic context within which other change can occur. In many respects, I view this alliance as the "anesthesia" necessary for an intervention to take place. Thus, whenever there is a disruption of an adequate working alliance, attention must be paid to repairing it before any other active intervention can take place.

Both Greenberg and I agree that it would be essential to

focus on helping Hal become more aware of his emotional experiences. This would hold true not only in his relationship with me but also in attempts he would make to develop his relationship with his son, particularly when he would disclose feelings. Unlike Greenberg, I would be very reluctant to focus on Hal's emotional awareness during the first session. Instead, I would wait until a good working alliance had been established—a view shared by Ujhely.

Ujhely and I also agree on the importance of obtaining some information that was not provided in the initial case description, such as relevant historical information. We also agree on the probable role of mid-life issues operating with Hal, and we share a concern regarding control issues as they may emerge within the therapeutic relationship.

I very much concur with Greenberg's suggestion that the focus of the therapy be placed on core organizing beliefs. This thematic emphasis would highlight cognitive-affective-behavioral components of Hal's idiosyncratic interpersonal scripts and the problems they create in his life. Although I typically make use of associative methods in trying to uncover significant aspects of these interpersonal scripts, I find the nonspecific use of free association methods advocated by Bachant to be too open-ended. Instead, I would have Hal's association focus more on specific interpersonal issues to obtain a better understanding of the implicit personal meanings he brings to such situations.

Gertrud B. Ujhely

Regarding points of contention, as I have pointed out in my comments about the case, I would not explore Hal's feelings early in the therapeutic process, since it seems to me that he is not sufficiently conscious of them. Focusing on unconscious material in someone who is already close to panic would only aggravate the situation, perhaps to a dangerous point. I would rather build a bridge to his feelings via modes of experience that are close to his consciousness—thoughts, sensations, images.

I do not think he is ready for a two-chair dialogue; he barely knows his own experience. At the level of consciousness on which he operates in relation to his subjective experience, allowing for the experience of the other person visualized in the opposite chair would mean he would have to repress his own, and he does enough of that already.

Nor would I assume the psychoanalytic stance, given Hal's lack of connectedness with his experience. Again, I believe, such an approach would only escalate his anxiety. I would rather address his ego and help his ego to become aware of his subjective reactions. Similarly, I would not use interpretations; rather, I would stay with what he brings up, not in terms of causality, but in terms of similarities to past experiences.

As for points of convergence, I agree with Greenberg and Bachant in wanting to establish a working alliance and wanting to focus on Hal's present experience and awareness. I also agree with working on his relationship to his son's mother via working on his relationship with his son. All these approaches would be nonthreatening to and strengthening for Hal's ego. I also agree with Bachant's exploration of the negative transference, for the reasons I pointed up in my comments on the case.

I agree very much with Goldfried's careful history taking, his points about mid-life crisis, his view of Hal's need for control, and his focusing the patient on bodily sensations. I believe I made rather similar points. I also liked Goldfried's emphasis on teaching Hal skills in relating. The patient has a learning deficit in the area of relationships—a deficit for which he needs to learn ego skills and which, I believe, cannot be rectified by exploration of his past and the unconscious.

8

The Make-Up Artist

◨

Stanley B. Messer
J. Kevin Thompson
Elisabeth A. Lederman
Bernard D. Beitman

Case Presentation

Mary first came to see the psychotherapist, accompanied by her parents, at age twenty-two. She had taken an overdose of pills and had cut her wrists. For five years, she had been going on destructive and self-destructive rampages, tearing up her room, thrusting her hands through windows, and banging her head against walls severely enough to leave visible contusions. When asked why she acted as she did, Mary blamed what she perceived to be her bad skin and general repulsiveness. The failure of her efforts to improve her skin had left her angry and wanting to die. The therapist describes her as an attractive young woman with no apparent skin problems. Her tone challenging and angry, she suggested he not waste his time; nevertheless, she agreed to return.

Mary was the eldest of four children. Except for her sister at college, they all lived in the parents' home. Her father had

Note: This case was contributed by Joel Weinberger of the Henry Murray Research Center, Harvard University, and the Center for Applied Social Sciences, Boston University.

been physically abusive as far back as Mary could remember; his attacks were unprovoked and unpredictable. As she approached adolescence, he began tearing off her bathrobe, calling her a slut, and so forth, but he never attacked her sexually. The attacks ended when Mary began injuring herself; her mother was unpredictably supportive or depriving. Mary's parents kept her indoors for her entire eleventh summer as punishment for fighting.

Mary was concerned about her looks as far back as she could recall. In kindergarten, she destroyed her lunch box because she thought it was pretty and she was not; she felt she did not deserve it. In elementary school, she thought that her hands were large and repulsive and, as puberty approached, that her hair was frizzy and unattractive.

She had been popular and active in high school, coleader of a singing group and cocaptain of the cheerleaders. When asked to lead these activities on her own, she deferred to a friend whom she idolized. She perceived the friend as beautiful, popular, and poised—all of the things she wished to be but felt she was not. The friend broke with her toward the end of high school in a sadistic manner. Characteristically, Mary felt she deserved it. When the therapist began seeing Mary, she had another best friend whom she idolized and deferred to in a like manner.

Until her seventeenth year, Mary avoided her male admirers. She deflected them in any way she could and disbelieved their compliments and advances. When she finally allowed herself a sexual encounter, her fears seemed confirmed. He was a man in his thirties who appeared to be upset that she was a virgin. He ignored her afterward and allied himself with the idealized friend. Mary felt that the two of them joined in mocking her. She remained fearful of men and shunned involvement.

Mary attempted college and achieved good grades, but anticipating failure, she dropped out. A series of employers liked her and wished to advance her, but in each job she became uncontrollably anxious that she was doing badly, and she quit. When the therapist began seeing her, she had held a job for six months. She was about to receive a third, substantial raise and an increase in responsibilities, but she felt she was doing poorly and experienced each day as an overwhelming, anxiety-filled struggle. Three weeks after therapy began, following a typically destructive episode in her room, her parents hospitalized her. Her behavior was no different than it had been on previous occasions, but the parents claimed to be "fed up." She was observed for three days and discharged. During this time, the mother called her employer and told him what had happened, adding that Mary would probably not return to work. The mother gave the employer the therapist's telephone number, and the employer called the therapist to say that he liked Mary, thought her an excellent worker, and would keep her position open for her.

Mary's employers liked her, most of her friends remained loyal, and she was often called for advice from her large circle of friends and acquaintances. She was able to disguise her feelings to a point where she was perceived as a bright, attractive, and enjoyable person. This was a strain on her, however, and she continually fought anxiety during her social and work interactions. She acted out only at home.

Mary was hospitalized several times, mostly after threats by the parents to do so—threats that Mary challenged them to carry out. The last hospitalization was a voluntary three-month stay in an inpatient program. The staff admitted to being perplexed by her. She was medicated and she received psychotherapy, but there was no improvement in her functioning. She was discharged on the understanding that she would continue therapy.

After some largely supportive and nonconfrontational treatment, Mary's destructive behavior and suicidal attempts ceased. But the therapist could not make progress against her delusion concerning her skin. Her parents would periodically refuse to continue paying for treatment, usually when she seemed improved, and at one point, they evicted her from their home. During this time, she stayed with a female friend, and she refused to see the therapist. But Mary did call him after two months to say that she had concocted a plan for suicide and that she felt much better. Then she hung up. The therapist did not have her current phone number or address, so he contacted her family, who refused to believe that she would "embarrass" them this way, despite her history. He finally located her, her parents took her back, and she began seeing the therapist again. This episode convinced her, she said, that he truly cared.

Early in therapy Mary reported the following dream: "I am on a train with a group of women. You are outside on the station platform. I try to attract your attention by tapping on the window, but you walk away. The train pulls into another station. Men get on and begin beating or having sex with the women; I am not sure which."

Mary showed considerable ability to take charge in crises. On one occasion, her sister was trapped on an island during a dangerous military operation. Mary kept in touch with the State Department, organized the relatives of others in the same situation, and arranged a way of exchanging information on a regular basis. Nonetheless, she felt constantly out of control and could barely conduct her daily activities. A journal I asked her to keep of her typical daily activity included the following:

1. Up at 8:00 A.M. feeling anxious.
2. In bed trying to fall back asleep for one hour while fantasizing about looks and sex.
3. Rush to mirror worrying about looks and staring for one-half hour.
4. Hair and skin care activities for one hour.
5. Overwhelmed by panic and screaming curses at self.
6. Outdoors in attempt to calm down but stopping before mirrors in shop windows.
7. Out with friends, acting "normal."
8. Home, staring in mirror obsessing over ugliness.
9. Panic and cursing again.

In a much more detailed account, from waking to sleeping over a period of a few weeks, Mary described her unsuccessful struggle against her fears and urges. Her failure to control her impulses increased her anxiety.

Mary developed very powerful feelings toward the therapist. She was reluctant to express them directly but alluded to them often. She harbored fantasies of "getting better" and running into him years later whereupon they would begin a serious relationship culminating in marriage. There were also sadomasochistic sexual fantasies in which he would abuse her.

Perhaps the most perplexing aspect of Mary's case is the high degree of insight she displays concerning the motives and actions of others, and even concerning some of her own behavior. Yet, she has not given any sign of abandoning her delusions concerning her skin.

The hospital diagnosis (with which Mary's therapist disagrees) is as follows:

Axis I: Obsessive-Compulsive Disorder
Axis II: Histrionic Personality Disorder

Formulations and Treatments

Stanley B. Messer (Psychoanalytic)

Let me start by putting my cards on the table. I do not view Mary primarily as a histrionic personality. I would not recommend psychoanalysis, brief dynamic therapy, behavior therapy, family therapy, or medication as the treatment of choice for her difficulties. I believe that Mary suffers from a narcissistic personality disorder, as understood psychoanalytically, and that she would respond best to a Kohutian self psychological approach with its stress on therapist empathy and support (Kohut, 1977, 1984; White & Weiner, 1986).

How are we to view Mary's major symptoms or maladaptive behaviors, namely, her self-destructive rampages and suicidal threats? Following Kohut, I would understand these as rage brought on by what she alternately perceives as an unresponsive or hostile environment. There is an urge to destroy those who thwart Mary's expectation of controlling them.

When her rage was met by a parent's counteraggression ("Father had been physically abusive as far back as Mary could remember") or by inconsistent nurturing or neglect ("Mother was unpredictably supportive or depriving"), her aggression was turned back on herself, leading to self-hate, depression, and masochism. The masochism, including giving up jobs at which she performed well, is itself a way of defending against her fear of unleashing still greater self-destructive rage in the form of suicide.

Mary's anxiety that she was doing badly at her job and that she was repulsive physically (in spite of realistic assurances to the contrary) suggests unconscious expectations of self-perfection. To self psychologists, the view of oneself as perfect is considered natural in early childhood; it is referred to as the *infantile grandiose self*. Grandiose beliefs of being able to exercise complete control over the environment are modulated through daily confrontation with reality, optimally in a gradual way, leading to healthy ambition and achievement.

As children's grandiosity is tamed, it yields to a second way in which they try to control the world and make it safe, namely, idealizing the parent. They assume that parents are all-powerful and that they can and will protect their children from feelings of helplessness and pain. Mary's parents, however, were poor figures for idealization; the father was more abusive than protective, and the mother (so far as we are told) did nothing to protect Mary from her father's violence. It is quite apparent that they were unable to help her transmute her natural grandiosity into healthy narcissism or self-love. Both Mary's grandiosity and tendency to idealize have taken a pathological turn due to failures in her environment. In this connection, note that she continues to feel the need to cope with the world either through her own perfectionism—being physically flawless or performing flawlessly at work—or by idealizing others ("She deferred to a friend whom she idolized" and "When the therapist began seeing her, she had another best friend whom she idolized"). Neither her self-perfectionism nor her tendency to idealize others currently contributes to a satisfactory life for Mary.

The therapist's initial and primary job is to provide the supportive environment lacking in Mary's development, thereby allowing her to identify with and internalize a very different kind of parent imago. Early in therapy, I would not confront, or try to direct, or even interpret Mary's self-destructive behavior. I would try to be, in Kohut's terms, a "selfobject" for Mary—someone who, she feels, is part of her in some way, who can help maintain, by virtue of the merger, the coherence, continuity, and positive affective coloring of her self. That is, she should be allowed to display her arrested grandiosity and idealization rather than be confronted with them. I would try to appreciate what it must be like to be Mary and to empathize with her dilemmas. There is no place here for Freud's (1921/1959, p. 327) model of the analyst as a surgeon "who puts aside all his feelings, even his human sympathy, and concentrates his mental forces on the single aim of performing the operation as skillfully as possible." I would take an introspective-empathic stance, always trying to remain sensitively attuned to the nuances of Mary's experience. I would admire her accomplishments—and she clearly is capable of considerable achievement as the case report indicates. She was coleader of a singing group and cocaptain of the cheerleaders; her employer thought her an excellent worker; she could take charge in a crisis. The model of a good parent to the patient is not a bad idea for the therapist to keep in mind in this kind of therapy.

Mary must feel that she has an ally in the therapist (which she did not have in either parent), someone whom she can idealize, at least for a time, and with whom she can bask in the glow of her accomplishments. Alongside his attunement and support, the therapist must show respect for Mary's autonomy and decision-making capacities. We would, I am sure, explore her view of men—graphically portrayed in the dream—as ignoring women or beating them. I would ask for her associations to the dream in order to explore more deeply the personal meanings and memories conveyed by its rich imagery. Because of the explicit reference to the psychotherapist, discussion of the dream would be an opportunity also to focus on Mary's developing transferential reactions to him. Eventually, if all goes well, Mary will be able to make use of interpretations of her self-destructiveness, anxieties, and idealizations.

Is there evidence that sustained empathic inquiry and support would work for Mary? I believe there is. Two kinds of interventions were salutary: (1) "After some largely supportive and nonconfrontational treatment, Mary's destructive behavior and suicidal attempts ceased." (2) When Mary called the therapist to say that she had a plan for suicide, the therapist's concerned, extensive efforts to intervene, consistent with the self psychological approach described above, convinced Mary that he truly cared, thus allowing therapy to resume.

In brief, the therapy I would recommend and conduct would try to provide Mary with a responsive and attuned environment emphasizing sustained empathic inquiry and, eventually, interpretation. I would expect her narcissistically based rage to surface whenever she felt that I was off the mark, inattentive, or in any way critical of her. And I would expect that these episodes would present opportunities to explore her reactions, eventually enabling her to modify them. Over time, she would come to put trust in, and internalize, a very different kind of "selfobject" in the figure of the therapist, an internalization that would result in a more cohesive, lovable, and enhanced sense of herself.

J. Kevin Thompson (Cognitive)

Mary has characteristics of several different diagnostic categories. In addition to the disorders cited in the hospital diagnosis, she has symptoms consistent with obsessive-compulsive personality disorder, borderline personality disorder, intermittent explosive disorder, and body dysmorphic disorder— extreme disparagement of physical appearance (Thompson, 1990). More information is needed before a specific diagnosis is made.

There is information lacking that might help explain Mary. It does not appear that other schizophrenic symptoms accompany her specific physical appearance delusion; however, I would like to be certain that there are no signs of other delusions and to be informed whether there are occurrences of schizophrenia in her family. I would also like to know the precipitating circumstances for the onset of her dissatisfaction with her looks (if available). Was she teased or insulted by family or peers? Also, what specifically are the "skin problems" of which she complains?

Other background information might be relevant. Was she often compared to her elder sister? Is she less attractive, and was this pointed out to her at an early age? Other aspects of their relationship would also be helpful, especially because her need to idolize a female friend may be a substitute for a failed relationship with her sister. Were either of her younger siblings female, and if so, what was their relationship? What about her parents' treatment of them—as Mary saw it? Finally, I would also like to know the specific medications and types of psychotherapy she has previously received.

The relationship that must be developed between the therapist and Mary is one of the utmost trust, based on unconditional acceptance, genuineness, and caring. Mary has never been accepted for herself—by parents, by peers, or by men (Thompson & Williams, 1987). I would suspect that the abuse she received as a child led to self-blame and increased efforts to please her parents. The need to please others was also present in her peer relationships.

Unfortunately, her desperate drive to be loved and accepted resulted in extreme acting out and attempts at suicide. The therapist's efforts to find her brought her (first?) realization that he "truly cared." The evolution of Mary's fantasies of involvement was foreseeable. The therapist must be completely up-front regarding these transference issues, which might allow him to suggest that if someone can "truly care," so can others—and that, therefore, she needs to give other men a chance. Acceptance of this model by the client could lead to interventions such as role playing and training in dating skills and relationship skills.

The therapist must deal aggressively with Mary's specific

problems of anger control and physical appearance delusion. Given Mary's past sexual problems with transference, a female therapist might be preferable. Once core aspects of the relationship—trust, acceptance, caring—have developed, the therapist would be more free to be openly directive and challenging (Thompson & Williams, 1987).

Let me review my conceptualization of Mary's case, based on the available evidence. Mary's problems are a consequence of pathological early socialization in the home. Her protective self-abuse and self-disparagement, leading to low self-esteem and inappropriate acting out, communicate her feelings of isolation and despair. Her acting out was initially both a way to escape from her father's abuse and an attempt to get attention from her mother. The attention from her mother was inconsistent (schizophrenogenic), and therefore Mary sought nurturance from peer-group women. However, her female friends tired of her idolization and rejected her. Her one attempt at trusting a male also met with rejection. Consequently, Mary developed as an individual who did not trust others and felt others were trying to control her. She rejected any evidence that she was a worthwhile person, or even the possibility that she might be bright, and tended to back away from imminent success at college or on the job. Her efforts to hide her low self-esteem and to act socially appropriate worked in some settings; however, on returning to her pathological home environment, she was unable to override her loneliness and lack of direction, and she gave way to further outbursts.

The delusion regarding her ugliness seems symbolic of her inability to accept herself. Comparisons with her sister and possible teasing or insults from her family may have contributed to this focus of self-disparagement. I do not see her delusion as schizophrenic, but rather as a learned obsession, which makes sense given her background. It protects her from experiencing the anxiety that might manifest itself if she had no reason for hiding from success, men, and independence. The fact that she still lives at home suggests that she may have difficulty breaking away from this crazy environment.

Treatment should be multifaceted and, if possible, should include family and individual therapy. The family intervention should focus on her need for true acceptance from her parents and on the necessity of a separate residence for Mary. In individual therapy, the therapist needs to work on her self-esteem, anger control, social and sexual relationships, and ugliness delusion. I would use desensitization procedures, thought stopping, and cognitive restructuring for the delusion (Thompson, 1990). Skills training, role playing, and cognitive therapy might be useful for issues of self-esteem and for social and heterosexual relationship issues. I would also work with her fear of success regarding college and employment, and I would use stress management strategies for anger control. It is essential that any directive intervention be in the context of a caring client-therapist relationship.

Mary's therapy is likely to include numerous ups and downs, especially when she feels misunderstood or unaccepted. I predict that she will slowly give up her delusion and begin to accept herself, but only if active interventions are begun with a therapist whom she trusts implicitly.

Elisabeth A. Lederman (Humanistic)

In the account of Mary's case, there are many signs of the likelihood of a hidden history, and these clues might be ignored by clinicians who follow a tradition of denying the reality of incestuous violation. The first line of defense, traceable to Freud, is to say that incest did not happen; it was all a fantasy that represents a desire of the victim. Since it did not happen, there is no need to ask the violator embarrassing questions or to disturb elements of society whose emotional security depends on keeping their heads in the sand. The second line of defense is to say that, yes, it happened, but it was the victim's fault because she was seductive. Both these defenses conveniently scuttle the facts of child development. All children need love (as expressed by warm hugs); they do not want or seek genital fondling or intercourse. In those rare instances when sexual fantasies or truly seductive behaviors (in contrast to healthy sensuality) occur in early years, it is because the children have already been denied loving warmth and then are taught by their violators that they can get contact only through sexual behavior.

Seven signs, taken together, signal a high probability of a hidden history in Mary's case. First, as Mary neared adolescence, the father "began tearing off Mary's bathrobe" (that is, he did it many times or regularly); but he is said not to have attacked her sexually. This repeated sexual harassment, it is implied by the form of the sentence, is not to be regarded as sexual. Yet, the act is sexual in itself and is unlikely to have been the only manifestation of the father's proprietary interest in Mary's body.

Second, as Mary's father tore off the bathrobe, he called the preadolescent girl a "slut." This word implies some prior sexual activity for which he is abusively blaming her.

Third, there is a history of physical abuse as far back as Mary can remember. We are not given the details; are we therefore to imagine that the father scrupulously avoided baring sexual parts of his daughter's body and that he avoided beating her on any part that might have had erotic connotations to either of them? The form of the physical abuse chosen by this father—who stripped his preadolescent daughter and accused her of being sexual—was therefore almost certainly implicitly sexual. It may also have been explicitly sexual.

Fourth, Mary has a dream in which she tries to get the therapist's attention, but he walks away. The glass window between them also indicates she has difficulties being heard (by her father or mother or therapist?); she is reduced to futile tapping. Let us hear what she is saying: "Men got on the train and began beating or having sex with the women; I am not sure which." When, and under what circumstances, would one not be able to tell whether she was having sex or being beaten? This dream, in the context of what we are told about Mary's history and symptoms, is an early memory of punitive sex or sexualized beating.

Fifth, Mary had masochistic sexual fantasies about her therapist. Thus, she recapitulates in the transference the "path to love" that her father taught her.

Sixth, Mary's self-destructiveness is typical of sexually abused clients, who maintain the feelings of abuse by head-banging, cutting their own limbs, tearing at their own faces, or ripping their clothing. The feelings are "I am bad, dirty, unworthy."

And seventh, Mary's distortions of reality strongly indicate that she is hiding something from herself. Her denial of early incestuous violation by her father is no more trustworthy than her blaming her problems on her supposed ugliness. The revulsion at her own hands (in elementary school) and face is typical of patients who have been required to perform manual and oral sex at an early age. Children repress the experience of sexual contact and transfer the feelings to their hands and faces, thus sparing the incestuous violators their feelings of revulsion (and maintaining the hope of being loved). Mary's choice of her lunch box as an object to destroy may be significant beyond the explanation Mary gave. The lunch box is a place to put food, like her mouth; it may also represent her vagina, and often appears as a symbol with that meaning in dreams. Vaginal intercourse may have occurred or may have been threatened.

How could vaginal intercourse have occurred if Mary's first sex partner scorned her virginity? We know about this pecul-iar reaction only from Mary's account. Is it not just as likely that Mary rejected herself because she was not what she was supposed to be and withdrew from the relationship?

Note that the loss of virginity may be regarded as occurring normally through gradual stages in adolescence. Whether or not Mary's father technically deflowered her, he appears to have taken her virginity in the more general sense of having initiated her sexually.

Mary's version is understandable as a triple denial of the loss of her virginity to her father. As Freud pointed out in other circumstances, the denying mind negates every element of the distressing scene. Mary says, (1) "My boyfriend rejects me" rather than "I reject our sexually intimate relationship" and "I reject myself," (2) "I was a virgin" rather than "My father deflowered me," and (3) "He rejects me because I am a virgin" rather than "I reject myself because I am not a virgin—because my father made me unfit for normal relations."

Mary may have been violated very early, beginning at an age before the capability for memory developed. All that would be left from these experiences would be vague feelings, defensive reactions, and a disordered mind.

The hypothesis of incestuous abuse, whether through fondling, any form of intercourse, or other means, would be corroborated or disconfirmed by the gathering of information, essential in any event. The following questions—and others—would be asked of the father in an individual session: Did he at any time sexually abuse Mary? If so, over what period of time did he sexually abuse Mary? Why did he rip Mary's bathrobe off, and what did he mean in calling his daughter a slut? What was his rationale for the physical abuse of his daughter? Why did he stop the physical abuse five years ago? What did he think of his daughter, and how did he feel toward her when she was a little girl (questions reiterated through the age range)? Does he love his daughter now? What does he mean by the word *love?* Why is Mary still living at home? What is his present relationship with his wife and with the children? And is he close to anyone in the family or outside?

The father would probably begin by denying sexual abuse; but the questions probably would elicit contradictions in his responses, opening up avenues for further confrontation. He might deny that pulling off his daughter's bathrobe was sexual, but I would say that I did not believe him, for there is no plausible alternative meaning to that act.

Perhaps a psychotherapist sensitive to civil rights analogies might ask, What right do we have to confront the father with the presumption of incestuous abuse? The answer is, first, that since we are not in court, the father is not entitled to a presumption of innocence; second, the risk to the patient of not uncovering the hidden history (by not grilling a guilty father) is far greater and more harmful than that of hurting the feelings of an "innocent" father who in this instance "merely" stripped his daughter and abused her physically and verbally; and third, the fact that Mary's parents brought her to a therapist itself presents an aspect of the family pathology. If they had not done so, let us say, if they had given Mary the therapist's telephone number and left it to her to call, they would not be part of the treatment process. (If Mary wished her parents to be involved later—and I might suggest this, depending on the evolution of the case—and if the parents agreed, then it would be up to Mary, with my support, to confront them.)

The following questions, among others, would be asked of the mother in an individual session: What made this attempted suicide, in contrast to Mary's preceding five years of self-destructive behavior, mobilize the parents to bring her to therapy? Was she aware of her husband's physical abuse of Mary? How did she feel about the bathrobe tugging? Did she ever intervene on her daughter's behalf? Did her husband ever abuse her—physically or emotionally? Why was she on and off with her daughter emotionally? Does she love her daughter now? What is their relationship? What is her relationship with her other children? Does she encourage her children to become individuals guiding their own destinies? How does she view herself within the family? Why did she phone her daughter's office and give them information of the attempted suicide? Why did she not just inform them that Mary was ill and would be in touch? What were her motives for giving information that could have jeopardized her daughter's job? What does she get out of controlling her daughter?

I would not be surprised to learn that the mother is cold to Mary and possibly to the other children. This would fit the picture of the incestuous family in which the mother is unavailable physically or emotionally to the abused daughter. On some level, mothers know about abuse but are incapable or feel incapable of doing anything about it. The first daughter is usually the target. Information is needed here to ascertain whether the other children, especially other daughters, were abused in the same years that Mary was—or if, after father's abuse of Mary ceased, he attempted to move down the line.

My sequence of treatment goals for Mary would be first, to help her become strong enough to face her feelings about herself and her family, and second, to enable her to separate from the family.

Digging out the truth by confronting the parents serves these two goals. First, Mary needs some basis in reality to which she can respond emotionally. If she does not know the truth, she will continue to substitute imaginary problems— such as her face. Second, the true history is needed to interrupt the family pathology that keeps her dependent.

In the first phase, I would see Mary in individual sessions. Time would be required to allow trust to develop between us; I would say to her that no matter what she told me about what had happened to her, I would believe her, and it would take still more time for her to find out that I meant that. As I show her that I care about her, that I find her face likable, that I find her (apart from her defenses) likable, her defiance and resentment of her face might temporarily become more intense; the more I accept Mary, the harder she would have to work to maintain the idea that her so-called ugliness precludes a relationship between us.

Since Mary presents her history as a consequence of defects in her appearance, we would start with them. I would not ask her to tell me what is wrong with her face, but rather how she feels about the supposed defects. My assumption is that feelings of any kind (except anxiety) are foreign to her and need to be brought into awareness. I would use the Gestalt two-chair method. As she allows more of her feelings to come to the surface, I would relate them to the physical abuse and her feelings about it.

I would use Gestalt and bioenergetics methods in working with Mary on her feelings within the train dream. That dream, describing both physical and sexual abuse, is her way of saying, "This is what happened to me. Now, how do I deal with it? Who is going to listen? I have tried, but there was a glass window between me and the one I wanted to hear me, and he just walked away."

I would ask Mary to lie on the mat, eyes closed, breathing deeply, relating the dream in the first person as if she were living it in the present, owning the feelings of the dream as hers. I would suggest that Mary allow whatever emotions she felt to come to the surface. This method would allow me to see where she stops her breathing, cutting off her emotions and (according to the teachings of bioenergetics) storing her repressed feelings. I would use similar methods for the bath-robe memories. Having Mary lying down allows body defenses to relax and stifled feelings and thoughts to emerge.

If Mary arrived for a session angry or suicidal, I would place a pillow in front of her, give her a plastic bat, and ask her to smash out the angry feelings. As she was doing this, I would ask her to scream, "I'm angry!" or "I hate myself!" or "I hate my face!" If the self-hating expressions were expressed loudly enough and long enough, the underlying issues would surface, since the feelings about her face are defenses against her emotional responses to what has happened to her. As she cries how she hates her face, she might recall, or I might prompt her to recall, her father's violations of her.

Mary would in time give up her self-abusive actions, expressing directly the feelings that behaviors such as head banging communicate dysfunctionally.

In the second phase, concurrent with individual sessions, I might attempt to see Mary together with her parents—not necessarily to resolve the issues, but to allow Mary to confront her parents in a positive and supportive environment. It concerns me that Mary, at age twenty-two, with adequate financial resources to maintain her own living space, is still living at home. In family therapy, we could explore how the parents are maintaining the dependency, and we could work to break it. Mary shows in her outside activities that she is a capable individual who can socialize and maintain a normal existence. She needs to extend these capabilities by leaving home and establishing her own life. I conjecture that the attempted suicides and the self-abusive actions would diminish once she was out of the family home, since these actions have not occurred anywhere else.

Bernard D. Beitman (Integrative)

My first concern is whether a *DSM-III-R* diagnosis would indicate an approach likely to be successful or to aid in my understanding of Mary's problem. It appears from the text and from her diary that Mary has panic attacks. She is self-destructive, has attempted suicide several times, and utterly depreciates herself in the face of work successes. These findings suggest a strong depressive element. I would therefore ask questions to confirm or disconfirm the diagnoses of panic disorder and depression. Also, it appears Mary may fit diagnostic criteria for narcissistic personality disorder or borderline personality disorder. The tendency to idealize others and devalue herself reflects interpersonal and intrapsychic dynamics that are critical for a therapist to address.

What else would I need to know? Mary's family is strongly implicated in the development of her difficulties. Her need to live with her parents, taken with their reactions to her hospitalization and her suicide threats, calls for an assessment of her difficulties in individuating and separating from them.

Since Mary does live at home, I would want to see her mother and father at least once to get some idea of their behavior with her. I would also instruct her to keep a triple-column diary, in the form suggested by Beck and his colleagues, to help recognize and discriminate episodes of panic, depression, suicidal thinking, and self-destructive behaviors. In this way, I might be able to isolate the situations giving rise to these episodes and then to track the associated cognitions. I suspect that many of these experiences are related to fears of abandonment, isolation, and her own rage. Another way I would begin to learn about Mary is through the manner in which her transference develops. I am assuming that she is not being transferred to me but that I am the presenting therapist, continuing to see her. It appears that she has developed a powerful transference in which the twin elements of idealization and self-depreciation are beginning to unfold.

As for the progress of therapy, I see that engagement was very difficult. Mary came to trust the therapist's ability to care for her through his response to her suicide plan; he sought her out despite her parents' lack of concern. I am sure his nonconfrontational and supportive approach to her was at variance with her previous experiences with men, whom she sees as exploiting her in violent and possibly sexual ways. I anticipate that she would make many attempts to run from therapy, fearing the therapist's violence against her. At this point, however, she appears to have given up some of those concerns.

Since Mary is fairly disorganized in her personal life, cognitive therapy for panic and depression might require more time and energy than she would be able to devote to this energy-intensive approach. Instead, I would consider using medication. Although Mary was receiving medication as an inpatient, what she received is not clear from the report. I would consider a tricyclic antidepressant and possibly a benzodiazepine for panic attacks (if that diagnosis is warranted). It is possible that during her episodes of aggression, she is simply attempting to release intense pressure within herself by banging her head, putting hands through windows, and destroying her environment. It is possible that a short-acting benzodiazepine might disrupt the spiral of intense emotion by relaxing her and distracting her from impulsive behavior. The prescribed medications, if successful, should help her engage more fully in therapy. Even if not successful, discussion of medications might provide a relatively objective way of describing symptoms and related cognitions and behavior.

I would engage Mary in a pattern search to define her interpersonal difficulties as seen both in her transference and in her relationships with others. I would anticipate a good deal of countertransference in the first part of the pattern search, and I anticipate that she would respond intensely to me with both fear and strong desire. She might have difficulty forming a self-observer alliance, at times falling into fantasy and wanting that fantasy to be reality. The vignette states that Mary fantasized about marrying the therapist and also about a masochistic involvement with him. I believe these wishes would not always be deferred to after the therapy, but would appear at some point in therapy (demanding to be acted upon at once!), creating anxiety and disorganization in the therapist.

The purpose of the pattern search is to define patterns in such a way that the possibility of change is implied. These patterns would be derived from Mary's transference reactions, from her narcissistic, grandiose, and depreciated self, and from the meaning of her perception of herself as having bad skin and being generally repulsive. I would expect that she would have difficulty receiving compliments from me: she would either exaggerate their significance to infer that I wanted a sexual relationship with her, or she would deprecate them, saying that they were silly or that I was lying or being insincere. I would be most concerned about the discrepancy between Mary's self-evaluations and the success of her actions, particularly in regard to work. I would repeatedly point out discrepancies between what Mary says about herself and what her actions show, and I would attempt to engage her in considering the possibility that the supposed bad skin was a reflection of her tendency to depreciate herself. I would remain aware that the notion of herself as having bad skin may be fixed in Mary's mind and difficult to remove, so I would not attack it as a single focus, but would consider it as an element of a major dysfunctional pattern of self-depreciation.

I see change as being extremely difficult for Mary and taking place over a long period of time. Will she be able to separate from home and live on her own? That would be one major objective. Will she be able to catch herself at depreciating herself? In the transference, will she be able to talk freely and easily about her fantasies toward me, maintaining a strong self-observer alliance with me?

Termination may be fraught with difficulty and danger. Mary may find me to be the first man who is kind and caring and who does not exploit her. Termination means she will have to go out into the world and attempt to establish such a relationship again. She may prefer simply to stay in the warm and secure therapy setting and not ever say good-bye. That inclination would have to be confronted and discussed, and its associated cognitions would have to be examined for change. One set of strongly associated thoughts and feelings would concern her difficulty in giving up her parents and leaving their home. Ideally, at termination, she will have made it out of their house. I would hope that she would not have rushed into another dependent relationship quite yet but that she would have had some experience of being out on her own.

Points of Contention and Convergence

Stanley B. Messer

There are both shared emphases and specific points of difference between my approach to Mary, based on psychoanalytic self psychology, and those of my counterparts, who are proponents of either cognitive-behavioral, experiential, or eclectic therapy. The clearest arena of convergence is the kind of relationship that we regard as necessary to engage Mary in a therapeutic process. Thompson aptly describes it as "one of utmost trust, based on unconditional acceptance, genuineness, and caring." Lederman also emphasizes the development of trust, adding the importance of believing Mary and conveying that the therapist cares about and likes her. Beitman refers, at least indirectly, to the value of a nonconfrontational and supportive approach, one in which the therapist might compliment Mary. In psychoanalytic therapy, too, caring, empathy, and support are advocated, especially when working with more severely disturbed clients like Mary (Messer, 1986, 1988).

All of my fellow psychotherapists, however, introduce practices stemming from their different theoretical positions that I would be hesitant to endorse. Once the relationship is established on a firm footing, Thompson advocates a more directive and challenging therapy. Because of Mary's fragility, I would be concerned about whether she could withstand confrontations without decompensating. That is, as a narcissistic personality, she may interpret confrontation as criticism and may view her difficulty complying with the therapist's suggestions as evidence of her badness. I would worry, too, about how the therapist's authoritative-directive role may affect Mary's efforts to establish herself as an autonomous person, one who is fully capable of making her own decisions. On a manifest level, she may comply with the psychotherapist to maintain his caring and attention, but she may then find it more difficult to become a person who possesses her own locus of initiative.

Although I am intrigued by Lederman's formulation and speculations about Mary having been sexually abused, I would not be as willing as she to probe the repressed emotions so directly. There is the possibility of Mary's unleashing more feeling than someone so unstable could handle. In addition, the bioenergetics approach, by attempting to bypass her defenses to produce a catharsis, does not allow her to learn how she uses various symptoms, behaviors, and defenses to protect herself from her own worst fears in her relationships to others. I believe that such awareness could help Mary integrate her feelings, cognitions, and behavior in a more adaptive fashion. Furthermore, I would not bring in her parents or encourage her to leave home, as Lederman suggests, because I would see this effort to increase her independence as, paradoxically, fostering her dependence on the therapist (cf. Lazarus & Messer, 1988). I would prefer to let her arrive at such decisions on her own when she feels ready to do so.

Beitman and I share a similar understanding of Mary's problems. I like the way he uses that understanding to anticipate the course of therapy, especially the obstacles that are likely to arise. Unlike Beitman, however, I would not refer Mary for medication until I had sufficient opportunity to observe how she responded to psychotherapy. My hope would be that a soothing relationship would calm her sufficiently to obviate the need for medication, which often brings unwanted side effects. In addition, medication shifts the perceived locus of change from the person's volitional capacities to an outside chemical agent. And Mary could interpret the use of medication to mean that she is not able to learn to deal with her feelings through her own psychological efforts. I should add, however, that if matters deteriorated in spite of my best efforts, I would consider medication.

All three instances of my divergence from the other commentators relate to their advocating measures outside a purely supportive or interpretative therapeutic framework. These measures include therapist suggestion and confrontation, involvement of the client's family, and medication. Although I agree that each has its place in a therapist's repertoire, my contention is they all have pitfalls that probably can be avoided in the case of Mary, who so much needs to come to believe in herself, in her abilities, and in her considerable adaptive capacities.

J. Kevin Thompson

Upon rereading the case, my own initial conceptualization, and the formulations of Messer, Lederman, and Beitman, I am struck by the complexity of the case and by the richness of our attempts to understand Mary. I found myself agreeing with the great majority of the other writers' recommendations, especially with regard to the need for Mary to separate from the family (Lederman, Beitman), the importance of a warm, empathic client-therapist relationship (Messer, Lederman), and the role of transference (Beitman). I was particularly affected by the case Lederman made for a sexual abuse component. I now see that this issue must be fully addressed. In addition, Messer's Kohutian model deserves attention as a possible explanation and treatment for Mary's problems. And Beitman makes a cogent argument for the further assessment of panic disorder and depression, the use of confrontation procedures (for her facial delusion), and the role of medication. My own analysis of this case has been broadened by the exposure to the opinions of colleagues who have backgrounds quite different from my own.

On the other hand, I am somewhat dismayed that the use of cognitive-behavioral techniques was not advocated by Messer and Lederman. While these procedures are not without limitations, they have certainly received more empirical validation than Kohutian analysis, Gestalt procedures, or bioenergetic methods. In addition, some of Mary's primary complaints are amenable to cognitive-behavioral procedures, including delusions, impulsivity, anxiety, and possibly depression. At the very least, cognitive-behavioral procedures, including cognitive restructuring, assertiveness training, relaxation methods, and desensitization, should be used as ancillary procedures for symptomatic relief, problem solving, stress management, and coping. I also concur with Beitman that self-monitoring procedures would add a wealth of assessment information.

I am also dismayed at the lack of parsimony apparent in our collective formulations of Mary. After rereading the case, I note that her initial explanation of her acting-out behaviors was her failure to improve her bad skin. She had always been concerned about her looks, including large hands, frizzy hair, and general unattractiveness. Accordingly, she idolized others she saw as more attractive, and she avoided men. With this background, a crazy family environment, and the possibility of sexual abuse, it is fairly clear how she became an angry, hostile young woman with low self-esteem, depression, and a high level of self-punitiveness. Thus, it seems logical to me that, regardless of the accompanying problems and etiology of her delusions regarding her appearance, we are faced with someone who meets the *DSM-III-R* requirements for body dysmorphic disorder. Even if other issues are involved and more in-depth psychotherapeutic approaches are considered, an immediate intervention of directive techniques is indicated for the modification of her physical appearance disparagement (see Hay, 1970; Thompson, 1990).

Elisabeth A. Lederman

Let me consider convergence first. We all agree that Mary needs time to develop trust and a sense of security. For this, the psychotherapist must provide an environment where Mary feels she can bring the feelings that are represented by her perception of herself as ugly and by the head banging and other self-destructive behavior. We all recognize this will be a long-term process, at least initially involving the parents because she is living at home.

Thompson notes that Mary needs someone who really cares. I agree with him and with Messer in his recommendation of support and empathy; but I also agree with Beitman when he says that Mary probably would attempt to run away from treatment numerous times if she became frightened that the therapist was getting too close or cared too much. Survivors of abuse find it extremely hard to accept that anyone cares about them. In some cases, to get a caring person "back to his or her senses," that is, "to respond to me as my parents do," survivors may go to great lengths to sabotage relationships. Love often means hurt to survivors, because even as it feeds into their strong desire to be loved, it rouses the feeling of being unlovable.

Messer's "introspective-empathic stance," sensitive to Mary's experience, is commendable. Most survivors of physical and sexual abuse have not had a healthy person to depend on or to reflect a sense of self. Instead, exploitation leaves them feeling nonexistent; they are expected to play roles in which they deny themselves. Mary needs a psychotherapist with whom she can begin to develop a sense of self, "a good parent," in Messer's words.

Themes of contention arise in looking at the same material from different perspectives. While I concur that Mary exhibits perfectionism (Messer), delusions (Thompson), and narcissism (Messer, Thompson, Beitman), I consider these symptoms not to be the primary issues, but defenses against underlying feelings. These feelings are responses to a reality that has been too painful and frightening for Mary to cope with.

I agree with Messer that Mary is not a case of histrionic personality and that her rage, elicited by a nonresponsive, hostile environment, has been turned against herself. However, I do not agree with diagnosing or characterizing Mary on the whole as narcissistic. As a brief example, let me examine perfectionism and show how it can be a symptom with different shadings.

A frequently observed manifestation of grandiosity is the child seeing herself as perfect. Such perfection implies the capability to do anything she wants if she puts her mind to it, and therein lies a wishful way for her to improve her milieu. However, to the abused child, perfectionism is also a magical means of self-protection. The abused child acts as though she follows an unconscious belief system that, in words, would sound like this: "If I'm good and do not do anything wrong and anticipate my father's or mother's wishes, then I can stop them from hurting me, because I won't have done anything to get him or her angry." Here is perfectionism deriving from feelings of guilt and self-blame. Since it is too dangerous for the abused child to say daddy or mommy is wrong, since she still needs whatever her parents can give her, she regards herself as faulty, and she then fantasizes and endeavors to improve herself to meet standards of perfection. Hence, perfectionism can be either narcissism or an archaic defense mechanism.

I see diagnoses such as depersonalization disorder or PTSD with borderline features as coming nearer to the underlying issue: What do the presenting symptoms that occur only at home—disorganization, head banging, window smashing, and suicide attempts—tell us about how Mary coped with abuse when it was actually taking place? Now, long after the first abuse, Mary has found a way of stopping her father from abusing her: she acts crazily self-destructive.

Thompson would look to family therapy to focus on Mary's need for acceptance by parents and the necessity of a separate residence. While I agree regarding the latter, Mary's need for parental acceptance seems to me to call for individual therapy, wherein Mary would be helped to recognize (1) how her parents treated her and (2) that her parents are unable to give her what she needs. If Thompson intends the conciliatory sort of family therapy wherein old abuses are covered over or "forgiven," then I disagree. Mary needs to realize the truth about her parents' behavior in order to individualize and separate. As Beitman stated, in effect, Mary's problems in individualizing and separating will continue as long as the therapist ignores the primary teaching of this family unit. Mary looks for others to reinforce her parents' teaching that she is bad and ugly, and when this is not corroborated, she goes back home. Mary's inner prerequisite for individualization is not to be accepted, though we all need that, but to recognize the truth about her past, to place the responsibility where it lies, and to decide to move on from there.

Beitman's idea of using a triple-column diary is a technique I have never used, nor would I begin in Mary's case. Mary has episodes of panic, depression, and suicidal ideation expressed in her head banging and other self-destructive actions, such as quitting her job because it gave her positive feelings that she could not handle. She needs to focus not on her symptomatic feelings and behavior, but on what they represent.

I take this position because the determination of cause and effect here is already evident. Mary's history tells what Mary and her therapist need to know; addressing the issue of Mary's self-abuse as a continuation of her parents' teachings would be more helpful. Mary needs to be confronted not on the surface (for example, not on the precipitating details of her episodes of harming herself), but on the underlying pattern— who taught her, by what means, and how she can at last express her feelings about it.

Bernard D. Beitman

Lederman offers powerful arguments for the possibility of incestuous contacts between Mary and her father, a conclusion with which I agree. Careful attention to the indirectly stated references to these likely events adds to the therapist's approach by encouraging the uncovering of sources of the crucial patterns governing Mary's self-destructive behavior and thinking. Lederman's questions for Mary's parents appear to be incisive and important, but in order to help Mary in her struggle to free herself from their external and internal domination, I would want to prepare the groundwork with Mary for the confrontation. Without such preparation, Mary could be confronted with the often terrible problems with which rape victims are faced when they are asked to testify against the accused in court. In order for the confrontation to be useful, Mary should help direct the inquiry. In reading her section, I sensed Lederman's fury with men and abuse. While I share some of her fury, I would want to balance the confrontation with the best interests of the patient, as I am certain she would in practice.

Mary's fragile self-concept makes me quite hesitant to consider the active approaches with bioenergetics and Gestalt techniques that Lederman advocates. Perhaps I am more cautious because I am a man and these techniques (which include having Mary lie down and fantasize) may too closely resemble the sexually abusive commands of her father.

One cannot argue with Messer's insistence upon a highly empathic approach to this patient. Mary is likely to be highly sensitive to therapeutic errors and deviations, so her negative reactions must be carefully anticipated and noted. Unfortunately, depth of empathic sensitivity is likely to be necessary but not sufficient for change. What is to get her through the next days and hours, tormented perhaps by panic attacks and major depression? How can Messer categorically deny the value of medications for this person when several studies and much clinical evidence suggest that borderline patients are often burdened with major depression that is responsive to antidepressants?

Thompson seems to share my belief that strong engagement through the establishment of trust may lead to more active work on the part of the psychotherapist. I do not see this emphasis on engagement in Lederman's description. While keeping in tune with Mary's strong need for empathic connections, I too would work on specific cognitive and behavioral problems in her life, but I would not be quite so active.

Clearly, one cause of my disagreements has to do with differences in training relative to the other respondents. The three other writers are psychologists having had much less experience with medication than I. More than 50 percent of the patients I see for psychotherapy are on medication. I have not been trained in bioenergetics or extensively in either cognitive-behavioral approaches or psychoanalysis. I am also not a woman. No point in this discussion deserves greater emphasis than the fact that in this exercise involving three men and one woman as commentators, only the woman clearly and forcefully made the case for the almost obvious sexual abuse of the patient. As a result, all of us, particularly male psychotherapists, should increase our sensitivity to this all too common and all too commonly neglected problem.

9

The Returning Hero and the Absent Wife

▣

Jeremy D. Safran
Martin R. Textor
Robert N. Sollod

Case Presentation

A marital crisis erupts after a few sessions in the therapy of Carl and Trudy, and Trudy expresses her readiness to quit the marriage and the therapy.

Carl is thirty-eight, a large man with impressive muscular development of chest and arms. He walks with a cane because of injuries sustained in Vietnam, for which he volunteered out of a sense of duty. He lived his childhood in an orphanage where no one had time for the children. "The food was handed in under the door," Carl said, "and the bigger boys got most of it. You had to fight for your share." Three times a year, he was allowed out to visit an aunt, who was affectionate. But when he was nine, he was told he would not be getting out for Easter; that was how he learned his aunt had married and moved away.

Trudy is thirty-two, a tall, slender woman with dark eyes and curly black hair. She was raised by her mother, a former Miss Arizona. Trudy's father was an Air Force test pilot who adored her. He died flying an experimental plane when Trudy was ten years old. Before his death, the family was transferred to a different base every few months; she has sparse memory of her childhood. Trudy learned not to make friends, because the family always expected to be moving again. Trudy's mother drank heavily and was (or became) irresponsible, but she demanded obedience and affection from her child. She married a man who claimed to be a minister, but Trudy guessed that he wanted to live off her mother's pension. As she became an adolescent, her stepfather sexually abused her and threatened to kill her if she told. Trudy hinted about it to her mother, who eventually caught them in bed. Her mother's first reaction was to take Trudy away. The stepfather came after them, and Trudy, believing (probably accurately) that her mother wanted to go back to him, ran away and got work as a waitress. She passed for eighteen, but in reality, she was a tall, precociously developed fourteen-year-old.

Carl eventually became an engineer, responsible for research and development of high-tech products. Aggressive on behalf of his company, Carl is never assertive for himself. He enjoys sex but is not at all affectionate to Trudy except in bed. He has severe hypertension and consented to go to psychotherapy at his physician's insistence. Trudy says that everyone takes advantage of him, that his boss manipulates him, and that his subordinates get him to do their work for them. Carl is strongly self-controlled, compulsive, ethical, laconic, and at least in our consultations, passive.

Trudy was first married at seventeen to a man who did not believe in birth control, but who discovered he was not ready for fatherhood and left her with three children when she was twenty-two. Carl married unwisely, too, and was left with two boys. Trudy and Carl also have a young child in common to complete the household.

Trudy has read widely to make up for her lack of formal education. She believes she fell into motherhood because of her insecurities. She describes herself as "street smart," but also as "scatterbrained," and as having "jumbled emotions," jealous rages, painful feelings of inadequacy, and numbness (terror). She says she cannot ever get out of her mind what her stepfather did to her. Often, she is sexually unresponsive to Carl because she is angry at him or because she just wants to be held, which he does not understand. She would like someday to have a career or small business of her own, "if I could handle it."

After a few sessions, Carl announced he would be out of town and would miss at least one session. Trudy said she would come to the session by herself, but she did not. Instead, she called afterward to say that she would not be coming back to therapy. She moved out of the family apartment, as she had done many times in the past, but vowed that this time she would not return. Leaving her young teenagers to fend for themselves, she dropped Carl's children with his ex-wife's family and took their baby with her to the apartment of some girlfriends. I talked Trudy into coming back for at least one final session, during which she expressed anger at Carl's lack of consideration in not calling her when he was on business trips, even to say when he would be back. From her voice and body language, and from her flight itself, I knew she was deeply frightened. She was so extremely angry and scared at once that it was hard to talk with her.

Trudy remarked that Carl thinks she ought to be glad to see him whenever he walks in the door. His fantasy is that she will drop whatever she is doing and that they will make love at once. Trudy hates this scenario. What actually happened the last time (and it had happened before) was that when Carl arrived home, Trudy and his children were gone, and hers were dirty, ill-fed, and "swinging from the ceiling."

Carl never expresses any emotion. One can see that he is suffering, but if one says that to him, he hardly responds—as though "it doesn't compute." Upon being asked why he does not call Trudy when he is away (and reminding him that he is extremely responsible in every other way), he gives only rationalizations. It appears that he avoids the pain of separation by cutting off and pretending to be emotionally self-sufficient.

Carl is willing to work at therapy because it is a medical necessity to lower his blood pressure. He wants Trudy to come back, but when he says without any feeling in his voice that he needs her, she retorts, "Get a maid!" She says she wants to stay in the marriage "only if Carl changes a lot," and she doubts therapy can do that.

If our panelists had conducted the first sessions themselves, they would have inquired more deeply along some of these lines or along different lines, as they have noted. The following *DSM-III* diagnoses were suggested, but the panel was invited to amend them or add other categories as they felt warranted.

Carl
  Axis I: Psychological factors affecting physical condition
  Axis II: Compulsive personality disorder, with masochistic tendencies
  Axis III: Hypertension

Trudy
  Axis I: Posttraumatic stress disorder

Formulations and Treatments

Jeremy D. Safran (Cognitive)

In considering the establishment of a therapeutic relationship, I find Ed Bordin's (1979) distinctions among the goal, task, and bond components helpful. I would want from the outset to establish whether the goal of therapy was to work on the relationship or on specific issues with either Carl or Trudy independently. It is not clear how Carl's referral due to hypertension led to relationship counseling, nor how willing either is to work on the marriage. The information provided on Trudy suggests that she may not be motivated to work toward improving the marriage at present.

Granted that Carl, because of his need to lower his blood pressure, may be more motivated than Trudy, it remains unclear what type of therapeutic task he would perceive as relevant to that goal. Does he want to work on the relationship as well as reduce his hypertension? Would he see the type of self-exploration common to insight-oriented therapies as relevant to whatever goals he decides are worth pursuing? Depending on the answers, I might wind up seeing one of them, both of them, or neither of them in psychotherapy.

In what follows, I will assume that both Carl and Trudy are interested in improving their relationship and that they both perceive some form of self-exploration as relevant to that goal.

From a cognitive-interpersonal perspective, psychological problems are maintained by a cycle. Individual expectations shape perceptions of interactions and influence behavior in a way that elicits behaviors from others confirming an individual's dysfunctional expectations. A corollary is that a two-person system can be understood as the complementary integration of individual cognitive-interpersonal cycles through which the dysfunctional patterns of the two individuals elicit and maintain one another, reciprocally confirming their associated dysfunctional beliefs.

To treat Carl and Trudy, I would want four interdependent pieces of information: (1) What is the primary, repetitive dysfunctional pattern that characterizes their relationship? (2) How can this interactional pattern be understood as the integration of specific interpersonal patterns characteristic of each of the spouses? (3) What are the key pathogenic beliefs linked to Carl's and Trudy's respective, dysfunctional interpersonal patterns? (4) How does their interactional pattern confirm each spouse's dysfunctional beliefs about relationships?

I have some information already. Carl has difficulty expressing intimate, warm, and caring feelings toward Trudy, and Trudy appears to interpret his behavior as exploitative and possibly rejecting. She expresses her anger both by withholding sexual intimacy and by threatening to abandon Carl. This response discourages emotional openness in anybody who has difficulty expressing feelings of need and vulnerability in the first place. Carl's lack of emotional openness, in turn, confirms Trudy's belief that she is being exploited.

From the biographical information available at this point, I can form only tentative hypotheses about what the important subjective construing processes and tacit beliefs might be for Carl and Trudy, and how these might be related to important developmental experiences. I might conjecture that Carl may have a fear of abandonment because of his early experiences in an orphanage and that he has learned not to express his feelings and needs because of his belief that to do so would be futile or would lead to rejection. Similarly, I might conjecture that Trudy's traumatic sexual experience with her stepfather might contribute to a general sensitivity to exploitation by men.

The truly important information would have to come from a detailed, emotionally live and experiential exploration of both clients' subjective interpretations of the interaction that constitutes the fabric of their relationship. I would obtain this information from both partners' moment-by-moment interpretations either of specific dysfunctional interactions that have taken place between the two of them in the recent past or of a dysfunctional marital interaction taking place in my office. The specific interactions I would want to focus on would be those that are most characteristic of their relationship. The more concrete, specific, and immediate the interaction, the greater the likelihood that both clients would be able to explore their actual feelings and thoughts in the situation. Hence, a dysfunctional marital interaction occurring in my office would be particularly useful for assessment purposes.

Recall the situation in which Carl tells Trudy in my office that he needs her, but without any feeling in his voice. Trudy responds, "Get a maid!" and starts talking about leaving him. This simple interactional sequence would provide a perfect opportunity to explore whether Carl is aware of the lack of emotion in his voice. If not, I could point it out to him or simply have him listen to himself. I would then help him explore how he inhibits his expression of feelings and what beliefs, expectations, and fears lead to the difficulty he has in expressing his desires and needs to Trudy. This process would gradually help Carl to become more aware of his feelings and needs and to be able better to express them. It might also help

Trudy to understand the fears and vulnerabilities that under-lie Carl's difficulty in expressing his needs spontaneously. This understanding might help to disconfirm her belief that she is being exploited by Carl and to soften her feelings toward him.

I would also explore Trudy's fears and feelings of vulnera-bility that underlie her angry response to Carl. It may be that Carl's lack of emotional expressiveness in the present context confirms Trudy's dysfunctional belief that people are out to exploit her. It may be that she believes herself to be ultimately unlovable and that she interprets Carl's lack of tenderness toward her as confirmation.

As Trudy becomes aware of and is able to articulate some of the fears and vulnerable feelings that underlie her anger and threats of abandonment, Carl may begin to feel somewhat safer about expressing his feelings and needs.

Ultimately, both partners must assume responsibility for the roles they play in their dysfunctional interactions and come to see the ways in which their own fears and beliefs about intimate relationships contribute to their own behavior. In addition, learning to see and understand fears and vul-nerabilities that underlie the other person's characteristic be-avior will help each of them to disconfirm his or her own dysfunctional beliefs about relationships.

Carl and Trudy must learn to communicate their underly-ing fears and vulnerabilities. Either partner, on encountering the other's expression of vulnerability for the first time in the relationship, would be confronted with new, powerful, and irrefutable evidence about the other.

This process will help to disconfirm the dysfunctional or pathogenic beliefs about intimate relationships that both spouses have. As these beliefs become disconfirmed, their behavior with respect to one another will continue to change. Carl will find it easier to communicate his feelings to Trudy as he realizes how his beliefs and fears inhibit his expression and as he is moved by Trudy expressing the vulnerable feel-ings underlying her anger. Trudy will soften her anger toward Carl as she becomes aware how her own fears and beliefs maintain her anger and as she begins to see that Carl does care about her and is not trying to exploit her.

At some point, it may be useful for Carl and Trudy to explore the role that various experiences played in the development of their respective beliefs about intimate relationships. This exploration may not be an essential component of the treatment process, but it can serve two useful functions. First, it can facilitate the acceptance of responsibility as both partners develop a clearer sense of their own contributions to the dysfunctional interaction and the influence of their own histories. Second, such an exploration can help both clients appreciate that the beliefs they hold about relationships, while perhaps accurate and functional in a certain historical context, may be dysfunctional and subject to revision in the context of the present relationship.

Martin R. Textor (Systems and Integrative)

To formulate a treatment plan for Carl and Trudy, I would need much more information. I would ask Carl and Trudy about their parents; their development in childhood and puberty; their first sexual experiences; Carl's time in the orphanage; Trudy's past relationship to her parents and present one to her mother; her assessment of the impact of the sexual abuse on her later fears, sexual experiences, and attitudes toward men; Carl's experiences during the war; the earlier marriages (including similarities and differences between old and new partners); their marital relationship and sex life; their relationships to the children; the development of the children and their problems; and involvement in the marital conflicts.

Lacking this information, I can only speculate on the individual and marital dynamics. Carl appears to have developed an identity as a lone wolf in the orphanage and in Vietnam. I surmise that he lost fights with older orphans. His experience was that when he expressed his needs and wishes, they were rarely or never satisfied. On the one hand, his self-assertiveness became impaired, and he allows others to take advantage of him. On the other hand, he became laconic and self-controlled. He might regard the expression of emotions, wishes, and needs (such as his need for Trudy and the pain of separation) as a weakness that will be exploited. His experience that he cannot rely on others and that they do not really care for him was reinforced by the sudden loss of his affectionate aunt, his divorce, and the short-term abandonments by Trudy.

Trudy's development led to her sense of herself as a homeless child. Because her parents were always moving, she did not feel at home anywhere; she felt like an orphan. She might regard her present marriage as another phase in an endless sequence of brief episodes that leave her anxious, insecure, and emotionally uninvested. Having had no friends in childhood and early adolescence, she did not learn to get involved with others and to trust them. Her mother's unreliability and failure to protect her from her stepfather reinforced her expectation that people will let her down. Like Carl, Trudy had to fend for herself from early on, but unlike him, she was not successful in the practical world, and she developed feelings of inadequacy, low self-esteem, and a poor self-image. She was afraid of getting a job and perhaps of Carl's expectations. Despite Carl's evident success, she did not have high regard for him, and she viewed him as exploited by others. She might have been comparing him to an idealized image of her courageous and loving father. Could there be object conservation and unresolved mourning?

Thus, we have two extremely lonely and untrusting individuals living together. Both are unable to express their feelings, thoughts, needs, and wishes. Moreover, Trudy cannot differentiate between emotions and often has no evident reasons for them (her jealous rages, for example), while Carl has strong defenses against emotions, cuts off his own, and avoids Trudy's. He wears the mask of the "super-reasonable" (Satir, 1972), while Trudy acts like an "irrelevant person" who talks a lot but says little of importance. Both suffer from disturbances in communication, such as exclusion of topics, ineffective verbal expression, and lack of feedback. These disturbances also impair their problem-solving capabilities.

Their unresolved conflicts are acted out in the sexual sphere, and Trudy probably fails to communicate how much she needs love and affection because of an incorrect assumption that her partner will know by himself.

Carl may feel that the world owes him a lot since nobody cared for him in childhood and because he was wounded fighting for his country. According to his "merit accounting" (Boszormenyi-Nagy & Spark, 1973), he no longer has to give, and he deems it fair to take. He expects a lot from Trudy, including her being ready for sex from the moment he enters the apartment. However, Carl's expectations are not fulfilled as Trudy's merit accounting shows she has given a lot and now has the right to take: she lost her father, and she had to meet the demands of her mother, to submit to the sexual urges of her stepfather, and to relinquish her self-fulfillment by caring for her children on her own after her first husband deserted her. Thus, she may be making Carl responsible for her happiness.

Carl is self-controlled, pretends to be emotionally self-sufficient, and tends not to say what he wants, and Trudy lacks self-control, is impulsive, immature, and extremely needy. Sometimes she acts like an anxious child who wants to be held and comforted. Since Carl does not show love or consideration, she becomes, at the same time, deeply afraid (that she will be left again or that the marriage is just another episode in her life) and extremely angry (because of not receiving her just share or because she feels unloved and exploited). She tries to escape from this situation, thereby punishing Carl for not giving to her. However, this step increases her fear and her anger, for Carl does not show his pain and suffering and does not express a strong need for her or beg her to return. He cannot allow himself to be dependent on her or to show weakness.

Their marital system suffers from a lack of restorative mechanisms. It is an "unstable unsatisfactory relationship," in the words of D. D. Jackson (1968). Their system is not well-defined because expectations and wishes are not verbalized, and since there is little problem solving, conflicts can easily get out of hand. Both spouses married unwisely (at least the first time) and do not fulfill their marital roles well. There is no information given on how Carl behaves as a father; Trudy, however, seems to follow the example of her irresponsible mother. She did not use birth control, thereby allowing herself to become pregnant for secondary reasons, and she does not care for her children consistently. She seems to be unsatisfied with her role as mother, and she wants a job.

Carl and Trudy are still willing to undergo psychotherapy. Since both individual and marital problems are of great importance, I would suggest continuing in one of two ways. The first possibility is *parallel psychotherapy*. If Trudy is still unwilling to return to Carl, I would offer her individual therapy. She accepted the suggestion to return for at least one session. I would use this opportunity to motivate her to discuss with me, or with a female cotherapist, the loss of her father, the sexual abuse, and her strong, undifferentiated feelings. Carl is motivated by the necessity to lower his blood pressure, and I would offer to treat him separately from Trudy, focusing on his experiences in the orphanage, in Vietnam, and on the job, as well as on his love life. Ideally, the parallel psychotherapy would lead to marital therapy in which common problems could be discussed.

The second possible method is *collaborative or serial psychotherapy*. If Trudy returns to Carl, I would offer them a sequence of individual and conjoint sessions. The individual sessions would be to discuss important events in their lives and their intrapsychic conflicts, and the conjoint sessions would be to discuss marital problems and child-rearing issues. I would prefer these sessions to be conducted with a woman cotherapist, an arrangement that permits role modeling and perhaps greater empathy by each therapist for the client of the same sex. Moreover, the relationship between the therapists can serve as a symbolic marriage in which marital and parental behaviors, joint problem solving and decision making, the acceptance of individual differences, and mutual respect are modeled.

I think that Trudy will be hard to keep in psychotherapy

because she has not learned to sustain longer-lasting relationships. If she gets a lot of support, positive regard, and warmth, she may continue the treatment. Carl is better motivated but may be hard to activate, especially with respect to expressing feelings and needs. Thus, I would act as a role model trying to help him learn how men express emotions and show affection and how they can be open without getting hurt.

Carl will also need some warmth and affection to help him stay in treatment; he needs help in making contact with inner experiences. I would often ask what he feels, thereby making emotions conscious, fighting defense mechanisms such as rationalization, broadening the range of his feelings, and increasing his sensibility. By modeling, shaping, and role playing, he could learn much about congruently expressing his thoughts, feelings, and wishes, and in the course of participating in these therapeutic processes, he may become more trusting. If it is true that he is exploited by his boss and subordinates, assertiveness training is indicated.

Trudy needs to learn to differentiate emotions and to identify unreasonable ones. I would help strengthen her self-control by showing that she is responsible for her feelings and that she can decide how to react emotionally. I would also challenge her negative self-concept by emphasizing her strengths and uniqueness. I would ask her to close her eyes and remember the traumatic events of losing her father and of being sexually abused—an exercise that would foster catharsis, interpret feelings, terminate unresolved mourning, and diminish object conservation.

Conjoint sessions would provide an opportunity to foster open and honest communication between Carl and Trudy. I would facilitate a dialogue about emotions, needs, attitudes, and expectations; ask Carl and Trudy to express everything they feel at a given moment; and encourage each partner to explore the other's inner world. Thereby, I would identify communication disturbances such as incongruence while teaching them listening skills and empathy. I would also clarify signals about sex, further the nonverbal expression of love and affection (maybe prescribing sensate-focus exercises), and attempt to enhance intimacy.

I would ask Carl and Trudy to discuss their so-called merit accounts and the resulting expectations that cannot be fulfilled. This discussion would lead to a more appropriate definition of their marital relationship—one that takes only realistic desires into account. I would also attempt to increase the stability of the marriage by teaching Carl and Trudy problem-solving and conflict-resolution skills. After they have taken responsibility for their marriage, family sessions might be indicated for the discussion of their relationships to their children and their child-rearing methods.

Robert N. Sollod (Integrative)

A core tenet of an integrative, pluralistic approach to psychotherapy is the acceptance of the validity of a number of experiential and therapeutic domains. In application to the presented case, this approach would require additional probing, especially of Carl. I would need more information about the couple's courtship, the positive aspects of their marriage, the couple's sexual behavior, the level of functioning of their children, the family dynamics, Carl and Trudy's patterns (if any) of use or abuse of drugs or medications, and any aggressive, violent, homicidal, or suicidal behavior they may exhibit. Information about these areas would help determine the appropriate types of therapeutic intervention.

Additional information on Carl's presenting problem, hypertension, should be obtained from both Carl and his physician. Is there a family history of cardiovascular problems? What is the history of Carl's hypertension? Has its severity been related to specific events or situations in his life? If there is a correlation, a chart summarizing it could be constructed. What medication, if any, has been prescribed? What side effects are present? (Common side effects of drugs that lower blood pressure include erectile dysfunction and mild to moderate depression.) Are there treatment compliance issues? What life-style and nutritional factors may contribute to

Carl's hypertension? How much fat, cholesterol, and salt does he ingest? Does he smoke? What patterns of physical activity and exercise does he engage in? Minnesota Multiphasic Personality Inventory (MMPI) results and assessment of Type A behavior might reveal personality patterns related to hypertension. Based on thorough, detailed information, I would decide whether hypertension should be a focus of treatment, how urgent the problem is, and what other factors might be addressed. Treatment modalities such as biofeedback, relaxation training, cognitive restructuring, reduction of Type A behavior through behavior modification, encouragement of emotional expression, and catharsis could all be helpful. I might refer Carl to other professionals for work in specific modalities or for obtaining assistance in diet and exercise.

Veterans who experienced combat in Vietnam have a high likelihood of distressing emotional sequelae. According to Laufer and Gallops (1983, p. 6), "Limiting of the emotional scope of the veteran is likely to limit his inclination to enter marriage or to find an acceptable partner . . . or to satisfy his mate's emotional needs and maintain the relationship over time." Carl's emotional numbness, lack of responsiveness, and inability to connect emotionally with his wife are typical symptoms of posttraumatic stress disorder (PTSD) in Vietnam veterans. His possible victimization at work (as reported by Trudy) may be connected to his war experiences. Wilson, Smith, and Johnson (1985) state that the survivor of a traumatic event begins to perceive his or her destiny as shaped by external forces over which he or she has little or no control and to see the world as hostile, threatening to inflict more pain and suffering.

Carl's hypertension may result from a state of constant vigilance and accompanying automatic arousal, often a symptom of PTSD in Vietnam veterans. Recent research has indicated that the various symptoms of PTSD in war veterans are directly related to the type and severity of stressors experienced during the war, as well as to preexisting problems.

It is ironic that Carl is referred to in the title of the case history as "the returning hero," because the status of hero has been denied Vietnam veterans, who were often treated as outcasts. Not only Carl's war experience, but also the nature of his subsequent reintegration into society should be explored.

Trudy's relational dynamics are consistent with a diagnosis of PTSD. She is a grown-up, sexually abused child. Ideally, she should participate in group therapy with other grown-up incest victims. In such a therapeutic atmosphere, she could get in touch with the intensity of her feelings about her incestuous experiences and could develop insights into how these traumatic events have affected her current relationships. Analogously, if Carl is found to have a traumatic-stress-related disorder, there could be significant benefit for him in participating in a Vietnam veterans group. Both of these forms of PTSD could be addressed in individual therapy, but the group method with participants who have undergone similar stresses has proven preferable. Perhaps this group approach could be supplemented by individual therapy. Trudy and Carl also appear to need help in the development of parenting skills. This parenting area should be explored carefully and some sessions should be devoted to assisting Trudy in acquiring more competence as a parent.

I would suggest that Carl and Trudy delay any decisions on their marriage. A moratorium—which could involve living together or apart—would give them the opportunity to deal with the tremendous emotional burdens that each is bringing to the relationship. They both need significant individual support during therapy, although Trudy appears to be the pivotal person at present regarding the continuation of the marital relationship. Developmentally, Trudy is struggling with issues at the trust-mistrust level, whereas Carl has not yet successfully resolved intimacy-isolation issues. The behavior of each reinforces the fears and suspicions of the other, and as a result of intrapsychic conflicts and preoccupations related to past traumas, both Trudy and Carl would likely discount positive changes in the other. To the extent that each is able to resolve his or her own issues enough to perceive the behavior of the other more objectively, couple counseling to resolve relationship issues would be warranted.

A beginning point in such couple counseling might well consist of aiding Carl and Trudy to become more sensitive to the emotional burdens that the other is carrying.

The case, as presented, leads one to consider strategies of treatment management rather than of therapeutic integration per se. Both clients would likely benefit from a combination of different therapeutic modalities. The primary therapist would have to provide Carl and Trudy with a clear rationale for the selection of therapeutic approaches, assess their impact, and modify them as warranted. Both Carl and Trudy eventually need to make a decision about their marriage, but it would be premature to try to resolve this problem at the outset.

Points of Contention and Convergence

Jeremy D. Safran

My impression is that the most important point of convergence among the three orientations is our common recognition that Carl and Trudy are caught in a dysfunctional interaction of their individual maladaptive cognitive interpersonal cycles. There appears to be an agreement that Carl has difficulty communicating his feelings directly and that Trudy has a tendency to interpret Carl's behavior as exploitative, even when it is not. There also appears to be an agreement that Trudy's style of angry withdrawal further aggravates Carl's difficulty in being emotionally open and vulnerable.

Also, all three panelists appear to agree that change will take place through both partners' becoming aware of the roles that their respective issues play in the marital problem, learning to communicate their feelings in a more honest and direct way, and coming to see the hurt, fear, and vulnerability that lies underneath their partner's problematic behavior.

Both Textor and Sollod recommend supplementing couples therapy with individual therapy. While this is a recommendation that I did not make, it certainly seems to be a reasonable one, particularly given the apparent severity of the clients' individual problems.

The most important differences between Textor's and Sollod's orientations toward the case and my own is the source of the information on which we base our formulations and the relationship between formulation and treatment. As I indicated initially, I am reluctant to develop an elaborated formulation on the basis of the information available to me at this point. My formulation would only come from an in-depth exploration of the way in which both clients construe the present situation.

Textor has also indicated a reluctance to develop an elaborate formulation on the basis of the information available to him. The difference between his perspective and my own, however, appears to be that he would want more historical or biographical information to formulate a treatment plan, while I feel much more comfortable giving weight to the information that emerges through a careful phenomenological exploration of both clients' present construing processes. I am concerned that an overreliance on historical information would blind me to the subtleties of both clients' inner worlds as they reveal themselves in the here and now. For this reason, I feel at a disadvantage when the case material is presented in the present format; I feel limited in terms of the inferences that I can draw and constrained to speak in tentative generalities.

Sollod appears to pay greater attention than either Textor or I do to diagnostic formulations. He reasons that if both Trudy and Carl are suffering from specific forms of posttraumatic stress disorder (sexual abuse in Trudy's case and war trauma in Carl's), assignment to relevant therapy groups would be helpful. I do not rule out the possibility of both partners benefiting from relevant groups. I am more inclined, however, to develop an evolving formulation of both partners on the basis of an ongoing assessment of the respective phenomenologies rather than to assign them to treatment modalities on the basis of my initial formulations.

The particular way in which the case is presented calls for

a rather static portrayal of the formulation and treatment process, and hence Textor's and Sollod's accounts probably do not do justice to the way in which they work in practice. Both therapists, however, appear to me to feel more comfortable than I do in speaking about predestined treatment programs or modules on the basis of their initial formulations. To me, however, so much of what goes on in therapy involves moment-to-moment process considerations, so talking about specific treatment programs in advance does not make much sense. A so-called treatment program seems to be too large a unit of analysis.

Martin R. Textor

For me, all psychotherapy approaches are "personal theories" (Textor, 1985, 1988). They are not scientific theories based on empirical data and serving as models of reality; rather, they serve as "manuals" guiding a therapist in his or her work. Because the therapeutic situation is extremely complex, a therapist has to focus on a small number of selected variables and neglect the others. Otherwise he or she would be overwhelmed by the multitude of verbal and nonverbal responses, by intrapsychic and interpersonal patterns, and by situational factors, not all of which can be perceived, considered, and evaluated. Thus, each therapist has to limit himself or herself to a reasonable and manageable number of variables. The therapist thereby arrives at a unique personal theory, which is strongly influenced by biography, personality structure, view of people, and attitudes.

Accordingly, I can accept all approaches to psychotherapy as long as they are well-founded and work with the respective clients. Thus, I agree with nearly all of Sollod's and Safran's thoughts on how to treat Carl and Trudy. Moreover, I did not notice great differences from what I wrote. Sollod made me more aware of the medical and life-style aspects of Carl's hypertension and of the characteristics of posttraumatic stress disorder (which is little discussed in West Germany). In hindsight, I think it worthwhile to consider suggesting that Carl join a Vietnam veterans group and that Trudy join an incest victims group. However, I might refrain from those suggestions for fear that Carl and Trudy might be overwhelmed by too many treatment formats (and therapists). Safran made me notice the importance of Carl's and Trudy's belief systems. In contrast to Safran, I would try another treatment format and put more emphasis on the life history of each client. I would also put more importance on improving the clients' (especially Trudy's) parental behaviors; but I assumed they would come around, so I did not mention it.

I believe that in each idiosyncratic case, hypotheses, strategies, and techniques from different schools of psychotherapy should be combined—those that best fit the characteristics of the case and that are most likely to be successful. Accordingly, in the case of Carl and Trudy, I refer to psychodynamic approaches (interpreting past relationships, traumas, and experiences as well as impact on the present), behavioral approaches (modeling, role playing, assertiveness training), Rogerian psychotherapy (furthering self-actualization, contact with inner feelings), and approaches of family therapy (merit accounting, improving communication and child-rearing skills).

While such personal, eclectic approaches in psychotherapy may always be the reality in practice, I also believe that we must achieve a theoretical framework for therapy more satisfying than is afforded by the present multitude of limited, one-sided conceptualizations. Therefore, I strive for the integration of effective approaches. To the extent that these approaches concentrate on different variables and focus on certain aspects of the client and therapist situation, they are mostly complementary and compatible. An integrative theory (Textor, 1989), more comprehensive than personal approaches to psychotherapy, takes into account the multicausality of phenomena, the complexity of reality, and the complex interplay of biological, psychological, interactional, systems, and sociocultural variables.

Robert N. Sollod

My main disagreements with the initial responses of the panel, and on some points with my own position, concern the level of knowledge and understanding of the clients, our attitudes toward the clients, and the establishment of a therapeutic bond. The case history, with its allusions to various events in the lives of clients, has a two-dimensional feel— possibly inevitable as a result of space limitations. It is possible that the information as originally presented is colored by a therapeutic attitude that led to major difficulties getting therapy off the ground. Whatever the cause, the panelists, including me, may not have fully spotted the problem.

I admit that, based on the information provided, I do not genuinely know or understand either Carl or Trudy. Rather, the events in their lives and their reported behaviors lead to probabilities generated in my own mind that these events or behaviors are connected to presumable personality characteristics. Carl was an orphan, Trudy had been sexually abused, Carl is a veteran, both were divorced, therefore, what?

Our psychological training and experience should have sensitized us to the proposition that such a series of facts in many cases can camouflage the true stories of the lives of people. Not all adults who were orphans as youngsters are alike, nor do they all have similar experiences and dynamics. Most of our conclusions are drawn from the questionable logic of reasoning from small parts to the whole. I wonder what we would think of clients who made major interpersonal commitments based on such a paucity of information.

It is difficult to escape this trap, both in the current endeavor and in actual practice, because we are often called upon to reach conclusions based on insufficient evidence (Sollod, 1982). Safran is more tentative and cautious in his conclusions than is Textor, who comes up with many speculations without adequately qualifying them. Until a clearer, fuller story emerges, the words of Socrates seem relevant— "One thing I know is that I know nothing."

One area of major disagreement I have with the other panelists is the likelihood of Carl's suffering from posttraumatic stress disorder, which I do not believe either mentioned. At the very least, I think there should be an attempt to interview Carl regarding his adjustment to the Vietnam war and to assess him carefully for signs of posttraumatic stress disorder. If he does turn out to have PTSD, then the choice of Trudy as a partner becomes more understandable. Perhaps she is acting out the fear and turmoil that Carl is hiding from in himself.

None of the panelists, including me, emphasized the areas of growth that Trudy has demonstrated. Survival is, in such circumstances, a major achievement. We are informed that Trudy has read widely and has, in a sense, made up for a lack of formal education by her own efforts. She is also interested in psychotherapy. The case presentation suggests that both married "unwisely" the first time since their marriages ended in divorce, and they were each left with children. Positive aspects of the first marriages of each are not presented, and they just might be doing some things right in their difficult chores of parenting. Textor views Trudy as following the example of her "irresponsible" mother. Does he appreciate, I wonder, the struggles she might have undergone to keep her family together and the sense of helplessness that might underlie her potential decision to leave her older children with Carl? Is it merely a question of irresponsibility? In general, I found Textor's approach to reflect a pathologizing attitude that would be less likely to facilitate the development of a therapeutic relationship.

I have a strong impression that the breakdown that seems to be occurring at the beginning of therapy is somehow the result of vagueness or confusion in setting up the therapeutic contract. Safran addresses the issue of sorting out these issues at the beginning of therapy, but he does not give them the needed level of attention. Textor more or less tries to bypass these issues. In my rereading of the case, these complications regarding the development of the therapeutic relationship now seem paramount (Beitman, 1987).

Hellmuth Kaiser, according to Shapiro (1989), said that

knowing what to do in therapy is much less important than the attitude of the therapist. An attitude of respect for the patient can emerge, according to Kaiser, only from understanding the patient. The lack of understanding and the paucity of indications of positives (Wiesen, 1977) in the narrative are both indications and continuing causes of the lack of a good, working therapeutic relationship with either client.

Assuming that a therapeutic contract could be negotiated and a good therapeutic relationship established, then one main question the case presents is that of sorting out each partner's lifelong difficulties, problems, and needs. Both Safran and Textor, I believe, are aware of this problem and address it well. Textor considers the possibility of different modalities as a partial solution. I suspect that much effort will be needed to help both Carl and Trudy resolve some of their own issues—prior to the possibility of a lot of work on the relationship. It might turn out, however, that some solution of relational issues can be reached without much progress on individual issues. Issues of basic trust or intimacy can often be resolved, in part, through positive relational experiences.

I especially like Textor's concept of merit accounting, and I believe that it does hold promise for this couple. I agree with the approaches and tactics that Textor and Safran would use once therapy actually got under way. I agree with their emphasis on improving the relationship and, at the same time, their sensitivity to the needs and concerns of both Carl and Trudy. Safran is more of a therapeutic optimist than I am regarding this case, since I am more convinced that individual limitations may severely affect what they can reach in their relationship. I agree with Textor's options of parallel therapy, collaborative therapy, and serial therapy and with Safran's options of individual therapy, couple therapy, or no therapy. Less pressure on the couple will result from the availability of such options.

One final suggestion is that *cognitive decentering* regarding the relationship be promoted for both Carl and Trudy (Sollod & Wachtel, 1980). In this process, each should become more able to sort out his or her own experiences from the problems of the other. If this sorting can be accomplished, there will be a lower likelihood of downward interpersonal spirals whereby each partner's problems would trigger excessive reaction from the other.

10

The Adopted Sister

□

Bernard G. Guerney, Jr.
Janus M. G. Fraillon
Diana A. Kirschner
Samuel Kirschner

Case Presentation

Ginny, a beautiful Vietnamese child of nine, was adopted by
the Banners when she was three months old. The Banners
have one daughter, Molly, who is five years older. Ginny can
be socially charming. She likes to engage her older sister's
friends and hang out with them, but, sometimes, having insin-
uated herself into the teenager's circle, she will wreck everyone's good feelings by "clowning" (Molly's word), talking
baby talk, or speaking in nonsense syllables. This behavior
embarrasses Molly when she is unable to get Ginny to stop or
to go away. The scene rapidly becomes an angry shouting
match between the sisters, who are unable to resolve their
differences or separate without adult intervention. In these
circumstances, Mrs. Banner tends to become hysterically
angry, mostly at Ginny, and her anger unnerves Molly, who
"goes to pieces."

The therapist has known the Banner family for three years,
but they have met with her regularly only during the past
four months. Mr. and Mrs. Banner are bright, attractive, and
successful. He is an engineer. She was formerly a busy interior

designer. Since giving birth to their older daughter, Mrs. Banner takes occasional jobs but prefers to devote her energies to home and church activities. After several miscarriages, the Banners adopted Ginny.

Ginny's parents are concerned that she might be hyperactive. She can be extremely difficult to deal with at home, refusing to obey, challenging requests, blaming her mother, thwarting family routines (by not going to bed on time, for example), staying in bed instead of dressing to go to school, and generally alternating between misbehaving and clinging. Mrs. Banner nearly always has to deal with Ginny's tantrums and immaturities alone, since her husband works long days at the office and is often out of town on business trips. When Mr. Banner happens to be home and is drawn into the family disputes, he also tends to become angry at Ginny for acting out.

Molly is a sensitive child. She is plainer than her sister, who has flashing black eyes and black hair. Aside from reacting to Ginny's provocations, Molly frequently expresses considerable unhappiness. Her parents do not understand her and feel a lack of closeness with her. When the family is at its most disrupted and angry, Molly expresses hatred toward Ginny, tells her she wishes she were dead, and strikes at her physically. At other times, the sisters enjoy being with one another. Both have mercurial changes of mood.

Ginny was disruptive in kindergarten and first grade. She would not wait her turn and sometimes would intrude on another's artwork or block construction. She was often the center of commotion in class. When she tipped her chair over backwards, flinging her coloring book and crayons in all directions, it appeared to be part of a pattern of drawing attention to herself. Although she followed her teacher around, evidently wanting her affection, Ginny would often ignore directions. Even when given ample notice, she would dig her heels in and refuse to leave an activity she was engrossed in to go to the next one.

During the therapist's classroom observations and in testing, Ginny did exhibit moderate hyperactivity. Intrapsychic conflicts involving fears of being abandoned, guilt, and fantasies about her real family appeared to underlie her disruptive behavior and rejection of limits. Despite her problems, she was liked by her peers. By contrast, Molly worried about being accepted. At her saddest, she withdrew and her parents did not know how to communicate with her.

Mr. and Mrs. Banner maintain that they have a good marriage, and they decline to talk about problems they may have in relating to each other. The therapist has the impression that Mrs. Banner may wish to say more but that she is inhibited by her husband. Mr. Banner is not especially intimidating, but his wife appears to feel she must respect his reserve. The Banners are somewhat ashamed of being involved with a therapist at all.

During the first year following their referral, the Banners wanted nothing more than help in understanding the test data on Ginny and guidance in terms of her school placement. The therapist encouraged them to keep her in the same school setting, and at the therapist's suggestion, school personnel kept Ginny in a mainstream class. During the second year, the Banners wanted behavioral recommendations from the therapist. They came sporadically to therapy and resisted becoming involved in an ongoing therapeutic relationship, hoping their problems would simply disappear. At the suggestion of the school psychologist, they took Molly to a different therapist in the Banner's community. Molly did not object but also did not open up; in fact, she became increasingly constricted.

Up to this point, the approach of the therapist submitting the case was to encourage whatever efforts the Banners made toward engaging in a therapeutic relationship. She openly shared her assessment of Ginny with them and recommended family therapy, but she felt they could not accept confrontation at that point. The family hoped that summer would bring respite, which indeed it did. Molly went away to camp and did well socially. Ginny went to day camp and also adjusted well. Soon after the start of school, however, matters deteriorated. In January, the Banners accepted the therapist's suggestion of a short series of family sessions to evaluate family needs and to consider how to proceed. During these sessions, Molly opened up to a degree that shocked her parents, saying that no one saw or cared how taking Ginny into the family had messed up her life. Ginny was far less expressive but responded well to behavioral contracts worked out by the family in the sessions. A token economy, instituted at the therapist's suggestion, worked well in getting Ginny to conform to family schedules.

Over the past four months, the Banners have become more aware that they need to commit themselves to family therapy. Mr. Banner's absences disrupt the process somewhat, and the specific approach has yet to be determined.

Formulations and Treatments

Bernard G. Guerney, Jr. (Systems and Integrative)

I read the case description to mean that an organic basis for Ginny's hyperactive behavior and the need for medication have been ruled out. If there still are serious problems in school, I would want to confer with school personnel to gain a better understanding of these problems. I also would want to get the perspective of all family members, especially Ginny, about such problems and to work with them toward their solution.

If family members have not already had brief, confidential individual interviews, I would do this in order to elicit problems they may be reluctant to discuss in the presence of other family members. This approach seems particularly important for Mrs. Banner, because it was noted that she appeared inhibited in Mr. Banner's presence. I also would conduct such interviews to discover or rule out sexual or physical abuse, alcoholism, serious depression, or other problems that might call for interventions adjunctive to family therapy—which is, I agree, the most appropriate treatment choice.

I gather that nothing was found requiring treatments other than family therapy. No mention was made of a requirement to supply diagnoses to a third-party payer, and I feel no need to apply even informal systemic diagnostic labels, such as *enmeshed* or *disengaged,* to the family.

As I practice family therapy, I do not rule out separate sessions with individuals or subgroups within the family. For example, if the wife called me for a confidential interview, I might agree. Issues discussed in such an interview would be brought up with other family members, if and when appropriate, and I would not be concerned about creating problems by sharing a so-called family secret. Rather, I would be concerned about a problem remaining unknown to me and having one or more family members know that I do not know it.

All members of this family would benefit greatly from learning to express their emotions and viewpoints to one another and to help one another resolve interpersonal and intrapsychic problems and conflicts. Hence, I would conduct *relationship enhancement* (RE) family therapy with all of them. A key question, however, is whether to use one or two types of RE therapy.

That decision depends on characteristics of Ginny's that are not entirely clear in the description. If Ginny is an articulate child with a reasonably long attention span for discussion of family issues, then the only type of family therapy needed would be family relationship enhancement (RE) therapy. If not, another type of RE therapy would also be introduced—*child RE family therapy* (CRE), also called *filial therapy.*

In CRE, parents of children (generally up to age ten) are taught the theory and methods of client-centered play therapy. The parents then conduct therapeutic play sessions with their children to help the children express themselves emotionally and to overcome traumas and intrapsychic and interpersonal conflicts. Ginny's feelings about her adoption could be worked through in play sessions. Parents also are taught certain behavior modification principles to help them socialize their children appropriately (Guerney & Guerney, 1985). If Mr. and Mrs. Banner were to engage in CRE with Ginny, they would offer Molly equivalent "special times" with them to avoid exacerbating rivalry (L. F. Guerney, 1983). Even if

CRE were used, we would want Ginny present in the RE family sessions when rivalry issues were discussed. Because her age limits her articulateness, a therapist would use a great deal of *doubling* (B. G. Guerney, 1977). That is, in discussing issues with other family members, the therapist often would speak as if he or she were Ginny, with Ginny confirming or denying what the therapist said on her behalf. Molly and the other family members are entitled, should the need or wish arise, to the same service from the therapist.

The processes of RE therapies are designed to resolve intra-psychic and interpersonal problems and conflicts of family members by transforming the family system from one that is neutral or pathogenic to one that is therapeutic. RE integrates psychodynamic, humanistic, behavioral, and interpersonal theories and methods of psychotherapy; it rejects some aspects of each of these schools and blends other aspects of each into a coherent therapeutic system (Guerney, Brock, & Coufal, 1986).

RE procedures have been explained in detail elsewhere (e.g., B. G. Guerney, 1977, 1984, 1987; Guerney & Guerney, 1985) and demonstrated on videotape (e.g., Figley & Guerney, 1976; Vogelsong & Guerney, 1977). By means of in-session training and home assignments—some of which make use of audiotapes (Guerney & Vogelsong, 1981), readings, questionnaires, and logs (B. G. Guerney, 1987)—the clients are systematically taught nine skills: empathy, expression, discussion/negotiation, problem/conflict resolution, facilitation, self-change, other change, generalization, and maintenance. The therapist provides direct, intensive, live supervision in the sessions and selective after-the-fact supervision (through audiotape or self-report) of the play or family sessions conducted at home. In both types of interaction, the family members use the skills they learn to achieve catharsis and insight—relevant both to intrapsychic and interpersonal problems—and to initiate and maintain behavioral changes.

If there were a crisis situation that required immediate resolution before the family had acquired sufficient skills to follow the usual procedures for resolving it, special RE procedures would be brought into play. Crises do not seem particularly likely in the Banner family, and the ordinary sequence of procedures of RE and CRE would be expected to suffice. These ordinary procedures would include trouble-shooting, social reinforcement, and vicarious reinforcement to improve the regularity of Mr. Banner's attendance (B. G. Guerney, 1977). As the family developed proficiency in RE skills, the therapist would guide their selection of issues toward ones progressively more difficult, more emotion arous-ing, and more fundamental.

To give the reader a flavor of RE, a brief imaginary seg-ment of the Banner's therapy will be presented. The annotated hypothetical transcript is from the tenth hour of RE family therapy. By then, the Banners would have enough skill to tackle highly emotional issues.

The family member initially adopting the expressive mode chooses by eye contact a particular family member to respond empathically. Discussion/negotiation skills allow the em-pathic responder to become the expresser if he or she so desires, after having given a response deemed empathic by the expresser. (Others in the family may interject comments into the dialogue under conditions not explained here.) The fam-ily member to the left of the expresser (exempting the empathic responder) acts as the facilitator (coach) for all the other family members. The children have the same privileges and responsibilities as the adults. At this stage of therapy, with exceptions as necessary, the therapist facilitates through the facilitator.

Let us assume that Ginny has chosen Molly to talk to and that she has expressed the view that Molly treats her unfairly, makes fun of her, and says mean things to her, especially in front of Molly's friends. Molly has already responded empath-ically to a series of such expressive statements from Ginny over a span of five minutes. Ginny's expressive performance and Molly's empathic performance have been assisted and socially reinforced by the facilitator, who happens to be Mr. Banner, and indirectly by the therapist, who also facilitates through Mr. Banner.

Our transcript begins with an empathic statement from Molly to Ginny.

Molly: It really bothers you a lot when I say something like "Beat it, creep" or "Get lost!" or "I hate you!" It makes you feel like I don't care about you at all. In fact, it makes you think I really do hate you.

[The therapist wants Molly to be further reinforced for her empathic responses and seeing that Mr. Banner has not spontaneously done so on this last occasion, sends a nonverbal signal to Mr. Banner, who understands the signal.]

Mr. Banner: Very good, Molly. [The therapist reinforces Mr. Banner's appropriate facilitation.]

Therapist: [to Mr. Banner] Good.

At the same time, Ginny, who is tearful, has nodded her head and shows no indication of wanting to continue talking. Molly correctly takes Ginny's head nod as meaning that her empathic response has been perceived by Ginny as being on target. Ginny's nonverbal acknowledgment of the appropriateness of Molly's empathic response means that it is all right for Molly to switch to an expressive stance now if she wishes to do so. She does switch, choosing Ginny by eye contact as her empathic responder. Molly makes the following unskilled statement.

Molly: Ginny, I just do that when you're being a baby. When you . . .

Therapist: [interrupting Molly] Molly, hold it, please. [turning to Mr. Banner] Mr. Banner, I'd like you to take over as facilitator on this one. You could help her correct the "baby" business, but I think it is important that we try to bring in some of the underlying positive feelings, and you have not had any experience in coaching that. So this time just watch me, and try to remember the way I go about trying to help so that you can do it in the future, OK?

Mr. Banner.   Sure.

[The therapist turns to Molly to troubleshoot, structure, and model.]

Therapist: Molly, you're frustrated and annoyed right now because it seems to you that Ginny is putting all the responsibility on you and not seeing her role in the problem. I'm sure that would make it hard for you to bring in some of your underlying positive feelings at this point, before you get into some of the negatives. But if you can do that, I think that it would really help you to get your own views across to Ginny. So, if it is true, and if it can fit in well enough with your overall feelings right now, I'd like you to say something like this to Ginny: "I feel really bad that you feel so hurt when I say things to you like 'creep' and all. I may want to hurt you at the moment, but overall I don't want to make you feel bad about yourself. But some of the things you do, especially when I am with my friends, make me furious." And go on from there, Molly. Tell Ginny some of the specific things she does that make you so mad. Following the specificity guideline will also help you follow the guidelines for avoiding generalizations and get you out of the "baby" comment. First, is what I said about your underlying positive feelings toward Ginny true?

Molly: [nodding her head vigorously] Yes.

Therapist: Do you feel you could say that to her now, in your own way, of course, and also tell her what, specifically, she does that makes you so very mad?

Molly: OK. [and she does.]

This gives some idea of the structure of the session and a few of the types of responses RE therapists make. It is important to note that the purpose of the intervention was as stated—to implement a guideline for expressive skill that calls for stating underlying positives (as well as to correct the "baby" generalization). The intervention very definitely was not intended to cut off the expression by Molly of angry feelings or simply to help relieve Ginny's depressed or hurt feelings.

In a prior hypothetical sequence, the therapist helped Mr. Banner to help Ginny go as deeply as possible in expressing negative feelings of anger, pain, and hopelessness over Molly's treatment of her; and, a few minutes after the transcript ended, the therapist helped Mr. Banner to help Molly freely express her strong anger and her momentary desire to hurt Ginny when Ginny behaved in certain ways. The therapist tried to deepen and facilitate the expression of such negative feelings as well as positive feelings. The RE therapist did so because he or she viewed the full expression of negative feelings (catharsis) when done in appropriate ways and contexts (and only then) as highly conducive to the expresser's insight, as freeing the expresser to make therapeutic changes, and as permitting other family members fully to appreciate the expresser's predicament and to show complete acceptance to the expresser. When the expresser harbors strongly negative feelings, he or she cannot feel fully accepted as a person by the object of those feelings if the latter does not even know about them.

Where would this dialogue likely go after Molly described what Ginny did that infuriated her? At the least, we would apply problem/conflict-resolution skills based on new perceptions, emerging feelings, and attitudes acquired during the dialogue. Specific agreements between Ginny and Molly about how each is to behave when Molly is with her friends would commit each to use self-change skills. Possibly, each family member would undertake to use other-change skills to help Ginny and Molly make the changes they agreed to make. Efforts toward such change would be regularly monitored and adjusted by the family, with the therapist supervising this application of their skills. Probably not immediately, but springing from this dialogue or another, issues of perceived parental favoritism and Ginny's feelings about her adoption would be discussed. We would expect such a discussion, with facilitation, to lead to highly emotional expressions of love and caring from both parents toward both children. The out-pouring of love and affection would have a dramatic effect on the self-esteem of the children, would sharply reduce their rivalry, and would result in a general improvement in family functioning.

I assume, especially in light of Mrs. Banner's reticence in Mr. Banner's presence, that problems additional to those already visible will need attention in the course of the therapy. However, I see nothing in this case to warrant unusual wari-ness—no anticipations of psychotic breakdowns, suicide, hom-icide, or child or spouse abuse. I expect that Ginny's school difficulties, her adoption problem, the excessive sibling rivalry, the mood swings of the children, Molly's distress, Mrs. Banner's lack of assertiveness regarding Mr. Banner, and struc-tural defects in the family will be resolved without more than the usual therapeutic interventions.

Janus M. G. Fraillon (Existential)

The Banner family is presented as living in a state of hostile dependency that is being addressed by family therapy. This may be a useful way to proceed, but it is important to know as much as possible about the family and its individual mem-bers, about their past and present, and about the existential problems they face, not only with the family, but also in the society in which they live. Specifically, I would like answers to the following questions.

How old are Mr. and Mrs. Banner? Is the age difference between them significant? Is religion a source of conflict, per-haps even inside a shared religious structure? Do Mr. Banner and Mrs. Banner share or integrate into each other's interests?: Is there conflict in their social consciousness?

What medical examinations of Ginny have been made, and what were the results? What could be learned of the Banners' psychological functioning by means of IQ testing, MMPI, Logo Test, and results of other psychometric instruments? Do the Banners form a hierarchy based on sex, color, body size, or whatever? Is Mr. Banner a rigid or flexible type, and so forth?

Are Mr. Banner's hours of work and traveling related to a precarious position? If so, who has put him there—himself, his wife, his parents or siblings, or economic forces affecting his work? Why is Mrs. Banner devoted to church work? Who blames whom for the miscarriages, and what share of the blame does Molly have to bear, if any? Why should Molly accept Ginny? What is the parent's attitude toward Molly?

What were the Banners' reasons for marrying? Have attitudes and values that originally attracted the Banners to each other become grounds for the present evident isolation? Are Ginny's problems a projection of an already failing marriage?

Did Mr. Banner sire Ginny while on a tour of duty in Vietnam? Even if not, does Mrs. Banner think he is her natural father? How did Mrs. Banner feel about an adopted child—a Vietnamese adopted child? Did she love this baby at the time of adoption? Did Mr. Banner? Does she now? Does he?

How do Mr. and Mrs. Banners' parents, siblings, and friends react to the children and to the present situation? How does the community accept a Vietnamese child? Is she called names, attacked, or made to feel different in school?

Has Mr. Banner been involved sexually with either or both daughters? Is his wife frigid? Does Mr. Banner have extramarital relations? If so, does Mrs. Banner condone them because she cannot cope with him sexually? Or is she having an affair with another man or woman—perhaps one in her church or PTA group? Are they hostile to therapy and therefore keeping these matters secret?

Does any of the family have an accessible sense of humor? Could any of them be trained to use *paradoxical intention* or *dereflection* to look at what can be done to cope with each person's reactions while pursuing a constructive goal?

This is an ideal situation for existential analysis and a logotherapeutic intervention once all these variables are assessed for presence and importance. I would explore with each family member the present choices available and the implications for him or her and for others in the family. The factors in such choices can be explored by the techniques of paradoxical intention and logical extension into absurdity. When counseling techniques falter, even at Ginny's age, this exploration is possible using stories, poems, role playing and drama, discussion of films, television dramas, and class events.

What harvests do the Banners reap? It could well be that the Banners' marriage is no longer of value to either of them and should be dissolved. If so, then both Molly and Ginny will need a great deal of support over a period of years, including allowing them to express anger and receive love and to express fear and find acceptance.

Diana A. Kirschner and Samuel Kirschner (Systems)

We can only admire the therapist's persistence with an obviously resistant couple. The therapist observed the identified patient in the classroom, saw the parents together, spoke to the older sister, and interviewed the family together. This flexibility may have ultimately paid off in her being viewed as a resource when the parents finally "gave up" in the second year and came in for treatment. In our view, the therapist's movement toward a stronger therapeutic contract that includes family therapy is entirely appropriate for this case. Adopted children and their families often have intrapsychic and interpersonal issues that can be dealt with effectively in a treatment integrating individual and family sessions. Here is a brief description of an integrative therapy model, followed by our assessment of this case and a possible treatment plan.

Comprehensive family therapy (CFT) (Kirschner & Kirschner, 1986) provides a theoretical framework that targets both psychodynamic and transactional processes in the family. The intrapsychic model is derived from psychoanalytic and object-relations theories. In this model, CFT postulates a three-level self-system. At the core of the self is the foundation of the ego (Guntrip, 1969), which is formed initially through the relationship with the mothering one. Basic and primitive issues of trust are generated in the mother-child dyad.

At the next level of the self-system, the child develops an even more separate sense of self—a sexual identity (Freud,

1975) based on identification with parental figures. Sexual identity is usually congruent with that of the parent of the same sex.

The third level of the self-system is the triangulation level, an internal model created by the child's experience of relating in a triad. The triad's features may include oedipal wins and losses, homoaffiliative coalitions against the opposite-sex parent, and scapegoating the child to avoid the issues in marital conflict.

Ginny manifests separation anxiety and abandonment terrors at the foundation level (following the teacher around, staying in bed, and refusing to go to school). At the level of sexual identification, Ginny manifests an infantile sense of self (talking baby talk, using nonsense syllables). She does not appear to be deeply identified with her adoptive mother, and she fantasizes about her biological family. This is quite common among adopted children in adolescence, although in our experience, children in the latency period do not usually do so.

We would hypothesize that Ginny is experiencing a reverse oedipal win. Mrs. Banner's energies go to her, albeit in a negative way, rather than to Mr. Banner. A reverse oedipal win typically engenders much guilt and self-hatred (as manifested in Ginny's protocol). Along with primitive fears of abandonment, Ginny suffers from an inadequate sexual identification and from being caught in an illicit coalition with her adoptive mother.

The self-systems of each family member are in dynamic exchange with the transactional components of the family. In CFT, we typically assess three systemic variables: the *rearing*, *marital*, and *vocational transactions*. In the Banners' rearing transaction, the mother seems to play an ineffectual role leading to conflict with Ginny, while the father plays a distant role. At times, Ginny sets herself up to be mother's companion by refusing to go to school and remaining at home. Both parents seem more distant from Molly, who is neglected. Parental teamwork seems weak or nonexistent. Neither girl is receiving adequate nurturing, discipline, or guidance. As a result, both girls are in distress. Ginny acts out more overtly, while Molly complains of "going to pieces."

The difficulties in the rearing transaction can be linked to signs of severe marital dysfunction. Mrs. Banner's signals about possible marital problems, followed by her subsequent reluctance to discuss them in front of her husband, suggest a lack of openness between the spouses. What other secrets are being covered up in the marriage? Is Mr. Banner, who is away much of the time, having an affair? Molly's complaints about being alienated and displaced can be heard as metaphors for the alienation in the marriage. And the siblings' conflict may be a manifestation of the latent marital conflict.

Systemically, Ginny's role as the identified patient keeps attention focused on her and away from the marriage. At times, Mrs. Banner can draw her disengaged husband back into the family through her helplessness in coping with Ginny. She can also vent her marital frustration through Ginny, thus maintaining the stability of the marriage.

In CFT, the marital transaction is viewed as the most powerful determinant of the emotional life in the family. The marriage shapes, and in turn is shaped by, the self-systems of the spouses. This dialectical exchange tends to control the other familial transactions. Because the spouses' self-systems are formed in their families of origin, information about their backgrounds is critical for the success of treatment. Data about the Banners' families are lacking in the write-up. We would certainly pursue this information in clinical interviews with each spouse individually.

In the area of vocational transactions, we also require more information. Why did Mrs. Banner not return to work after Molly was of school age? Did Mr. Banner feel threatened by her competency outside the home? These questions would be addressed both in individual and conjoint sessions.

The therapist would work with all members of the family using both individual and conjoint sessions. Initially, the therapist would focus on the presenting problems while bonding with the family and seeding for later marital work. In family sessions, Ginny's behavior would be reframed as bringing the family closer together. Ginny's fears of abandonment and Molly's despair as metaphors of family alienation would be communicated to the spouses. The therapist might remark that in this family, no one has a sense of belonging. The parents would then be joined together with the therapist to provide a greater feeling of community for the parents and the girls. It would be suggested to the parents that, with the therapist, they could straighten out their daughters' problems as well as their own.

Following the CFT model of healthy family functioning (Kirschner & Kirschner, 1986), the therapist would place Mrs. Banner in charge of the girls. She would be the primary disciplinarian and programmer, while Mr. Banner would function more as the facilitator and nurturer. This triangulation model serves to promote same-sex identification while promoting a positive view of the opposite sex.

In individual sessions with each spouse, the therapist would elicit material about his or her family of origin and explain how such an upbringing contained the seeds of the marital conflict and alienation. We have found that clients are open to this interpretation because it seems to shift blame from them to the preceding generation. As the therapist is perceived as more understanding and empathic, each spouse becomes more open to a reparative relationship. The therapist can then tailor a more nurturant or confrontational stance with each spouse—a stance designed to fill gaps and heal wounds from childhood.

This type of reparative relationship is the cornerstone of CFT, supporting all the individual-behavioral and structural-strategic family techniques. As the work continues, both spouses will regress in relation to the therapist while progressing in their marital and parental roles.

Marital intimacy would be encouraged through initiating dating and other courtship activities. Communication skills to enhance self-disclosure and active listening would be taught to the spouses in conjoint sessions. As the spouses grew together, their parental teamwork would become stronger and the children healthier. Occasional individual sessions with both Ginny and Molly would assist the parents to monitor their progress. In particular, Ginny would need to be able to discuss her longing for and fantasies about her biological family.

In the final phase of therapy, the spouses would learn to become therapeutic agents for each other (Kirschner and Kirschner, 1989a, 1989b). By then, better acquainted with each other's needs, they would be asked to be more active in fulfilling them. For example, Mrs. Banner might have a fantasy about a career that Mr. Banner could help her make a reality. The couple's teamwork would be promoted in all areas of their lives—as parents, as lovers, and as promoters of each other's independent careers.

Points of Contention and Convergence

Bernard G. Guerney, Jr.

The major point of convergence is our agreement with the Banners' psychotherapist that family therapy is the treatment of choice here; at least none of us objected to it. A couple of decades ago, this agreement almost certainly would not have occurred. Of equal interest, in terms of agreement, is that none of us objected, as some family therapists might, to the idea that some separate interviews would be permissible, and perhaps desirable.

A convergence between the Kirschners' approach and mine can be found in their last paragraph. They say there that in the final phases of therapy, the spouses would learn to become therapeutic agents for one another. I was very excited and joyful about this, because promoting the use of family members as psychotherapeutic agents in family therapy has been my major "cause" for some thirty years (e.g., B. G. Guerney, 1964, 1969).

Upon calmer reflection, it seemed to me that although there doubtless is overlap, the Kirschners and I probably do not think of the term *therapeutic agents* entirely in the same way. In considering the Kirschners' use of the term, I wondered, "If family members are to act as therapeutic agents, why wait until the final phase of therapy to teach them how to do it?" I would think that by the final phase, by definition, there would be little therapy left to do. I infer from this statement about timing, and also from the statements and examples that followed it, that the Kirschners mean they encourage family members to be helpful to one another in meeting clearly expressed, already known, and nonconflicting wishes. Such a role is important, but to my way of thinking, it represents only the happily wagging tail of the therapeutic dog. We view the rest of the dog—the hardworking parts—as being represented by family members directly helping one another in the tough work of digging out the family's deepest fears, desires, and feelings and helping one another to resolve the often-conflicting intrapsychic and interpersonal expectations, desires, and goals that cause individual and systemic distress. To accomplish this digging out, the RE therapist generally starts training family members to be psychotherapeutic agents during the very first hour of therapy. In short, we expect mutual therapeutic assistance to become an integral part of the new "family rules" that we install to displace the old nontherapeutic or pathogenic family rules. (Of course, we encourage this type of hardworking therapeutic dog also to wag its tail when that is appropriate.)

Although it is not explicit in the responses, I believe there may be another related point of convergence among the three of us—one that distinguishes us as a group from many family therapists. I refer to our view that family therapy provides not only an acceptable but also a highly effective setting in which to help individual family members to work on personal problems in an intrapsychic fashion. By *intrapsychic fashion,* I mean exploration of such things as self-concept issues, feelings, and relationships—including those that may go back to childhood experiences and conflicts. These explorations can lead to the cathartic expression of deep emotion to help individuals achieve psychological insight.

Fraillon and I agree in our lingering concern about the possibility of an organic factor contributing to Ginny's hyperactivity. We also share a concern about the necessity to rule out the possibility of severe disorders and dangers such as suicide and abuse. However, Fraillon and the Kirschners seem to share the desire to pursue at once a great many diagnostic questions and decisions having to do with individual and family dynamics. And that brings me to a major area of divergence: the others have a diagnostic orientation; I do not.

As implied in my comments above about the need to discover organicity, suicidal tendencies, and the like, I am acutely aware of the need to make broad-gauged action-oriented diagnostic judgments that might immediately call for treatment strategies different from or in addition to family therapy. And, of course, diagnoses may be made for administrative purposes such as insurance requirements or for clinical research. For convenience, let us call all such diagnostic efforts *Type I diagnosis*. Let us call all other quests, not only for the best *DSM-III* label, but also attempts to determine the genesis, nature, causes, prognoses, and dynamics of an individual's or a family's problems, *Type II diagnosis*.

An RE therapist is as much concerned with Type I diagnosis as is anyone else. However, following an educational model as opposed to a medical one (B. G. Guerney, 1982; Guerney, Stollak, & Guerney, 1971), RE therapists do not concern themselves very much with Type II diagnosis.

Instead of trying to figure out what is wrong—so it can be eliminated with the expectation that family members will then know how to do what is right without having to be taught what is right (medical model)—RE therapists try to teach what is right with the expectation that doing so will eliminate all that is wrong (educational model). Reflecting this difference in orientation, by count of paragraphs, the Kirschners devote about 50 percent of their original response to Type I and II diagnoses combined, Fraillon about 80 percent, and I about 5 percent. These percentages may provide a measure of how much time and energy we each think worthwhile to devote to the diagnostic quest of figuring out what is wrong and why.

Even though not explicit in the three responses, it seems

fairly safe to conclude that RE differs from the other two therapeutic methods under discussion in the following respects: (1) RE working more directly and systematically with the family toward specified positive goals, (2) the method of determining the duration of therapy and structuring its phases, (3) termination procedures, (4) home assignments, and (5) topic selection and control. Space does not permit an elaboration of such differences here, and the reader can find elucidation elsewhere (e.g., B. G. Guerney, 1977; Guerney & Guerney, 1985).

Comparing therapeutic strategies and methods with esteemed colleagues in this manner has been an extremely stimulating and valuable experience. I much appreciate having had the opportunity to participate.

Janus M. G. Fraillon

What can we do to unfurl the Banners? It seems that a whole panoply of different therapies is open to us, and yet are they not perhaps cut from the same cloth?

Guerney's RE approach is obtainable, it would seem, from any reputable bookseller. However, the psychotherapist uses a form of social or behavior training to lead the family members into the light by means of audiotaping or even videotaping of family interactions. Who would actually operate the various recording devices—while Mrs. Banner refuses her tired husband's advances once more in the intimacy of the bedroom—is not actually stated.

The Kirschners' approach, CFT, is strongly based on the driven nature of the Freudian mechanistic model. Oedipus blindly drives the children even more dangerously in reverse. CFT, too, would seem to involve the therapist in social manipulative games with the parents trying, as in RE, to play roles with which they could become eventually at ease and so lighten the burden on the children. The problems that arise as a result of shifting the blame onto the preceding generations are not as bad, it seems, as those current ones with which the therapist is trying to deal.

Both RE and CFT lead invariably to the present and to the hopes of the individual family members for the future. They want freedom—freedom from the demons that have been driving them—and social-behavioral manipulations provide means to that end. But each silver lining has a cloud. In these situations, each family member must take responsibility for his or her own actions, despite the blameworthiness or not of the generations of the past. Almost as in the old Alcoholics Anonymous (AA) mode, each member of the family must make restitution for any costs incurred as a result of his or her behavior. Also, as in AA, an individual must acknowledge that he or she needs help to find the way to deal with the problems with which each day confronts him or her.

Many psychotherapists rely on typical Freudian transference to become this external source of power for the clients. Some of us try to tap the power inherent in the conscience of the clients themselves through seeking with them the meaning of the moment in any situation—any warm interaction as well as any disaster. Through the cumulation of these meanings, we hope to find the real purpose that keeps the individual alive, against all reason at times.

Ginny may have no real reason to wish to live with her adoptive parents. Indeed, the burden of being indebted to her supposed benefactors, who also expect her to like their older daughter, may be the last straw. The primal pains of her experiences in Vietnam, which led her to being adopted into an alien culture, may never be resolvable by the Banners under any flag. Ginny must eventually take the responsibility for resolving the mess herself, at her age in her way, in order to get on with her own life as a contributor to the society in which she now lives and from which she benefits.

Molly must also come to terms with her hostile dependency on her unlovable mother and absentee landlord of a father. It is awful to hate a do-gooder, especially an artistic one, particularly if that do-gooder is your mother. So Molly must resolve her anger in constructive ways that her conscience will allow.

The questions raised about the family and the possible complications of their situation described in my original contribution were meant to inspire therapists to seek the broadest canvas for the protagonists to paint their life pictures upon and to integrate with one another's vision. The psychotherapist then may become not only the art historian for that family but also somewhat of an entrepreneur recognizing the particular genius of each of them and encouraging them, individually and as a family, to realize their special potentials.

Diana A. Kirschner and Samuel Kirschner

There appears to be a consensus among the authors that intrapsychic and interpersonal issues need to be resolved in the Banner family. In this respect, we all agree that Ginny, the symptomatic child, can best be helped by broadening the treatment focus to include other members and other aspects of family life. For example, Guerney suggests that enhancing the communication skills of the girls will reduce conflict between them, and Fraillon believes that Ginny's problems may reflect other, more serious issues, including a failing marriage. In sum, then, all the authors agree that a unidimensional treatment approach to the Banners cannot adequately deal with the individual and family problems they present.

However, the authors clearly diverge in implementing a treatment plan. These divergences take several forms: framework for sessions, focus of treatment, and treatment goals.

Guerney advocates conjoint sessions for the therapy while using individual sessions "if necessary," and Fraillon recommends individual existential analysis for each family member. We suggest using a combination of individual sessions with each spouse as well as conjoint family or couple sessions. The differing frameworks arise out of the second divergence—the focus of treatment.

While stating that intrapsychic issues are important in this case, nowhere does Guerney really address them. Both our response and Fraillon's delineate specific hypotheses and concerns that we have about the spouses and their history—concerns we could address in individual sessions. For example, we would deal with Mrs. Banner's poor self-esteem and lack of assertiveness in the family and in the world.

In addition, like Fraillon, we have serious concerns about the marriage. Unlike Guerney, who ignores the issue, Fraillon would deal with the marital rift on an individual basis. We would take Fraillon's view one step further. As we have indicated in our response, we consider the marriage and the intra-psychic functioning of the spouses to be the most powerful dynamic in shaping all of family life. The spouses are, after all, the models and executives for the children. Thus, after restructuring the parenting relationships (especially reengaging Mr. Banner), we would concentrate on individual and marital work conducted in concurrent and conjoint sessions with the spouses.

The differences concerning frameworks and foci for treatment appear to grow out of differing goals for therapy. In comprehensive family therapy, our goals include a clear parent-child hierarchy and a marriage in which the spouses serve as growth agents for each other and for the children. As such, the therapy with the Banners requires restructuring the parent-child relationships through conjoint family sessions; building self-esteem, assertiveness, and self-awareness through individual sessions; and promoting sexuality, intimacy, and a "win-win" mutuality through conjoint couples work.

In contradistinction, Guerney's goals appear to involve a more diffused parent-child hierarchy in which each family member develops communication and facilitative skills so that there is clear empathic communication and negotiation in the family. As Guerney writes, "The children have the same privileges and responsibilities as the adults."

We disagree with Guerney that the hierarchy of parents and children is somehow not important in family life. Indeed, we view the Banner family as a dysfunctional one in part because the hierarchy between parents and children is unclear and because the boundaries between the marital couple and the children are diffuse. Mrs. Banner often plays the role of the hysterical child and is much more in the children's camp than she is a partner with her husband at the spousal or parental level. Without a strong parental coalition to guide and structure the daughters and to help them resolve conflict, the girls are left to flounder on their own. Reestablishing the proper hierarchy and boundaries in this family would be our first task. As a consequence, good communication between parents and children and between siblings would then be possible, and the symptomatic behaviors would tend to abate.

Fraillon's approach, on the other hand, seems to emanate from yet another set of treatment goals that include the individual family member's understanding and accepting his or her choices and realizing the implications of these choices for the family. We agree with Fraillon that insight into and acceptance of oneself is an important goal of therapy. We believe, however, that promoting behavioral change in the rearing, marital, and vocational transactions is also needed. In fact, it is our contention that in many instances, insight follows rather than precedes behavioral change.

11

Contention and Convergence
in the Psychotherapies

▣

John C. Norcross
Nolan Saltzman
Lucia C. Giunta

Observing patterns in the nine clinical exchanges and inter-preting their significance is at once exciting and daunting. We are excited by the rich insights of thirty-three clinicians, the remarkable amount of information, the vigor of the exchanges, and particularly the novelty of the entire enterprise. Simultane-ously, we are daunted by the challenge of doing justice to it all in a brief, concluding chapter.

Of the many topics that might have been addressed in an epilogue, we have selected three. First, we review the mission of the book, and we address, from several perspectives, the success in fulfilling it. Second, we share qualitative impressions formed while organizing, reading, and editing the contributions. Third, we present quantitative data from statistical analyses of the contributions. In these three ways, we hope to inform future dialogues on clinical material as well as research studies on psychotherapy integration.

Has Our Mission Succeeded?

Of diverse voices is sweet music made
So in our life the different degrees
Render sweet harmony among these wheels.

Dante (*Paradiso* Canto VI)

Have the diverse voices in this volume made sweet music? We must ask whether these clinical exchanges produced the intended benefits.

An affirmative response comes from the contributors. Behaviorally, all but one of those invited to contribute to the book agreed and subsequently did. These are busy and eminent clinicians, for whom a writing assignment is more often a chore than a prize. They offered a number of unsolicited remarks that, in our editorial experience, exceeded the norm for collegial compliments: "In all my years, I have never had such an opportunity"; "exciting project"; "very innovative idea"; "extremely stimulating"; "very valuable"; and so on.

A similarly positive response comes from the editors. We were particularly pleased that our emphasis on the process of exchange, as opposed to the outcome, was apparently evident to the contributors and to early readers.

To reiterate, the mission was not necessarily to produce rapprochement or synthesis. Neither exaggeration nor minimization of genuine differences was sought. Rather, the process of the exchange—encountering alternative, even rival, perspectives—was valued, and that may or may not eventuate in integration. Where differences remain, they should affect the world of human experience and clinical practice.

Now, for a few of the rewards of editing the Clinical Exchange section of the *JIEP* over the past four years and developing this book from it. We were surprised ourselves at how stimulating and downright educational for us the project could be at times. We have been apprised of unfamiliar techniques, and we have learned much about the range of therapist stances toward clients—from delicate and self-effacing to abrasive and directive.

When Alvin Mahrer (Chapter Three) responded to Michael's excuse for being late—that he had been up for two nights anticipating the session—with the remark, "That's something! You started to leave for here two nights ago?" we laughed and knew Michael was in good hands.

When Janet Bachant (Chapter Seven) interpreted Hal's dread of dying as a feeling that his life was already over, that his mortality was not just something that would happen to him, but was present within as his experience of himself, we felt the shudder of insight.

When Janus Fraillon (Chapter Ten) queried, "What harvests do the Banners reap?" we were boosted to a higher philosophical perch from which to think about the assumptions of therapy. And so on throughout the book.

Similar moving moments occur elsewhere in the literature, but they are rare. Clinicians, like other people, do not appear at their best while controlling all the variables to create a favorable impression. When psychotherapists provide themselves with the perfect illustration of their own therapies, they tend to be less spontaneous and convincing than they appear here, where the challenge of responding to cases not of their own choosing evidently opened the window of inspiration. It has been a joy to share that inspiration with our contributors and to pass it along to our readers; and we hope that our gratifying experience may inspire future symposia on clinical cases.

Qualitative Impressions

We expected the clinical exchange to be an interplay of discovery and justification in which one's formulations and intuitions were provisionally advanced without denying the possibility of alternatives. No recommendation was to be beyond cavil, but the discord would be respectful and factual. Many responses were indeed in this vein. However, we received something different in some cases; some exchanges were more hostile, more divisive, and less provisional than we had anticipated.

In this section, we share consensual impressions formed while organizing, reading, and editing this volume—the excessively critical tone of several exchanges, the miscomprehension among some panelists, and the paucity of informed pluralism or integrative attempts in the exchanges. In so doing, we are acutely aware of the irony of criticizing our collaborators for being overly critical at times. The objective is not to place blame, but to illuminate barriers to genuine comprehension and possible integration of disparate psychotherapies. Alexis de Tocqueville once wrote, "Men will not receive the truth from their enemies, and it is very seldom offered to them by their friends." Our intent is to offer friendly and constructive criticism.

The occasionally hostile tenor of the exchanges was manifested in the word choice: "social manipulative games," "therapeutic misadventure," "wildly speculative," and "superficial interpretation." These do not convey the respectful disagreements one hopes to hear from eminent clinicians. The propensity for hostile discord is apparently ingrained in many of us from our earliest professional socialization and reinforced throughout our careers—so ingrained, in fact, that there is an implicit expectation that one should find cardinal disagreements. This expectation led to an ironic apology from one of our panelists: "Sorry, but I did not find many points of contention with respect to my fellow contributors' responses."

We had an overall impression that many psychotherapists shun approaches with which they lack experience, or for which they have a temperamental disinclination. There were moments as we read the "Points of Contention and Convergence" section concluding each chapter when it appeared that the more some clinicians are exposed to what others are thinking and doing, the more defensive they become to protect the purity of their own approaches (Goldfried, 1980). In these instances, *Therapy Wars* seemed an appropriate title as proponents of other views were indeed treated as opponents and as the tone of debate turned petulant.

Sometimes our panelists' theoretical orientations not merely kept them from appreciating their colleagues' views, hence foreclosing integrative possibilities, but also, apparently, caused them actively to misread their colleagues' responses. One of the pernicious effects of theoretical orientations (Adams, 1984; Norcross, 1985) is that inveterate proponents consciously or unconsciously miscomprehend alternative perspectives. We fully expect that many contributors, upon reading the contentious remarks made about their treatment recommendations, will complain that they were misunderstood. As Goethe put it, the world has not really known me.

Miscomprehension breeds debate on the misrepresented version. If the reader did not catch these lapses, there is a good reason: we generally deleted them or added a phrase to correct them. It may have been worthwhile, for the sake of accurately reflecting the state of our movement, simply to observe that a misreading had occurred, without mentioning the culprit by name. But we declined in several instances to let the misreading pass where it would have detracted from an otherwise valuable debate. We were not entirely consistent in this policy, because there were instances in which the necessity to preserve contention won out. Still, our focus was on the contributors' many valid points of contention (and convergence), not on these occasional excursions to fence with straw men. Here are three instances of the latter.

1. An author in the panel on "The Diplomat" (Chapter Three) misrepresented Mahrer by alluding to "instincts closer to the center of Michael's conflicts"; but *instincts* is not a word that Mahrer used or would be inclined to, even if some mean editor rationed the number of times he would be allowed to write *inner experiencing* in any one paragraph.
2. A panelist on the case of "The Survivor" (Chapter Six) ignored that Saltzman states that he elicits climactic expression as part of a learning experience, "never for ventilation." Further, the panelist also cites a dearth of evidence for the therapeutic value of "ventilation without redirection," and relatively good evidence for harmful

effects of "such escalation." Since Saltzman does not propose ventilation, but a different process—emphasizing
spontaneous validating responses—with a different theoretical basis, it is not relevant evidence that is being
invoked against his approach, but a conclusion probably
extended beyond its range of applicability.

3. A respondent found the presenting psychotherapist for
    "The Returning Hero and the Absent Wife" (Chapter
    Nine) to have a rather patronizing and pathologizing
    attitude toward the couple, even going so far as to say
    that the description of Carl as "ethical" was conde-
    scending. In fact, Carl and Trudy were much admired
    by the presenting therapist as survivors and vital
    human beings. An objective reading does not detect
    condescension here.

Nor can the lively debate be solely attributed to disparate
pure-form psychotherapies. The discord in Chapter Four, in
which three eclectic/integrative therapists responded, demonstrates the fallacy of the "uniformity myth" (Kiesler, 1966).
Competent clinicians can always locate deficiencies in a colleague's work, even one of the identical theoretical orientation. We echo Beutler's belief (Chapter Six) that generic
categorization of psychological treatments into brand names
is of little value.

Another overall impression of the exchanges is that they
did not adequately exhibit modest and informed pluralism.
The definitive nature of the formulations and the warlike
quality of the debate are hardly justified in the absence of
broad consensus on the psychotherapies of choice for most
mental disorders. More provisional recommendations would
be more consistent with our knowledge base. This modest
attitude could be modeled on Saltzman's (Chapter Six) admis-
sion that, since he had not treated clients by the means he
declined, his preference is nothing more than his preference.
We—any of us—could be wrong.

Surprisingly few contributors acknowledged the well-vali-
dated finding that tested psychotherapies tend to work equally

well with most clients (Lambert, Shapiro, & Bergin, 1986; Luborsky & Singer, 1975; Smith, Glass, & Miller, 1980). Technically diverse psychotherapies produce approximately equivalent outcomes—the *equivalence paradox,* as it has become known (Stiles, Shapiro, & Elliott, 1986).

Several contributors did, however, explicitly recognize in their remarks the potential efficacy of disparate approaches. Milton Kline emphasized the selection of intensive dynamic psychotherapy using hypnosis in the case of "The Spaceman," but he did "not feel that other therapeutic modalities would not be effective." Douglas Powell was struck by how many ways there were to do right by "The Diplomat"; significant benefit would occur by working with any of the panelists in that case. By the same token, both Martin Textor and Robert Sollod in Chapter Nine embraced integrative pluralism in accepting the validity of a number of experiential and therapeutic domains. As editors, we were delighted by these respectful and integrative remarks.

In the panels' responses to the case vignettes in the *JIEP,* integration did not come easily, and often it did not come at all. Early on, "Clinical Exchange" editor Saltzman wrote editor-in-chief Norcross, "How long before my colleagues ask me, 'What are you trying to do, prove integration can't work?' " A similar sense is reflected by Douglas Powell considering the other three panelists' responses to the case of "The Diplomat" (Chapter Three). Yet, if his own integrative approach is more efficacious than it would have been years ago, we are making progress. Beyond rational attempts to assimilate, the psychotherapist, like an artist in any medium, will be subconsciously influenced by what others are doing and thinking. In this vein, Carlo DiClemente (Chapter Five) observed, "Psychotherapy continues to elude formal consensus and integration, while becoming more homogeneous at the level of practice."

Quantitative Data

The psychotherapy integration movement, by common decree, lacks empirical research on both the process of synthesizing various approaches and the outcomes of these integrative or eclectic treatments (Beitman, Goldfried, & Norcross, 1989; Lambert, 1986; Wolfe & Goldfried, 1988). Indeed, inadequate empirical research on integration is rated one of the most severe impediments to psychotherapy integration (Norcross & Thomas, 1988). Proposals to advance therapeutic rapprochement and the integrative process typically stem from battle-weary experience, questionnaire surveys, or armchair speculation. Further, there is little unambiguous evidence of the clinical superiority of a theoretically integrative or technically eclectic approach over a pure-form or "brand-name" approach. However, it is important to note that the reverse is true as well (Wachtel, 1983).

Integration without clinical and research documentation is likely to fail (Prochaska & Norcross, 1986). Integration becomes an academic exercise by ignoring the clinical realities and complexities of psychotherapy. Conversely, integration becomes a clinical exercise by slighting empirical discovery and verification. Hence, clinicians and researchers both have critical roles to play in documenting the applicability and efficacy of integrative models of practice.

We conducted a quantitative analysis of the thirty "Points of Contention and Convergence" responses to provide preliminary empirical data on the integrative process and to complement our qualitative impressions of the same responses. We did so, however, only after considerable reflection and friendly debate on honing the questions and on establishing the criteria prior to "crunching the numbers," because in the desire to make observations scientific, it is easy to make them too narrow.

Many are the potential pitfalls of transforming complex clinical reasonings to countable yeas and nays. The results can depend on implicit grouping decisions or unconscious biases. Gross categories of accord and discord can wind up comparing plates of apples and crates of oranges. As one breaks down the questions into finer probes, the discriminations become more meaningful, but the numbers get smaller and less representative. Moreover, reasonable humans can arrive at reasonably different conclusions as to what constitutes contention or convergence. A case in point is Paul Wachtel's remark (Chapter Four) that a psychoanalyst's "interpretation" can really be behavioral—a punishment of the patient.

With our ambivalent mix of distaste for simplistic number crunching and respect for empirical research, we proceeded to examine two broad questions related to convergence and divergence in clinical practice. First, what content areas are most likely to lead to accord or discord among clinical practitioners? Our experience in editing the "Clinical Exchange" and in reviewing fifty publications that proposed therapeutic commonalities (Grencavage & Norcross, 1990) led us to believe convergence was possible, more often than not, on the recommended therapeutic relationship. Alternatively, Goldfried (1980) observed that it is unlikely we can ever hope to reach common ground at the theoretical or philosophical level, and he contended that the search for commonalities across approaches in the realm of specific techniques would probably not reveal much more than trivial points of similarity. Goldfried suggested that the possibility of finding meaningful consensus exists at a level of abstraction that he labeled *clinical strategies,* somewhere between global theory and specific technique. The experimental method and coding system of the following analyses (see Table 11.1) were designed as a provisional test of Goldfried's proposition and ours.

The second broad question we attempted to address concerned what might be termed the rhetoric of justification. Specifically, if you reject a formulation or a technique of another panelist, why? What are the sources of evidence for your disagreement? From the research literature? From your theoretical underpinnings? From clinical experience? (See Table 11.2 for the coded sources of accord and discord.)

Method. True to clinical realities and our fears, problems were encountered both in counting agreements and disagreements and in classifying them into mutually exclusive categories.

It was difficult to discern on occasion whether agreement

Table 11.1. Frequency of Agreements and Disagreements by Content.

Content	Agreements		Disagreements	
	Frequency	Percentage	Frequency	Percentage
Obtaining particular information	12	4%	3	1%
Patient characteristics/Case formulation	72	27%	48	23%
Therapist qualities	11	4%	7	3%
Treatment structure/Therapy format	26	10%	16	8%
Therapeutic relationship	39	14%	16	8%
Treatment goals	28	10%	12	6%
Specific techniques	33	12%	48	23%
Clinical strategies/Change processes	34	13%	14	7%
Global theory	3	1%	24	12%
Not codable	13	5%	18	9%
Total	271	100%	206	100%

Table 11.2. Explicit Sources of Agreements and Disagreements.

Source	Agreements		Disagreements	
	Frequency	Percentage	Frequency	Percentage
Clinical experience	0	0%	6	3%
Research literature	1	<1%	14	7%
Clinical intuition	0	0%	0	0%
Theoretical orientation	8	3%	36	17%
Personal values	10	4%	1	<1%
Combination of above	4	1%	6	3%
Not specified	242	89%	125	61%
Not codable	6	2%	18	9%
Total	271	100%	206	100%

or disagreement was intended by the respondent. For example, how does one code Larry Beutler's statement (Chapter Six) "I do not disagree . . . but I urge caution"? (We took him at his word and did not count it as evidence of discord.) Arnold Lazarus (Chapter Four) provided another illustration with his comment that a particular case formulation was "debatable." This was considered a disagreement, as was Marvin Goldfried's statement (Chapter Seven) that "nonspecific use of free association . . . was too open-ended."

The objective was to record the number of fellow panelists

with whom each agreement or disagreement was made, offering no distinction between a major or minor point. We often experienced difficulty in differentiating between a central disagreement and a corollary or extension of that same point of contention. Moreover, there was no attempt on our part to account for the magnitude of agreement or disagreement. Thus, Milton Kline's (Chapter Two) mild and tentative reframing—"Perhaps the use of indirect rather than direct advice might be more consistent with my overall approach"— received the same weight as Albert Ellis's (Chapter Two) strong and definitive "Hogwash!" Our quantitative ratings do not reflect these differences.

Several psychotherapists expressed general accord or discord with the other panelists without specifying individual points. Alvin Mahrer (Chapter Three) stated, "On all other points, I seem to differ with all three other respondents." Martin Textor's (Chapter Nine) section proved to be a unique instance of collegial affirmation: "Thus, I agree with nearly all of Sollod's and Safran's thoughts on how to treat Carl and Trudy." Janus Fraillon (Chapter Ten) tartly but indirectly took exception to the clinical formulations and treatments of his fellow respondents. However, the abundance of oblique criticisms and the absence of specific disagreements made it a particularly difficult response to code. As a final example, Janet Bachant (Chapter Seven) implied agreement and disagreement based on the theoretical perspectives of the other contributors to the case. In this and other instances, we made consensual judgments on the basis of the theoretical orientation of the contributors.

A final coding problem embodies the inseparability of technique, strategy, and relationship in actual practice. Specific delineation among these categories was not always evident. When George Stricker (Chapter Three) and Bernard Beitman (Chapter Eight) shared a colleague's emphasis on empathic responding, were they agreeing with a technique, a strategy, a stance toward the therapeutic alliance, or all three? Similarly, are exposure and psychoeducation specific techniques, clinical strategies, or entire theories?

These coding quandaries reminded us that the value of a clinical intervention is inextricably bound to the relational context in which it is applied. Hans Strupp (1986a) offers the following analogy to illustrate the inseparability of the constituent elements of psychotherapy: Suppose you want a teenage son to clean his room. One technique for achieving this is to establish clear standards. Fine, but the effectiveness of this technique will vary depending upon whether the relationship between you and the boy is characterized by warmth and mutual respect or by anger and distrust. This is not to say that the technique is useless, merely that how well it works depends upon the context in which it is used.

Results and Discussion. These methodological problems and prefatory caveats notwithstanding, the statistical analyses yielded interesting data on general patterns and preliminary answers to our two broad questions. The length of the "Points of Contention and Convergence Responses," defined as the word count prior to light, prepublication editing, averaged 830 words, with a standard deviation of 374. On the low end were Milton Kline, Gertrud Ujhely, and Shridhar Sharma with fewer than 400 words each. Unquestionably at the upper extreme was Albert Ellis with more than 2,000 words—over 600 more than the closest wordsmith.

Did accord or discord win the day, numerically speaking? For individual respondents, the average number of coded agreements was 9.0 (SD = 6.2), with a range between 0 (Janus Fraillon) and 27 (Douglas Powell). The average number of coded disagreements was 6.9 (SD = 4.9), with a range between 2 (Shridhar Sharma) and 26 (Alvin Mahrer). Sixteen of the thirty psychotherapists expressed more agreements than disagreements; three therapists expressed exactly the same number of each. For the entire group, as shown in Table 11.1, total agreements numbered 271 and total disagreements totaled 206. Individually and collectively, convergence was more frequent than contention.

Why, then, are many readers, including us, left with the impression of more quarrelsome and contentious exchanges?

One reason lies in the differential length of the agreements and disagreements. Accord is typically expressed briefly by words to the effect that "we all agree that . . "—in contrast to the lengthy explication of discord and presentation of an alternative. The differential length is probably attributable to professional socialization, which rewards promulgation of distinctive elements but accords little glory to identification of common features (Frank, 1973), and to our editorial instructions, which enjoined contributors to provide short explanations for agreements and disagreements so that we could move beyond glib generalizations. Few contributors elaborated on the convergence; however, virtually all elaborated on their divergence. Unless the reader attends closely to the text—or literally counts as did we—then length alone can mask genuine accord and exaggerate discord.

To test this hypothesis, we correlated the number of words in a contribution with both its number of agreements and number of disagreements. The correlation with frequency of accord ($r = .05$, $p = .39$) was statistically and clinically insignificant. However, the correlation with frequency of discord was highly significant ($r = .46$, $p = .006$), confirming our impression that length was systematically related to discord.

Table 11.1 presents the frequency of explicit agreements and disagreements among contributors by specific content area. To illustrate our coding system for content area, we present a representative example for each of the nine categories in which agreements and disagreements were counted.

Obtaining Particular Information. In the case of "The Spaceman," Marmor expresses the need for more information abou the client's developmental history and personality patterns "before arriving at a definitive diagnosis." Ellis agrees that more information is necessary; however, he disagrees with Marmor on the type of information needed. Specifically, Ellis highly values information on Ken's main irrational beliefs and his reactions to the first few therapy sessions.

Patient Characteristics/Case Formulation. The case of "The Diplomat" provides an excellent example of this category. For example, Stricker agrees with Rice's assessment that Michael is appealing, with Powell's overall formulation of the case, and with Mahrer's interpretation of Michael's fantasies.

Therapist Qualities. Sollod, in "The Returning Hero and the Absent Wife," expresses concern about his own (and others') incomplete understanding of the case and encourages a more empathic and tentative stance. He also addresses the therapist's attitude toward clients, criticizing Textor's account as reflecting a "pathologizing attitude."

Treatment Structure/Therapy Format. In the case of "The Adopted Sister," we scored an agreement and several disagreements on structure and format. All the panelists would arrange separate sessions with each individual in the family (besides the other formats). Both Guerney and the Kirschners propose a conjoint family format; however, the Kirschners specifically recommend individual or couple sessions, or both, to address marital problems.

Therapeutic Relationship. There is some agreement among the psychotherapists on being relatively nondirective for "The Envious Lover," although their reasons for being nondirective vary. Bugental advocates an approach that is less therapist focused than that of Davidson. Davidson, however, says his approach would be the same regardless of diagnosis, implying that the diagnosis is secondary to the relationship.

Treatment Goals. In the case of "The Returning Hero and the Absent Wife," all the panelists delineate goals of their therapeutic encounters. Safran would like to see the clients become more aware of their feelings and learn to communicate them to one another. Textor hopes to help improve the parental performance of the clients. Sollod proposes helping Carl and Trudy understand their own and each others' disorders.

Specific Techniques. In the case of "The Make-Up Artist," Beitman and Messer decline Lederman's bioenergetic techniques, and Lederman declines Beitman's triple-column diary. These and other disagreements on specific techniques probably reflect deeper differences in assessing the patient and in the role of therapy.

Clinical Strategies/Change Processes. In the case of "The Survivor," there are several instances of accord and discord on clinical change strategies. Eth and Harrison agree with Beutler's warning against "mobilizing" volatile emotions. They also agree with Saltzman's proposal to confront Anne's use of the word "punishment."

Global Theory. In "The Don Juan," Bachant's orientation emphasizes a "focus on the development and emergence of unconscious material" and on the analysis of transference. By contrast, Greenberg and Goldfried adopt substantially different theoretical approaches to the case—approaches that reject Bachant's focus.

Looking at agreements again in Table 11.1, we found that patient characteristics, therapeutic relationships, and clinical strategies received the most endorsement. Specific techniques, patient characteristics, and global theory, on the other hand, were the most frequent areas of disagreement.

Both our and Goldfried's predictions on the content areas most amenable to consensus received moderate empirical support. Agreements on the desirable therapeutic relationship accounted for 14 percent of all agreements, but only for 8 percent of all disagreements. Similarly, accord on clinical strategies accounted for 13 percent of the agreements, but only for 7 percent of the disagreements. This pattern was reversed, as Goldfried (1980) predicted, on specific techniques and global theory. These content areas accounted for 12 percent and 1 percent, respectively, of total accord, but for 23 percent and 12 percent of total discord.

A failure of research such as that represented in Table 11.2, which was intended to show the sources of agreement and disagreement, is customarily not published. When a preponderance of the data falls into the "not specified" category, the routine "scientific" treatment is to blot out any trace of the original query. However, in research as in life, one can learn from one's failures. Here, the fact that clinicians did not articulate (in 89 percent of their agreements and in 61 percent of their disagreements) the requested rationale for the acceptance or rejection of their colleagues' recommendations turns out to be an unexpected value of the research.

One searches in vain for explicit justifications in many exchanges. Frequently implicit was the message "I disagree because I personally wouldn't do it that way." This pattern is problematic, in our view, for many reasons. First, although exchanges of this type promote diversity and intellectual stimulation, they are often not productive because they essentially pit one person's opinion against another's. Second, there is no opportunity for confirmation or disconfirmation. Everyone does his or her own clinical "thing," and who or what is to say one is better than the other? Third, we find the paucity of explicit justification for clinical preferences dismaying in that psychotherapists' treasured proficiencies, rather than outcome research and client needs, seem largely to dictate clinical decision making.

Correspondingly, the research literature was rarely brought to bear on the rhetoric of justification. Only 8 percent of the disagreements—7 percent coded as research literature plus 1 percent included in the combination category—cited literature to justify a contrary position. Put another way, only seven of the thirty respondents in the "Points of Contention and Convergence" sections made even one explicit use of the extant research to defend their points of view. Albert Ellis (Chapter Two) and Larry Beutler (Chapter Six) were encouraging exceptions to this pattern in that both repeatedly turned to the empirical literature.

Of course, the lack of a compelling empirical base for differential treatment decisions is hardly limited to this volume (Beutler & Clarkin, 1990). Several years ago, Norcross and Prochaska (1983) examined how hundreds of clinical psychologists, the plurality (31 percent) of whom were eclectic, selected their theoretical orientations. Of a list of fourteen possible influences on this selection process, outcome research ranked a disappointing tenth. The average rating fell between "weak influence" and "some influence." Our hope for future replication studies and future clinical exchanges is that the influence of outcome research will rank much higher.

Returning to Table 11.2, we discover that theoretical compatibility was employed as an explicit justification twice as frequently as research literature for both coded agreements (3 percent versus 1 percent) and coded disagreements (17 percent versus 7 percent). The contributors admit relying on theory far more than on research or even the circumstances of the client. John Davis, in his response (Chapter Four), articulated basic differences among the recommended approaches, probably owing to the therapists' conceptual, ideological, and personal commitments and having little to do with the client. Carlo DiClemente (Chapter Five), in similar fashion, acknowledged that we are directed by our theoretical frames, however broad or limited they are, more than we are by particulars of the case.

Disparate theoretical orientation and professional discipline clashed in "The Make-Up Artist" for a full-fledged therapeutic conflict. Kevin Thompson, a cognitive-behavioral psychologist, expressed dismay that the use of cognitive-behavioral techniques was not advocated by his fellow panelists. Bernard Beitman, an integrative psychiatrist, voiced incredulity that his colleagues would deny the value of medication in this case. In turn, Elisabeth Lederman, a humanistic psychotherapist, and the only woman on the panel, was the only one to articulate the real probability that the patient had been sexually abused.

Largely ignored in our quantitative analysis are client factors. Are some clients more likely to create contention or convergence? We cannot bring empirical data to bear on this question since the client factors presented in this volume are hopelessly confounded within individual cases and by unequal representation of contributors' theoretical orientations. Systematic manipulation of client variables in a case format or a survey questionnaire completed by large numbers of psychotherapists would be required to address this issue empirically.

Nonetheless, it is our distinct impression that achieving a consensus will be most difficult until we agree more specifically on therapeutic goals. A transtheoretical analysis of psychotherapy systems shows how much they agree on the processes producing change while they disagree on the content to be changed (Prochaska, 1984). In other words, different orientations probably do not dictate the specific interventions to use as much as they determine the therapeutic goals to pursue (Beutler, 1983).

Convergence will be facilitated to the extent that we can agree on client problems to be treated, on mediating therapeutic goals, and on the kinds of evidence to be accepted for successful therapy. For example, on a panel discussing treatments of choice for a specific disorder—a simple phobia—proponents of disparate psychotherapy persuasions agreed that psychoanalysis was contraindicated for efficient removal of phobic behavior. However, if the phobia was conceptualized as reflecting an underlying characterological problem, then a different therapeutic goal—and thus a different treatment recommendation—was advanced (Norcross, in press).

Concluding Remarks

We shall not cease from exploration
And the end of all our exploring
Will be to arrive where we started
And know the place for the first time.

T. S. Eliot

Having now arrived at the end of this volume, we have a final opportunity to share what we learned on our journey. Like the tireless traveler in Eliot's poem, we have rediscovered our origins, especially a few fundamental lessons about the practice and integration of psychotherapy. We knew in principle before we began that a science advances when its hypotheses are set forth in a way that invites their disproof; but our thwarted effort to count sources of agreement and disagreement, as revealed in Table 11.2, brought us home to this implication for clinicians: we had better strive to articulate our rationales. Otherwise, psychotherapy integration will remain dependent on each practitioner's personal preferences. We also confirmed, as shown in Table 11.1, that the therapeutic relationship and broad clinical strategies are two fruitful areas of convergence among clinicians.

Furthermore, our appreciation of the need for respect for professional differences has been enhanced; the clash of views we refereed has made us more provisional in our conceptualizations and inclines us toward more modesty in our claims. We find ourselves more acutely aware than ever that our profession must stay open to new data and nascent perspectives. No one who has been involved with the material of this book over the past four years would be likely to suppose that the future of psychotherapy can or should be limited to integrating just the canon of theories and procedures that have prevailed in recent decades.

We began with a fantasy that became the "Clinical Exchange," so it is fitting that we conclude with a fantasy. We look forward to a series of books, perhaps modeled in some respects on this one—say, a new book each passing decade. In the sequels to *Therapy Wars,* the panel members would take progressively greater responsibility for their motives in convergence and divergence—and for receptivity to comparative evaluation of procedures, as well as to theories and practices not within their immediate repertoire. The future editors and contributors would consider, perhaps regard as likely, that better ways to conceive psychotherapy, to practice it, to integrate what is known, and to study what is unknown may yet be waiting to be discovered by clinicians born in the twenty-first century.

References

Abend, S. M., Porder, M. S., & Willick, M. S. (1983). *Border-line patients: Psychoanalytic perspectives*. New York: International Universities Press.

Adams, H. E. (1984). The pernicious effects of theoretical orientations in clinical psychology. *The Clinical Psychologist, 37*, 90–93.

American Psychiatric Association. (1980). *Diagnostic and statistical manual of mental disorders*. (3rd ed.). Washington, DC: Author.

American Psychiatric Association. (1987). *Diagnostic and statistical manual of mental disorders* (3rd ed., rev.). Washington, DC: Author.

Arkowitz, H. (1989). The role of theory in psychotherapy integration. *Journal of Integrative and Eclectic Psychotherapy, 8*, 8–16.

Balint, M. (1968). *The basic fault: Therapeutic aspects of regression*. London: Tavistock.

Beitman, B. D. (1987). *The structure of individual psychotherapy*. New York: Guilford Press.

Beitman, B. D., Goldfried, M. R., & Norcross, J. C. (1989). The movement toward integrating the psychotherapies: An overview. *American Journal of Psychiatry, 146*, 138–147.

Berger, L. S. (1985). *Psychoanalytic theory and clinical relevance*. New York: Analytic Press.

Bergmann, M. (1987). *The anatomy of loving*. New York: Columbia University Press.

Beutler, L. E. (1983). *Eclectic psychotherapy: A systematic approach.* Elmsford, NY: Pergamon.

Beutler, L. E. (1986). Systematic eclectic psychotherapy. In J. C. Norcross (Ed.), *Handbook of eclectic psychotherapy.* New York: Brunner/Mazel.

Beutler, L. E. (1989). Differential treatment selection: The role of diagnosis in psychotherapy. *Psychotherapy, 26,* 271-281.

Beutler, L. E., & Clarkin, J. (1990). *Systematic treatment selection: Toward prescriptive psychological treatments.* New York: Brunner/Mazel.

Beutler, L. E., Frank, M., Scheiber, S. C., Calvert, S., & Gaines, J. (1984). Comparative effects of group psychotherapies in a short-term inpatient setting: An experience with deterioration effects. *Psychiatry, 47,* 66-76.

Bordin, E. S. (1979). The generalizability of the psychoanalytic concept of the working alliance. *Psychotherapy: Theory, Research and Practice, 16,* 252-260.

Boszormenyi-Nagy, I., & Spark, G. M. (1973). *Invisible loyalties: Reciprocity in intergenerational family therapy.* New York: Harper & Row.

Brabeck, M. M., & Welfel, E. R. (1985). Counseling theory: Understanding the trend toward eclecticism from a developmental perspective. *Journal of Counseling and Development, 63,* 343-349.

Brehm, J. W. (1966). *A theory of psychological reactance.* Orlando, FL: Academic Press.

Bugental, J.F.T. (1978). *Psychotherapy and process: The fundamentals of an existential-humanistic approach.* New York: McGraw-Hill.

Bugental, J.F.T. (1987). *The art of the psychotherapist.* New York: Norton.

Bugental, J.F.T. (1988). What is "failure" in psychotherapy? *Psychotherapy, 25,* 532-535.

Burstein, A. (1986). Treatment length in post-traumatic stress disorder. *Psychosomatics, 27,* 632-638.

Casriel, D. H. (1972). *A scream away from happiness.* New York: Dutton.

Colby, K. M., & Stoller, R. J. (1988). *Cognitive science and psychoanalysis.* Hillsdale, NJ: Erlbaum.

Daldrup, R. J., Beutler, L. E., Greenberg, L. S., & Engle, D. (1988). *Focused expressive psychotherapy: Freeing the over-controlled element.* New York: Guilford Press.

Davis, J. D., Schroder, T. A., Davis, M. L., Francis, V. M., Kelman, J. E., Binns, M., & Elliott, R. (1989, April). *Correlates of therapist difficulties and coping strategies.* Paper presented at the annual conference of the Society for Psychotherapy Research (U.K.), Ravenscar, England.

Davison, G. C., Robins, C., & Johnson, M. K. (1983). Articulated thoughts during simulated situations: A paradigm for studying cognition in emotion and behavior. *Cognitive Therapy and Research, 7,* 17–40.

De Forest, I. (1954). *The leaven of love.* New York: Harper & Row.

Driscoll, R. (1984). *Pragmatic psychotherapy.* New York: Van Nostrand Reinhold.

Ellis, A. (1958). Hypnotherapy with borderline psychotics. *Journal of General Psychology, 59,* 245–253.

Ellis, A. (1962). *Reason and emotion in psychotherapy.* Secaucus, NJ: Citadel Press.

Ellis, A. (1969). A weekend of rational encounter. *Rational Living, 4*(2), 1–8. (Reprinted in A. Ellis & W. Dryden, *The practice of rational-emotive therapy.* New York: Springer, 1987).

Ellis, A. (1986). Anxiety about anxiety: The use of hypnosis with rational-emotive therapy. In E. T. Dowd & J. M. Healy (Eds.), *Case studies in hypnotherapy* (pp. 3–11). New York: Guilford.

Ellis, A. (1988a). *How to stubbornly refuse to make yourself miserable about anything—Yes anything!* Secaucus, NJ: Lyle Stuart.

Ellis, A. (Speaker). (1988b). *Unconditionally accepting yourself and others* (Cassette Recording). New York: Institute for Rational-Emotive Therapy.

Ellis, A. (1989). Rational-emotive therapy. In R. J. Corsini &

D. Wedding (Eds.), *Current psychotherapies* (4th ed.). Itasca, IL: Peacock.

Ellis, A., & Dryden, W. (1987). *The practice of rational-emotive therapy.* New York: Springer.

Ellis, A., & Grieger, R. (Eds.). (1986). *Handbook of rational-emotive therapy* (Vols. 1–2). New York: Springer.

Ellis, A., & Harper, R. A. (1975). *A new guide to rational living.* North Hollywood, CA: Wilshire Books.

Engel, G. L. (1980). The clinical application of the bio-psychosocial model. *American Journal of Psychiatry, 137,* 535–544.

Eth, S., Randolph, E. T., & Brown, J. A. (1989). Post-traumatic stress disorder. In J. G. Howells (Ed.), *Modern perspectives in the psychiatry of the neuroses.* New York: Brunner/Mazel.

Ettedgui, E., & Bridges, M. (1985). Post-traumatic stress disorder. *Psychiatric clinics of North America, 8,* 89–103.

Ferenczi, S. (1952). *Further contributions to the theory and technique of psychoanalysis.* New York: Basic Books.

Feyerabend, P. (1970). Consolations for the specialist. In I. Lakatos & A. E. Musgrave (Eds.), *Criticism and the growth of knowledge.* Cambridge, England: Cambridge University Press.

Figley, C., & B. Guerney, Jr. (1976). *The conjugal relationship enhancement program* [Film or videotape]. University Park, PA: Individual and Family Consultation Center.

Fox, R. C. (1957). Training for uncertainty. In R. F. Merton, G. G. Reader, & P. L. Kendall (Eds.), *The student physician: Introductory studies in the sociology of medical education.* Cambridge, MA: Harvard University Press.

Frances, A. (1988, May). *Sigmund Freud: The first integrative therapist.* Invited address to the annual convention of the Society for the Exploration of Psychotherapy Integration, Boston.

Frances, A., Clarkin, J., & Perry, S. (1986). *Differential therapeutics in psychiatry: The art and science of treatment selections.* New York: Brunner/Mazel.

Frank, J. D. (1973). *Persuasion and healing* (2nd ed.). Baltimore, MD: Johns Hopkins University Press.

Freud, S. (1895). The psychotherapy of hysteria. In J. Strachey (Ed. and Trans.), *The standard edition of the complete works of Sigmund Freud* (Vol. 2, pp. 255-305). London: Hogarth Press.

Freud, S. (1959). Recommendations for physicians on the psycho-analytic method of treatment. In *Collected papers* (Vol. 2, pp. 323-333). New York: Basic Books. (Original work published 1921)

Freud, S. (1975). Some psychical consequences of the anatomical distinction between the sexes. In J. Strachey (Ed. and Trans.), *The Standard edition of the complete psychological works of Sigmund Freud* (Vol. 19, pp. 248-258).

Garfield, S. L. (1980). *Psychotherapy: An eclectic approach.* New York: Wiley.

Garfield, S. L. (1986). An eclectic psychotherapy. In J. C. Norcross (Ed.), *Handbook of eclectic psychotherapy.* New York: Brunner/Mazel.

Gendlin, E. (1981). *Focusing.* New York: Bantam Books.

Goldfried, M. R. (1980). Toward the delineation of therapeutic change principles. *American Psychologist, 35,* 991-999.

Goldfried, M. R., & Davison, G. C. (1976). *Clinical behavior therapy.* New York: Holt, Rinehart & Winston.

Goldfried, M. R., Greenberg, L. S., & Marmar, C. M. (1990). Individual psychotherapy: Process and outcome. *Annual Review of Psychology, 41,* 659-688.

Goldfried, M. R., & Newman, C. (1986). Psychotherapy integration: An historical perspective. In J. C. Norcross (Ed.), *Handbook of eclectic psychotherapy.* New York: Brunner/Mazel.

Goldstein, A. P., & Stein, N. (1976). *Prescriptive psychotherapies.* Elmsford, NY: Pergamon Press.

Greenberg, J., & Mitchell, S. (1983). *Object relations and psychoanalytic theory.* Cambridge, MA: Harvard University Press.

Greenberg, L. (1979). Resolving splits. *Psychotherapy: Theory, Research, and Practice, 16,* 310–318.

Greenberg, L., & Johnson, S. (1988). *Emotionally focused therapy for couples.* New York: Guilford Press.

Greenberg, L., & Safran, J. (1987). *Emotion in psychotherapy.* New York: Guilford Press.

Greenberg, L., & Safran, J. (1989). Emotion in psychotherapy. *American Psychologist.*

Greenberg, L., Safran, J., & Rice, L. (1989). Emotion and its relation to cognitive therapy. In A. Freeman, H. Simon, L. Beutler, & H. Arkowitz (Eds.), *Comprehensive handbook of cognitive therapy.* New York: Plenum.

Grencavage, L. M., & Norcross, J. C. (1990, March). *Where are the commonalities among the therapeutic common factors?* Paper presented at the annual meeting of the Eastern Psychological Association, Philadelphia.

Grinker, R., & Spiegel, J. (1945). *Men under stress.* Philadelphia: Blakiston.

Gruenwald, D. (1974). Analogues of multiple personality in psychosis. *International Journal of Clinical Experimental Hypnosis, 26,* 1–8.

Guerney, B. G., Jr. (1964). Filial therapy: Description and rationale. *Journal of Consulting Psychology, 28,* 303–310.

Guerney, B. G., Jr. (Ed.). (1969). *Psychotherapeutic agents: New roles for nonprofessionals, parents, and teachers.* New York: Holt, Rinehart & Winston.

Guerney, B. G., Jr. (1977). *Relationship enhancement: Skill-training programs for therapy, problem prevention, and enrichment.* San Francisco: Jossey-Bass.

Guerney, B. G., Jr. (1982). The delivery of mental health services: Spiritual vs. medical vs. educational models. In T. R. Vallance & R. M. Sabre (Eds.), *Mental health services in transition: A policy sourcebook.* New York: Human Sciences Press.

Guerney, B. G., Jr. (1984). Relationship enhancement therapy and training. In D. Larson (Ed.), *Teaching psychological skills: Models for giving psychology away.* Monterey, CA: Brooks/Cole.

Guerney, B. G., Jr. (1987). *Relationship enhancement: Marital/ family therapist's manual.* State College, PA: IDEA.

Guerney, B. G., Jr., Brock, G., & Coufal, J. (1986). Integrating marital therapy and enrichment: The relationship enhancement approach. In N. Jacobson & A. Gurman (Eds.), *Clinical handbook of marital therapy.* New York: Guilford Press.

Guerney, B. G., Jr., Stollak, G., & Guerney, L. F. (1971). The practicing psychologist as educator: An alternative to the medical practitioner model. *Professional Psychology, 2,* 276–282.

Guerney, B. G., Jr., & Vogelsong, E. (1981). *Relationship enhancement demonstration tapes.* University Park, PA: Individual and Family Consultation Center.

Guerney, L. F. (1983). Introduction to filial therapy. In P. Keller & L. Ritt (Eds.), *Innovations in clinical practice: A source book* (Vol. 2). Sarasota, FL: Professional Resource Exchange.

Guerney, L. F., & Guerney, B. G., Jr. (1985). The relationship enhancement of family therapies. In L. L'Abate & M. A. Milan (Eds.), *Handbook of social skills training and research.* New York: Wiley.

Guntrip, H. (1969). *Schizoid phenomena, object relations and the self.* New York: International Universities Press.

Gurman, A. S. (1980). Behavioral marital therapy in the 1980's: The challenge of integration. *American Journal of Family Therapy, 8,* 86–96.

Hay, G. G. (1970). Dysmorphobia. *British Journal of Psychiatry, 116,* 399–406.

Held, B. S. (1986). Toward a strategic eclecticism: A proposal. *Psychotherapy, 21,* 232–241.

Hersher, C. (Ed.). (1970). *Four psychotherapies.* East Norwalk, CT: Appleton-Century-Crofts.

Hogben, G. L., & Cornfield, R. B. (1981). Treatment of traumatic war neurosis with phenelzine. *Archives of General Psychiatry, 38,* 440–445.

Horney, K. (1945). *Our inner conflicts.* New York: Norton.

Horney, K. (1950). *Neurosis and human growth.* New York: Norton.

Horowitz, M. J. (1986). Stress-response syndromes: A review of post-traumatic and adjustment disorders. *Hospital and Community Psychiatry, 37,* 241–249.

Howard, G. S., Nance, D. W., & Myers, P. (1986). Adaptive counseling and therapy: An integrative eclectic model. *The Counseling Psychologist, 14,* 363–442.

Jackson, D. D. (1968). Family interaction, family homeostasis, and some implications for conjoint family psychotherapy. In D. D. Jackson (Ed.), *Therapy, communication and change.* Palo Alto, CA: Science and Behavior Books.

Jansson, L., & Ost, L. (1982). Behavioral treatments for agoraphobia: An evaluative review. *Clinical Psychology Review, 2,* 322–336.

Kiesler, D. J. (1966). Some myths of psychotherapy research and the search for a paradigm. *Psychological Bulletin, 65,* 110–136.

Kirschner, D. A., & Kirschner, S. (1986). *Comprehensive family therapy: An integration of systemic and psychodynamic treatment models.* New York: Brunner/Mazel.

Kirschner, D. A., & Kirschner, S. (1989a). Couples therapy: A new look. *Journal of Couples Therapy, 1*(1).

Kirschner, S., & Kirschner, D. A. (1989b). Love and other difficulties. *Family Therapy Today, 4,* 1–4.

Kline, M. V. (1984). Multiple personality: Facts and artifacts in relation to hypnotherapy. *International Journal of Clinical Experimental Hypnosis, 29,* 189–209.

Kluft, R. P. (Ed.). (1985). *Childhood antecedents of multiple personality.* Washington, DC: American Psychiatric Press.

Kohut, H. (1977). *The restoration of the self.* New York: International Universities Press.

Kohut, H. (1984). *How does analysis cure?* New York: International Universities Press.

Kuhn, T. S. (1970). *The structure of scientific revolutions* (2nd ed.). Chicago: University of Chicago Press.

Lambert, M. J. (1986). Implications of psychotherapy outcome research for eclectic psychotherapy. In J. C. Norcross (Ed.), *Handbook of eclectic psychotherapy.* New York: Brunner/Mazel.

Lambert, M. J., Shapiro, D. A., & Bergin, A. E. (1986). The effectiveness of psychotherapy. In S. L. Garfield & A. E. Bergin (Eds.), *Handbook of psychotherapy and behavior change.* New York: Wiley.

Laufer, R., & Gallops, M. (1983). *Life-course effects of Vietnam combat and abusive violence: Marital problems.* Paper presented at the meeting of the American Sociological Association, Detroit, MI.

Lazarus, A. A. (1967). In support of technical eclecticism. *Psychological Reports, 21,* 415–416.

Lazarus, A. A. (1981). *The practice of multimodal therapy.* New York: McGraw-Hill.

Lazarus, A. A. (1986a). From the ashes. *International Journal of Eclectic Psychotherapy, 5,* 241–242.

Lazarus, A. A. (1986b). Multimodal therapy. In J. C. Norcross (Ed.), *Handbook of eclectic psychotherapy.* New York: Brunner/Mazel.

Lazarus, A. A. (1989a). Multimodal therapy. In R. J. Corsini & D. Wedding (Eds.), *Current psychotherapies* (4th ed.). Itasca, IL: Peacock.

Lazarus, A. A. (1989b). *The practice of multimodal therapy* (rev. ed.). Baltimore, MD: Johns Hopkins University Press.

Lazarus, A. A., & Messer, S. B. (1988). Clinical choice points: Behavioral versus psychoanalytic interventions. *Psychotherapy, 25,* 59–70.

Lieberman, M. A., Yalom, I. D., & Miles, M. B. (1973). *Encounter groups: First facts.* New York: Basic Books.

Loewald, H. W. (1979, February). *Regression: Some general considerations.* Paper presented at the annual meeting of the Midwest Regional Psychoanalytic Association, Detroit, MI.

London, P. (1983). Ecumenism in psychotherapy. *Contemporary Psychology, 28,* 507–508.

London, P. (1988). Eclectic psychotherapy gets "uppity." *Contemporary Psychology, 33,* 697–698.

Luborsky, L., & Singer, B. (1975). Comparative studies of psychotherapies: Is it true that "Everybody has won and all must have prizes?" *Archives of General Psychiatry, 32,* 995–1008.

Lunde, D. T. (1974). Eclectic and integrated theory: Gordon Allport and others. In A. Burton (Ed.), *Operational theories of personality*. New York: Brunner/Mazel.

Mahrer, A. R. (1985). *Psychotherapeutic change: An alternative approach to meaning and measurement*. New York: Norton.

Mahrer, A. R. (1986). *Therapeutic experiencing: The process of change*. New York: Norton.

Mahrer, A. R. (1989a). *Experiencing: A humanistic theory of psychology and psychiatry*. Ottawa: University of Ottawa Press. (Original work published 1978)

Mahrer, A. R. (1989b). *Experiential psychotherapy: Basic practices*. Ottawa: University of Ottawa Press. (Original work published 1983)

Mahrer, A. R. (1989c). *How to do experiential psychotherapy: A manual for practitioners*. Ottawa: University of Ottawa Press.

Mahrer, A. R. (1989d). *The integration of psychotherapies: A guide for practicing therapists*. New York: Plenum.

Mahrer, A. R. (1990). *Dream work in psychotherapy and self-change*. New York: Norton.

Marmor, J. (1974a). Dynamic psychotherapy and behavior therapy. Are they irreconcilable? In J. Marmor, *Psychiatry in transition*. New York: Brunner/Mazel.

Marmor, J. (1974b). The nature of the psychotherapeutic process. In J. Marmor, *Psychiatry in transition*. New York: Brunner/Mazel.

Marmor, J. (1974c). Psychoanalytic therapy as an educational process. In J. Marmor, *Psychiatry in transition*. New York: Brunner/Mazel.

Marmor, J. (1975). The nature of the psychotherapeutic process revisited. *Canadian Psychiatric Association Journal*, December.

Marmor, J. (1982). Psychoanalysis, psychiatry and systems thinking. *Journal of the American Academy of Psychoanalysis, 10*.

Marmor, J. (1983). Systems thinking in psychiatry: Some theoretical and clinical implications. *American Journal of Psychiatry, 140*.

Maultsby, M. C., Jr. (1971). Rational-emotive imagery. *Rational Living, 6*(1), 24–27.

Maultsby, M. C., Jr., & Ellis, A. (1974). *Techniques for using rational-emotive imagery.* New York: Institute for Rational-Emotive Therapy.

Meares, R. A., & Hobson, R. F. (1977). The persecutory therapist. *British Journal of Medical Psychology, 50,* 349–359.

Messer, S. B. (1986). Behavioral and psychoanalytic perspectives at therapeutic choice points. *American Psychologist, 35,* 818–827.

Messer, S. B. (1988). Psychoanalytic perspectives on the therapist-client relationship. *Journal of Integrative and Eclectic Psychotherapy, 7,* 269–277.

Miller, W. R. (1985). Motivation for treatment: A review with special emphasis on alcoholism. *Psychological Bulletin, 98,* 84–107.

Millon, T. (1988). Personologic psychotherapy: Ten commandments for a posteclectic approach to integrative treatment. *Psychotherapy, 25,* 209–219.

Moultrup, D. (1986). Integration: A coming of age. *Contemporary Family Therapy, 8,* 157–167.

Norcross, J. C. (1985). In defense of theoretical orientations for clinicians. *The Clinical Psychologist, 38,* 13–17.

Norcross, J. C. (Ed.). (1986). *Handbook of eclectic psychotherapy.* New York: Brunner/Mazel.

Norcross, J. C. (1987a). Special section: Toward a common language for psychotherapy. *Journal of Integrative and Eclectic Psychotherapy, 4,* 165–205.

Norcross, J. C. (Ed.). (1987b). *Casebook of eclectic psychotherapy.* New York: Brunner/Mazel.

Norcross, J. C. (Ed.). (in press). Prescriptive matching in psychotherapy: Psychoanalysis for simple phobias? *Psychotherapy.*

Norcross, J. C., & Grencavage, L. M. (1989). Eclecticism and integration in psychotherapy: Major themes and obstacles. *British Journal of Guidance and Counselling, 17,* 227–247.

Norcross, J. C., & Napolitano, G. (1986). Defining our Journal and ourselves. *International Journal of Eclectic Psychotherapy, 5,* 249–255.

Norcross, J. C., & Prochaska, J. O. (1983). Clinicians' theoretical orientations: Selection, utilization, and efficacy. *Professional Psychology, 14,* 197–208.

Norcross, J. C., & Prochaska, J. O. (1988). A study of eclectic (and integrative) views revisited. *Professional Psychology: Research and Practice, 19,* 170–174.

Norcross, J. C., Strausser, D. J., & Faltus, F. J. (1988). The therapist's therapist. *American Journal of Psychotherapy, 42,* 53–66.

Norcross, J. C., & Thomas, B. L. (1988). What's stopping us now?: Obstacles to psychotherapy integration. *Journal of Integrative and Eclectic Psychotherapy, 7,* 74–80.

Orlinsky, D. E., & Howard, K. I. (1986). Process and outcome in psychotherapy. In S. L. Garfield & A. E. Bergin (Eds.), *Handbook of psychotherapy and behavior change* (3rd ed.). New York: Wiley.

Perls, F. (1969). *Gestalt therapy verbatim* (J. O. Stevens, Ed.). Lafayette, CA: Real People Press.

Perls, F., Hefferline, R., & Goodman, P. (1951). *Gestalt therapy.* New York: Julian Press.

Pine, F. (1985). *Developmental theory and clinical process.* New Haven, CT: Yale University Press.

Pope, K. S., & Bouhautsous, J. C. (1986). *Sexual intimacy between therapists and patients.* New York: Praeger.

Powell, D. H. (1988). Spontaneous insights and the process of behavior therapy: Cases in support of integrative psychotherapy. *Psychiatric Annals, 18,* 288–294.

Prochaska, J. O. (1984). *Systems of psychotherapy: A transtheoretical analysis* (2nd ed.). Homewood, IL: Dorsey Press.

Prochaska, J. O., & DiClemente, C. C. (1984). *Transtheoretical therapy: Crossing the traditional boundaries of therapy.* Homewood, IL: Dow-Jones Irwin, 1984.

Prochaska, J. O., & DiClemente, C. C. (1986). The transtheoretical approach. In J. C. Norcross (Ed.), *Handbook of eclectic psychotherapy.* New York: Brunner/Mazel.

Prochaska, J. O., & Norcross, J. C. (1982). The future of psychotherapy: A Delphi poll. *Professional Psychology, 13,* 620–627.

Prochaska, J. O., & Norcross, J. C. (1986). Exploring paths toward integration: Ten ways not to get there. *International Journal of Eclectic Psychotherapy, 5,* 136–139.

Pynoos, R. S., & Eth, S. (1986). Witness to violence: The child interview. *Journal of the American Academy of Child Psychiatry, 25,* 306–319.

Rice, L. N. (1983). The relationship in client-centered therapy. In M. J. Lambert (Ed.), *Psychotherapy and patient relationships* (pp. 36–60). Homewood, IL: Dow Jones-Irwin.

Rice, L. N. (1984). Client tasks in client-centered therapy. In R. L. Levant & J. M. Shlien (Eds.), *Client-centered therapy and the person-centered approach* (pp. 261–277). New York: Praeger.

Rice, L. N., & Greenberg, L. S. (Eds.). (1984). *Patterns of change: Intensive analysis of therapeutic process.* New York: Guilford Press.

Rice, L. N., & Greenberg, L. S. (in press). Two affective change events in client-centered therapy. In J. D. Safran & L. S. Greenberg (Eds.), *Affective change events in psychotherapy.* New York: Academic Press.

Rice, L. N., & Kerr, G. P. (1986). Measures of client and therapist vocal quality. In L. S. Greenberg & W. M. Pinsof (Eds.), *The psychotherapeutic process* (pp. 73–105). New York: Guilford.

Rogers, C. (1961). *On becoming a person.* Boston: Houghton Mifflin.

Ryle, A. (1982). *Psychotherapy: A cognitive integration of theory and practice.* Orlando, FL: Academic Press.

Saltzman, N. (1983). Paracatastasis and exorcism in bio psychotherapy: Treating shame, guilt, and bad feelings about the self. *International Journal of Eclectic Psychotherapy, 2*(2), 14–30.

Saltzman, N. (1989). Integrating intensely emotional methods with psychodynamic, gestalt, cognitive, and behavioral therapeutic elements (Part 1). *Psychotherapy in Private Practice, 7*(1), 57–67.

Satir, V. (1972). *Peoplemaking*. Palo Alto, CA: Science and Behavior Books.

Scoggin, F., Jamison, C., & Gochneaur, K. (1989). Comparative efficacy of cognitive and behavioral bibliotherapy for mildly and moderately depressed older adults. *Journal of Consulting and Clinical Psychology, 57*, 403–407.

Scrignar, S. (1984). *Post traumatic stress disorders*. New York: Praeger.

Shapiro, D. (1989). *Psychotherapy of neurotic character*. New York: Basic Books.

Shapiro, D. A., & Firth, J. A. (1987). Prescriptive vs. exploratory psychotherapy: Outcomes of the Sheffield Psychotherapy Project. *British Journal of Psychiatry, 151*, 790–799.

Siberschatz, G., Curtis, J. T., & Nathans, S. (1989). Using the patient's plan to assess progress in psychotherapy. Psychotherapy, 26, 40–46.

Sichel, J., & Ellis, A. (1984). *RET self-help form*. New York: Institute for Rational-Emotive Therapy.

Smith, M. L., Glass, G. V., & Miller, T. J. (1980). *The benefits of psychotherapy*. Baltimore, MD: Johns Hopkins University Press.

Sollod, R. (1982). Non-scientific sources of psychotherapeutic approaches. In P. Sharkey (Ed.), *Philosophy, religion and psychotherapy*. Washington, DC: University Press of America.

Sollod, R., & Wachtel, P. (1980). A structural and transactional approach to cognition in clinical problems. In M. Mahoney (Ed.), *Psychotherapy process: Current issues and future directions*. New York: Plenum.

Spence, D. P. (1982). *Narrative truth and historical truth*. New York: Norton.

Stiles, W. B., Shapiro, D. A., & Elliott, R. (1986). Are all psychotherapies equivalent? *American Psychologist, 41*, 165–180.

Stone, L. (1961). *The psychoanalytic situation*. New York: International Universities Press.

Stricker, G. (1986, May). *Some viable suggestions for integrating psychotherapies*. Paper presented at the annual conference of the Society for the Exploration of Psychotherapy Integration, Toronto.

Strupp, H. H. (1986a). The nonspecific hypothesis of therapeutic effectiveness: A current assessment. *American Journal of Orthopsychiatry, 56,* 513-520.

Strupp, H. H. (1986b). Psychotherapy: Research, practice, and public policy (How to avoid dead ends). *American Psychologist, 41,* 120-130.

Textor, M. R. (1989a). The "healthy" family. *Journal of Family Therapy, 11,* 59-75.

Textor, M. R. (1989b). *Integrative familientherapie (Integrative family therapy).* New York: Springer.

Textor, M. R. (in press). Models of abnormal behavior and treatment approaches: A call for an integrative theory. *Social Work/Maatskaplike Werk.*

Thompson, J. K. (1990). *Body image disturbance: Assessment and treatment.* Elmsford, NY: Pergamon.

Vogelsong, E., & Guerney, B. G., Jr. (1977). *The relationship enhancement program for family therapy and enrichment* [Film or Videotape]. University Park, PA: Individual and Family Consultation Center.

Wachtel, E. F., & Wachtel, P. L. (1986). *Family dynamics in individual psychotherapy: A guide to clinical strategies.* New York: Guilford Press.

Wachtel, P. L. (1977). *Psychoanalysis and behavior therapy: Toward an integration.* New York: Basic Books.

Wachtel, P. L. (1982). Vicious circles: The self and the rhetoric of emerging and unfolding. *Contemporary Psychoanalysis, 18,* 259-273.

Wachtel, P. L. (1983). Integration misunderstood. *Journal of British Clinical Psychology, 22,* 129-130.

Wachtel, P. L. (1987). *Action and insight.* New York: Guilford.

White, M. T., & Weiner, M. B. (1986). *The theory and practice of self psychology.* New York: Brunner/Mazel.

Wiesen, A. (1977). *Positive therapy: Making the very best of everything.* Chicago: Nelson-Hall.

Wilson, J. P., Smith, W. K., & Johnson, S. K. (1985). A comparative analysis of PTSD among various survivor groups.

In C. Figley (Ed.), *Trauma and its wake*. New York: Brunner/Mazel.

Wolfe, B. E., & Goldfried, M. R. (1988). Research on psychotherapy integration: Recommendations and conclusions from an NIMH workshop. *Journal of Consulting and Clinical Psychology, 56,* 448–451.

Yost, E., Beutler, L. E., Corbishley, M. A., & Allender, J. R. (1986). *Group cognitive therapy: A treatment approach for depressed older adults.* Elmsford, N.Y.: Pergamon Press.

Zeig, J. K., & Munion, W. M. (Eds.). (1990). *What is psychotherapy?* San Francisco: Jossey-Bass.

Index